SCRIPTS OF TERROR

BENEDICT WILKINSON

Scripts of Terror

The Stories Terrorists Tell Themselves

OXFORD

UNIVERSITY PRESS

OXFORD
UNIVERSITY PRESS

Oxford University Press is a department of the
University of Oxford. It furthers the University's objective
of excellence in research, scholarship, and education
by publishing worldwide.

Oxford   New York

Auckland   Cape Town   Dar es Salaam   Hong Kong   Karachi
Kuala Lumpur   Madrid   Melbourne   Mexico City   Nairobi
New Delhi   Shanghai   Taipei   Toronto

With offices in

Argentina   Austria   Brazil   Chile   Czech Republic   France   Greece
Guatemala   Hungary   Italy   Japan   Poland   Portugal   Singapore
South Korea   Switzerland   Thailand   Turkey   Ukraine   Vietnam

Oxford is a registered trade mark of Oxford University Press
in the UK and certain other countries.

Published in the United States of America by
Oxford University Press
198 Madison Avenue, New York, NY 10016

Library of Congress Cataloging-in-Publication Data is available
Benedict Wilkinson.
Scripts of Terror: The Stories Terrorists Tell Themselves.
ISBN: 9780197521892

Printed in Great Britain by Bell and Bain Ltd, Glasgow, on acid-free paper

For my father, my great storyteller

CONTENTS

ACKNOWLEDGEMENTS

This book is based on research I conducted for my PhD. It had always been my intention to publish it in 'book form', but as I finished the PhD and moved into the newly formed Policy Institute at King's College London, other projects and priorities had to come first. Much has happened since then, not least the rise of ISIS and near-complete overshadowing of al-Qa'ida. In these years, whilst I should probably have been writing this book, I have instead been focusing on other issues. Nevertheless, this volume represents several years of thinking and work, and the slowness to 'convert' it into a formal book—along with all mistakes and errors—is purely my own. I am hugely indebted to Michael Dwyer and his fantastic team at Hurst, who have stuck with me, despite my slow progress.

The sheer amount of time it has taken me to do that means that I am in debt to an inordinate number of people and institutions. First and foremost, to the ESRC and to the British-Yemeni Society without whose generous funding the research which underpins this book would not have been possible. I also owe a great deal to King's College London and the colleagues I have met there. King's has been my intellectual home for more than a decade, first in the Department of War Studies as an MA and PhD Student, and then in the Defence Studies Department, before I moved to the Policy Institute at King's in 2013.

During my time at King's, I have met brilliant colleagues, without whom this book would not have been possible. First and foremost, my thanks go to Lawrence Freedman, my teacher, mentor, advisor and friend, whose ideas have so inspired me and without whom this book would never have been begun, let alone been completed. But in addition to Lawry, King's has given me a host of advisors. James Gow has been a fabulous and hugely insightful mentor since we first met. His kindnesses are legion. Matt Uttley, as well as being a brilliant colleague and collaborator, has always provided great humour and brilliant advice. John Bew (along with Rob Gleave of Exeter) kindly examined the doctoral thesis and gave much counsel on how to turn it into a book. It is my fault it took so long. Michael Sanders has taught me more about behavioural science than I deserve. I also owe a deep debt to Jonathan Grant, Jennifer Rubin, Sarah Rawlings and the whole team at the Policy Institute. Over the years, they have developed my thinking in ways beyond measure.

A PhD that takes five years to turn into a book means that there are countless people who have helped in ways too complex to explain fully. This book would be far poorer without all of you: Alistair Maclellan, Tony Basford, Chris Sawyer, Claire Yorke, Heather Williams, Jeff Michaels, Mark Allen, Toby Feakin, Michael Clarke, Noel Brehony, Amelia Morgan, John Scarlett, James Spencer, Sarah, Rania and Mohammed, Manu, Ilham Salimane, Amal Ali, Amal Ayoubi, Carl Miller and Martin Moore.

On a more personal note, my special thanks to three people in particular: first, to my mother who took such an interest in the research that she cut out newspaper clippings, forwarded links which might be of interest and, having proofed it numerous times, proceeded to pose the most difficult questions. I am certain she is far more expert than I! Secondly, to my wife, Anna. This book could not have happened without her: she provided constant counsel, gentle encouragement and great patience, particularly while I was writing it so painfully slowly. Thirdly, to my father, who sadly died whilst I was writing this book. He was the greatest storyteller I have known and for that reason, this book is dedicated to him.

PREFACE

THE DILEMMA OF TERROR

If you visited Mosul at some point in the last 850 years or so, you would almost certainly have seen the spectacular minaret of the Great Mosque of al-Nuri adorning the skyline. Looking rather like an Iraqi version of the leaning tower of Pisa, you would have seen the mosque's curved minaret rising up on the western edge of the river Tigris, peering over the city like a monumental watch keeper. Locals call it 'al-hadba' ('the hunchback'), and say that the minaret became curved when it bowed in reverence to the prophet Muhammad as he ascended to heaven. Mosul may have seen its fair share of conflict and trouble over the last eight centuries or so, but through all that the Great Mosque has survived, a constant through times of peace and a bulwark in times of conflict.

However, the great bastions survive no longer. In 2017, Islamic State militants, driven back by Iraqi government forces, blew both monuments up. Footage shows a black flag flying from the curved minaret, then multiple scattered explosions which seem to dissolve the leaning tower into the ground beneath, as huge plumes of dust engulf the scene. The destruction of the Great Mosque was a critical moment for ISIS: for it was here, in July 2014, that Abu Bakr al-Baghdadi announced the establishment of the Caliphate and in so doing, ushered in a new era for the organisation and a new strategy for achieving the establishment of 'an Islamic state that doesn't recognize borders, [established] on the Prophetic methodology'. In demolishing the very same building just three years later, the leadership of Islamic State symbolically ushered in a new phase for the organisation. And, simultaneously, ushered in a(nother) new strategy—one which was less about occupying territory and controlling it through a core set of leaders, and more about Islamic State as an idea.

Multiple changes in strategy may smack of desperation—after all, why change something that works?—but in practice, terrorism is a pretty desperate strategy. It is a strategy of the weak and therefore one which demands repeated shifts in strategy to avoid getting stopped (at best) or obliterated (at worst) by one's enemies. Every terrorist group that has ever existed, regardless of creed or colour, has faced this very same dilemma: how do you bring about the political changes you want to when your opposition is overwhelmingly more powerful? How do you avoid the inevitable backlash of the state you are damaging and the citizens you are killing? How do you beat a more powerful opposition? Solving this dilemma is at the heart of all terrorism (indeed, all strategy). It is the constant problem that terrorists try to resolve. For them, mindless violence, and the fear that such violence engenders, tilts the balance of power in their favour; by being unpredictable and targeting citizens or the state, governments will give in just to keep order and peace.

This book explores that dilemma, charting the ways that different groups in the Middle East have tried to resolve it. As we shall see, terrorists tend to be faced with this dilemma at particular moments in their evolution. Every group has to figure out a way through the problem at the beginning of their organisation's life, when they are considering their first attack or set of attacks. It inevitably arises after terrorist groups have been on the receiving end of government reprisals, when they are on the backfoot and their carefully gathered financial and military resources have been reduced or lost. For those groups that survive for some time, it inevitably re-emerges towards the end of their lifespan, too, as they consider the last options available to them.

Although this book focuses on a set of organisations operating in the Middle East, the dilemma is one experienced by all groups. Bin Laden struggled with it in the late 1990s, as he sought to challenge the West, and again after al-Qa'ida's military defeat in Afghanistan in late 2001. Hamas grappled with it after the First Intifada, and again after the Second Intifada. Hezbollah faced it at the end of the 2006 Lebanon War, after Israeli Defence Forces pushed into southern Lebanon and established an air and naval blockade. Groups of different political leanings equally face the problem: in the early 1990s, Sendero Luminoso, who had previously controlled large portions of the south and centre of Peru, faced it when they found themselves bereft of their charismatic leader, Abimael Guzmán, and on the verge of complete military defeat. France's Action Directe struggled with the problem after the arrest of most of its members in 1981. The messianic doomsday cult, Aum Shinrikyo, faced it in the 1980s, and tried to solve it with the use of sarin in 1994 and 1995 in an effort to bring salvation to humanity before the Armageddon.

The core argument at the heart of this book is that terrorism, in all its guises, is an attempt to solve the same dilemma: how to achieve hugely ambitious goals when one has very little power. At some point—whether when embarking upon a new campaign of violence or on the cusp of destruction—every terrorist tries to resolve the conflict between their ambitions—often far-reaching, elaborate and grandiose—and their relatively limited resources. If terrorists cared less about their political objectives, other, less violent paths might be open to them; if they had greater means—fighters, equipment, finances—more conventional forms of conflict would probably be a better route. It is precisely because they have grand political objectives and few resources that every group from the Russian anarchists, through the leftist and ethno-nationalist groups, to today's violent Islamists, has sought to find ways to bridge the gap between the two. Some have tried to attack governments head on; others have tried attacking populations instead; some have sought to globalise, and some have gone underground to avoid detection; some, after long campaigns of violence, have even demobilised and sought to create political movements and parties to achieve their aims. At heart, however, the trajectory of every terrorist group is shaped entirely by its approach to this dilemma before it is wiped out by its opponents.

This book is an attempt to chart the ways that some groups have tried to solve this dilemma, and what happened when they tried. It examines what terrorists do when their options are limited or when they have no options at all. In so doing, it asks why terrorists choose terrorism, why it appeals, and whether it works. It explores why groups choose violence over other methods, and how they envisage violence bringing about their objectives. By drawing on the case studies, I identify a series of strategies of terrorism (which I term scripts) to which the violent Islamist groups returned time and again: survival, power play, mobilisation, provocation, de-legitimisation, attrition, co-operation and de-mobilisation.

One of the odd inevitabilities of writing a book of this kind is that I have had to (try to) take on the uncomfortable task of 'getting inside' the terrorist's mind, trying to understand what they were attempting to do, and why they thought it might work. In getting inside the terrorist's mind, one clear theme emerged throughout the research. Terrorists truly think terrorism works—and they are largely wrong. This is why terrorism is not just an abhorrent choice, but a foolish one. It is based on a strategic calculus that is broken. Terrorists have little in the way of weaponry or personnel to call on; they have enemies that are far stronger and better equipped; they have hugely ambitious political ends. This is a circle that cannot easily be squared. As the history of terrorism suggests, it is rarely very successful in meeting their stated objectives. And yet, for some reason, it is a strategy that is still returned to time and again. For all its failures, people still continue to choose violence in the face of overwhelming odds to achieve their ends.

In trying to piece together answers to some of these questions during the research, I kept butting up against one critical—and largely unresolved—question. Although it had come to mind at the beginning of the research, I did not realise its importance until I was diving into the case studies. Looking across the host of organisations, I kept asking 'why?'; why, if terrorism is so rarely successful and so hard to pull off, does it appeal as a strategy to terrorists? Or to put it more crudely, why do terrorists bother at all? The history of terrorism shows its outcome is known almost before they start: that terrorism will fail. The standard answer to this is that terrorists are mad, or suffer from a series of psychological traits that drive them to this kind of behaviour. But much of the literature on terrorists shows that they suffer from no greater incidence of psychological illness than any other group of randomly selected individuals. In short, they are normal. My own research also backs this up: terrorists, as far as I could tell from reading their work and speaking to them, seemed to be rational actors.

And so I returned to this core question: why do terrorists 'choose' terrorism? I eventually found some answers in the world of behavioural economics. This field, not often applied to the study of terrorism, explores how different factors influence decision-making, and how this differs from classical economic theory. Richard Thaler, winner of the Nobel Prize for Economics, gives a useful example. In the 1970s, he hosted a dinner party for some friends. They all came around twenty minutes before dinner was ready; there was a bowl of cashews on the table, and everyone helped themselves, devouring all the cashews. Thaler thought this was surprising, because dinner was only twenty minutes away. Why would rational people eat all the cashews when they knew dinner was imminent? Clearly there was some kind of cognitive dissonance at play; perhaps people were overestimating the amount they could eat, or underestimating how much they were eating before dinner. Perhaps they simply lacked self-control.

One of the preoccupations of the field of behavioural science is with the host of cognitive biases and heuristics (mental rules of thumb) that permeate all human decision-making. Amongst the long lists of biases is the narrative fallacy—the idea that humans believe stories all too easily. We are obsessed with books that tell stories of how investors 'cracked' the stock market, or got the best jobs, or quit their jobs and found the perfect life. We are passionate about fictional stories of spies who seemingly never die, of good wizards and bad wizards. But, as the narrative fallacy suggests, stories should also come with a health warning. Humans are highly susceptible to stories. We find stories compelling and convincing.[1]

Even credible stories can mislead by smothering the role played by luck, shortening the distance between cause and effect or oversimplifying the impact of human agency.

Behavioural economists provided at least some of the answer to the 'why do terrorists choose terrorism' question but are no less immune to cognitive biases than the rest of us. They are just as susceptible to stories—just as likely to be gulled into believing a story—as the rest of us. Each of the different strategies I found terrorists talking about and using were, in essence, a story. Each one had a plot, with different characters and different agendas. Each one had an end point, an articulation or vision of the future in an ideal world. Each one had cause, followed by effect. In short, each strategy or script was a story, a narrative about the future, used by terrorists (like other strategists) to show where they wanted to go and why. Indeed, as I continued the work, I found terrorists using different scripts to model different end points from different actions, using them to consider the likelihood of different reprisals and different actions from other players in the scenario and to test how successful different actions might, or might not be, in achieving their ends. They are, if you like, thought experiments, which allow the strategist to explore different options, and how they might unfold.

In some sense, then, the very process of thinking about terrorism was deluding terrorists into following that path. In devising and telling stories about how terrorism might work in achieving political ends, they essentially persuaded themselves that it could—indeed, might—work. In charting the different scripts, I found terrorists describing single attacks on governments that could bring down whole regimes, attacks on civilians that could persuade them to adopt different religions and different politics, attacks on infrastructure that would show whole nations just how wrong they were. I found terrorists talking about violence as a way of mobilising populations, demobilising armies, and inciting such reprisals that the terrorists would be the object of sympathy, rather than contempt and abhorrence. Needless to say, many of these outcomes never happened, but terrorists honestly believed they could. This book shows that they were wrong—and why.

1

THE SEDUCTION OF TERROR

Strategy is endlessly enthralling, exhilarating, subtle and complex. But, more so even than these, strategy is an innately frustrating activity. Like umbrellas, buses and words, strategies are elusive when you need them the most. When things are easy—that is, when resources are plentiful and goals limited—strategy is relatively straightforward, often involving little more than the judicious application of resources. But if resources are stretched and goals ambitious, strategy is both more complex and potentially more rewarding. It involves careful deliberation over the use of resources, the creation of unity of action and purpose amongst one's followers and friends, the premeditation of a rival's reactions. Often, it involves using cunning, speed, flexibility or deceit to out-play an enemy. Playing poker for matchsticks or for fun does not really require a strategy, because the stakes are low; put your house and everything you own on a game, however, and the stakes grow along with the need for, and complexity of, a good strategy. Start playing games with nuclear weapons, countless lives and the very existence of states, and creating a strategy can become so challenging as to confound even the most brilliant of minds.

Whether easy or hard, elusive or ready-to-hand, deliberative or instinctive, strategy is essentially about choices under uncertainty, choices about the future, choices which influence the behaviour of others and get you to your objectives—or at least get you to a middle stage where they are more attainable. Strategy is a way of bridging the gap between means and ends—it is about converting what you have into what you want. Or, to quote Lawrence Freedman, 'the realm of strategy is one of bargaining and persuasion as well as

1

threats and pressure, psychological as well as physical effects, and words as well as deeds... It is about getting more out of a situation than the starting balance of power would suggest. It is the art of creating power'.[1] Strategy is a choice, a particular type of decision that takes place when the stakes are high, when other players have both power and agency, when we can lose, as well as win.

Terrorism as a Strategy

It may seem strange to start a book about terrorism by discussing what strategy is and why it is hard, but the intellectual and philosophical starting point of this book is that terrorism is a strategy. It is a strategy that is designed to perpetrate acts of violence that create and perpetrate fear within populations who then pressurise governments into changing policies and bringing about the ambitions of perpetrators. Or, to put it more succinctly, terrorism is a strategy that involves deploying violence to terrify people into demanding specific political changes. And, because terrorism is such a carefully thought out strategy, it is also a rational choice—that is, it is a choice rationally made, even though its effects may seem to be mindless and its proponents fanatical.

If terrorism is both a strategy and a choice, then it is clearly one of the weak. Powerful, well-resourced groups do not need terrorism to achieve their goals: they have far more successful and safer strategies for achieving their ends to hand. Terrorism, however, is for those with little in the way of resources who need to coax every last ounce of coercive force from violence. To do this, they resort to creating fear. Regardless of which terrorist group it is, or what ideology they espouse, all terrorists use violence to create fear. This is why explosions and mindless acts of violence have been the hallmark of terrorists since they first acquired revolvers and bombs. Granted, each has sought to shock, appal and terrify by resorting to more unusual or unexpected forms of violence, but in the end they all use violence in an attempt to provoke fear and panic: it is only through panic that objectives can be reached.

In arguing that terrorism is a strategy and a rational choice, this book is in something of a minority. Perhaps surprisingly, bearing in mind the deluge of research on terrorism since 9/11, there is a dearth of material on terrorism as strategy. Indeed, not much has really changed since M.L.R. Smith and Peter Neumann noted back in 2005, 'among [the] flood of (often forgettable) books [on terrorism], what stands out is the absence of any meaningful examination of terrorism as a military strategy'.[2] The handful of studies which do view terrorism as strategy, however, tend to agree on how terrorism works strategically. For Freedman, terrorism is designed to create 'a psychological effect—terror—with a view to creating a political effect that will be manifest in changes in the target's strategy'.[3] For Smith and Neumann, terrorism is 'the deliberate creation of a sense of fear, usually by the use or threat of use of symbolic acts of physical violence, to influence the political behaviour of a given target group'. Ariel Merari quotes the definition of terrorism found in the United States Code: 'premeditated, politically motivated violence perpetrated against noncombatant targets by subnational groups or clandestine agents, usually intended to influence an audience'.[4]

Taking these together, it is possible to distinguish between terrorism's primary, long-term goals such as the establishment of a caliphate or the expulsion of a colonial power, and the shorter-term goals such as eliciting a government reaction, creating fear or mobilising a population. Kydd and Walter argue that 'individuals and groups often have hierarchies of objectives, where broader goals lead to more proximate objectives, which then become specific goals in more tactical analyses'.[5] More recently, Abrahms has differentiated between 'process' goals and 'outcome' goals; the former 'intended to sustain the group by securing financial support, attracting media attention, scuttling organization-threatening peace processes or boosting membership and morale', where the latter are their 'stated political ends'.[6]

Terrorism, then, can be seen to be a particular kind of strategy, one used (normally by underdogs) to create power by maximising the potential of resources in an effort to reach political ends.[7] As with any other strategy, communication and signalling is at the heart of terrorism. Violence is essentially a high-value political statement aimed to achieve ambitions through coercion.[8] Indeed, the communicative aspect is acknowledged by terrorists themselves. Khaled Mesha'al, for example, when leader of Hamas' Political Bureau, proclaimed, in the aftermath of 9/11, that 'the Zionist enemy... understands only the language of *jihad*, resistance and martyrdom; that was the language that led to its blatant defeat in South Lebanon and it will be the language that will defeat it on the land of Palestine'.[9] Al-Qa'ida showed itself to be equally aware that to engage in terrorism is to communicate in a particularly high-value language when other dialogues have brought little success.[10] Bin Laden similarly saw terrorist violence as a form of coercive communication which could redress the balance of power between terrorists and their oppositions:

> I cannot forget those unbearable scenes [from the First Lebanon War] of blood and severed limbs, the corpses of women and children strewn everywhere, houses destroyed along with their occupants and high rise buildings burying

their residents, rockets raining down on our land without mercy. It was as if a crocodile had seized a helpless child, who could do nothing but scream. Tell me: does the crocodile understand any language other than that of force?[11]

Al-Zawahiri was similarly explicit that his followers should be 'sure to inflict maximum casualties on the enemy, kill the greatest number of people, for this is the only language understood by the West'.[12]

Of course, strategic terrorism is not simply an attempt to send coercive messages to an opposition—it is also an attempt to communicate one's ideology and political ambitions to friends, allies and potential recruits in an effort to maintain or mobilise support.[13] In this sense, violence can be seen in terms of what Thomas Thornton referred to as an 'advertisement of the cause'; terrorism provides a spectacle that communicates a movement's commitment to violence, its political vision and, in so doing, incites others to join.[14] Like the coercive aspects of terrorism, this proselytising element has been well acknowledged by other terrorist groups. Bakunin, the great proponent of the 'propaganda of the deed' model, famously wrote that violence spreads 'principles, not with words but with deeds, for this is the most popular, the most potent, and the most irresistible form of propaganda'.[15] Or, to put it in the oft-quoted words of Brian Michael Jenkins, 'terrorists want a lot of people watching and a lot of people listening, not a lot of people dead'.[16]

There is no question that terrorism is ruthlessly efficient at sending political signals, both high-profile, coercive messages to targets, and advertisements of the cause to supporters. But how effective is it in bringing about the political goals terrorists so dearly want? For some scholars, terrorism can be effective. Based on his analysis of the gains of Palestinian terrorist organisations, for example, Alan Dershowitz famously argued that terrorism can be successful and is therefore 'an entirely rational choice to achieve a political objective'.[17] Sprinzak provides a more circular argument that 'the prevalence of suicide terrorism during the last two decades testifies to its gruesome effectiveness'.[18] Robert Pape asserts that, of the eleven suicide campaigns between 1980 and 2001, six 'closely correlate with significant policy changes by the target state toward the terrorists' major political goals'.[19]

But, more often, scholars have seen it as partially effective, at best, arguing that it can be useful in getting to an intermediate stage, from which to change strategy. Indeed, this point was made by Thomas Schelling, who suggested that terrorists frequently accomplish 'intermediate means toward political objectives... but with a few exceptions it is hard to see that the attention and publicity have been of much value except as ends in themselves'.[20] David Lake argued that terrorism is 'rational and strategic' because it increases the means available to 'extremists' and thus improves their bargaining position.[21] Gould and Klor similarly suggest that there is an intermediate point past which terrorism becomes self-refuting, noting that 'terror activity beyond a certain threshold seems to backfire on the goals of terrorist factions by hardening the stance of the targeted population'.[22] Kydd and Walter contend that terrorism is effective when the aim is to sabotage peace deals; they argue that of the fourteen agreements negotiated between 1988 and 1998, only one in four were implemented in the face of terrorist campaigns, whereas six out of ten were successful against a backdrop of peace.[23]

But, for more scholars, terrorism rarely works. In his study of twenty-eight terrorist organisations, Max Abrahms calculated that terrorism achieved policy objectives only seven per cent of the time, and naught per cent of the time when they attacked citizens.[24] Paul Wilkinson agreed with this conclusion, finding that the 'track record in attaining major political objectives abysmal'.[25] To put it more simply, a brief glance at the history of terrorism suggests that terrorism, for all its coercive potential, rarely achieves long-term political aspirations, although it might be more successful at gaining the upper hand temporarily or in producing concessions. Clearly, there are notable exceptions to this—the Algerian *Front de Libération Nationale* (FLN), the Irgun and Stern Gang, *Ethniki Organosis Kyprion Agoniston* (EOKA), the African National Congress all spring to mind. Nevertheless, these are exceptions to the rule; in the words of Lawrence Freedman, 'terrorism, when used on its own with the intention of transforming whole societies in order to achieve grandiose political objectives, is almost destined for futility'.[26]

Scripts of Terror

One of the questions that underpins this book is why terrorists choose terrorism at all. Recent work on decision-making provides some potential answers. Work in the behavioural sciences has focused heavily on the irrationality of what appear to be perfectly rational choices—the cognitive biases and heuristics that drive all decision-making. Behavioural economists argue that human decision-making is riddled with biases, heuristics and shortcuts which can be hugely insightful when we need to be instinctive and fleet of foot, but let us down enormously when precise, deliberative answers are needed. Daniel Kahneman, for instance, describes two types of decision-making: System 1 and System 2.[27] System 1 is 'unconscious, rapid, automatic and high capacity'.[28]

This form of impulsive or intuitive decision-making is a 'mental shotgun' that can be very powerful, particularly when situations really are stereotypical and formulaic. System 2, by contrast, is conscious, slow, deliberative and 'effortful', but unlike System 1, it 'can follow rules, compare objects on several attributes and make deliberate choices'.[29] System 2 is triggered when 'an event is detected that violates the model of the world that System 1 maintains'—that is, when questions posed are too complex for System 1 to solve, when situations are unusual or when answers require a high level of precision.[30]

System 1 thinking is good at handling simple, but stereotypical situations. If you think you see a poisonous snake, your instinct will be to run or recoil, rather than to carry on as before. Ordering coffee in a café is a simple, but fairly formulaic scenario, as is asking for directions. These formulaic situations—the ones which our impulsive System 1 mindsets are very adept and successful at handling—are called scripts. They are highly stereotyped sets of actions and reactions between players in a given scenario; or, as Schank and Abelson put it, 'a script is a predetermined, stereotyped sequence of actions that define a well-known situation'.[31]

Simple scripts can form the basis of dealing with more complex situations. If you were a regular coffee drinker, but had never eaten out, you may well use the 'café' script as a basis for dealing with ordering in a restaurant the first time around. Granted, you might make the odd faux pas but, in all probability, you would be able to get to the end of the situation. Simple scripts can also become the basis for dealing with more complex problems as well. If an office worker felt their pet project was about to be axed by a new boss, they might simply leave the organisation (flight), or may decide to confront the new leader (fight). Scripts can also be developed over time, as humans learn what series of actions work in a given context and return to them time and again. In the office worker example, other (perhaps more subtle) decision-makers will explore different reactions to the threatened termination of a pet project; they may use political capital, or seek to create it; they may form complex coalitions, or seek to bargain. In short, there are countless scripts: they are created as situations emerge, and as different courses of action show themselves to be effective, but in essence scripts are simply 'rules for handling particular types of situations'; they allow decision-makers to 'select from the available alternatives by generating expectations about how the other side will react to various policy options'.[32]

Scripts, whether complex or simple, are a key tool in decision-making. Knowing a series of scripts allows a decision-maker to model different futures, to test what effects an initial action will have, and where things might end up.

In short, they are thought experiments: they allow a decision to interpret a situation, identify the best available actions or reactions and provide expectations about the likely sequence of events and likely outcome of that sequence. System 1 scripts are likely to be short, simplistic and largely stereotypical. They provide intuitive or instinctive readings of a situation alongside essentially automatic responses. System 2 scripts are the product of 'effortful' thought and deliberation; they require conscious consideration, recognition of a range of factors, actors and constraints in a given situation and the identification of multiple possible actions. System 2 scripts may have their origins in System 1 scripts, or may be influenced by the decision-maker's knowledge of analogous situations or personal experience, but 'they have to take the present as a starting point and project forward... [they] are stories about the future, starting with imaginative fiction but with an aspiration to nonfiction.'[33]

Terrorists—like any decision-maker—also rely on scripts in their strategic calculations. Just like other decision-makers faced with a problem, terrorists use scripts to test out potential courses of action and see how different actors in the scenario might respond. Conceivably, scripts are infinite in number; strategists can formulate new scripts as they so desire: these can be idiosyncratic, unrealistic and occasionally absurd; they can also be insightful, predictive and meaningful. Terrorists, because they usually have ambitious political aspirations and only meagre means to pursue those aspirations, invariably have access to an even smaller number of scripts than those with greater materiel.

As we shall see in the case studies, violent Islamist strategic options were similarly restricted by their lack of military, human and financial resources. For these cases, fourteen more or less discrete organisations, active in three different countries and operating at some point during a sixty-year period, were explored. Only eight scripts were identified in the case studies: survival, power play, mobilisation, provocation and polarisation, de-legitimisation, attrition, co-operation, and de-mobilisation. To be clear, whilst the terminology is my own, each of these scripts represents a relatively stereotyped structure through which violent Islamists interpret situations, envisage interactions with their oppositions and allies, and, most importantly, through which they formulate their strategies. It is useful to examine the nature of the scripts and the sequences of events they describe in advance of the case studies not only to provide further clarity to the theoretical approach but also to simplify identification of the scripts in the case studies.

The first script, which I refer to interchangeably as the survival script and the fight or flight script, involves doing 'whatever it takes' to ensure the continued existence of the organisation. Although much emphasis has been laid on terrorism as a strategy for achieving largely grandiose political aims, in practice, this can be difficult: often the resources are simply not available for a major confrontation or the environment is so hostile that political goals cannot be pursued in safety. Thus, in spite of all their lofty rhetoric about political ends, terrorists frequently have the far simpler aim of 'getting to the next stage' so that the situation can be reappraised and new choices made.[34] As the fight or flight moniker suggests, this is an intuitive, impulsive System 1 script which emerges when terrorist organisations are particularly vulnerable—normally when they are embryonic, violent movements or when they have lost a particularly charismatic leader or large portions of their membership to counterterrorism efforts. The script occurs in two forms: organisations lash out at their oppositions with violence in an effort to force them to back away; alternatively, groups go into hiding, waiting for the environment to become more amenable to the pursuit of loftier aims.

Like survival, the second script aims to sustain the movement when it is struggling. In the power play script, violence is essentially inner-directed in that it is more concerned with (re-)acquiring resources—fighters, money, credibility, weapons—rather than achieving ends. The power play script envisages deploying violence in order to cement a leader's authority in the face of impending group fracture or with a view to establishing an organisation's reputation over that of rivals. In the inter-group sense, terrorist violence smothers growing internal dissent or averts potential organisational splits by constructing a persuasive narrative that a failing leader still has control or that an unpopular leader retains their commitment to violence and is not as weak as dissenting elements considered.[35] At the organisational level, where the power play script is normally referred to as 'outbidding', violence broadcasts a statement of intent to the public 'that the terrorists have greater resolve to fight the enemy than rival groups, and therefore are worthy of support'.[36]

The third script is provocation.[37] The standard formulation is that terrorist violence stings an opposition into a repressive or aggressive reaction which is out of proportion to the original act and which, in turn, increases public sympathy for the terrorists and reduces the government's own popularity. The script is not without its risks, however; while repression may well increase support for the organisation, it may also mean that the majority of its members are caught up in mass arrests, endangering the group's continued survival.[38] In this sense, provocation to over-reaction is decidedly a means-oriented script: its immediate aim is not to overthrow the government, but to gain resources in the form of broad political support and, potentially, new recruits. Although the provocation script normally involves over-reactions, it can, in relatively rare circumstances, produce under-reactions.[39] Here, violence is used, often against minority communities, to stretch governments when they are faced with other, more pressing, security threats. Stretched as they are, governments are unable to counter yet further challenges to the security of the state and target communities are left to fend for themselves. For the terrorist strategist, the script aims simultaneously to de-legitimise the authority of government, and to polarise large sections of the population. The point about both strands of the provocation script is that they force target governments to make choices between two options: over-react or under-react. In each case, the outcome is favourable to the terrorist organisation because it provides resources at the expense of government support.

The fourth script, de-legitimisation, similarly forces governments to make decisions they would rather avoid.[40] In this script, particular acts of violence, often against unpopular foreign presence on home territory, force a government to choose between supporting its allies and its opposition.[41] On the one hand, defending foreign presence is widely unpopular but it is a necessary task if powerful allies are to be maintained; on the other hand, doing nothing will inevitably be interpreted as weakness, or worse, complicity with the terrorist organisation.[42] From the terrorist perspective, this is, once again, about accruing means in the form of political support and recruitment: if the government sides with its allies rather than its own people, then the terrorist organisation has an opportunity to convert substantial sections of the opposition support base into supporters of its own cause. Of course, if the government decides not to defend its allies then it implicitly confers legitimacy and approval onto the terrorist cause, once again aiding it in terms of support.

The fifth script is mobilisation and it is both means- and ends-focused, making it particularly popular amongst terrorist movements.[43] For most scholars of terrorist strategy, it is a by-product of government responses, repression in particular.[44] Based on the theory of scripts, this research, however, views mobilisation as a strategic goal in its own right. It is a way of balancing the need to acquire resources with the desire to pursue ends. By mobilising others, the strategist envisages a genuinely global and largely autonomous movement fighting, both at home and abroad, for the same political ends. The strategic vision is as follows: spectacular acts of terrorism have the capacity to inspire fringe elements of the movement to construct their own campaigns of low-level violence; attempts to clamp down on these violent enterprises produce dissatisfaction among more moderate elements of the movement, who are similarly inspired to violence; further attempts to extinguish multiple fires result in even harsher terrorist responses, in turn, creating further grievances and continued mobilisation for the terrorists. In this (rarely attained) form, mobilisation is decidedly a product of System 2 decision-making, in that it envisages the actions of multiple players numerous moves ahead.

The most ends-oriented script is that of attrition. Normally, terrorist strategists who opt for this script have access to substantial resources (significant personnel, extensive finance, considerable military supplies and, most importantly, sizeable political support from non-violent moderates) in order to conduct a long-term campaign and to survive in the face of reprisals.[45] Terrorist organisations with means on this scale anticipate a long-term campaign of strategic violence against their opposition; although they recognise that no attack is likely to achieve their desired political ends they also recognise that no government response is sufficiently lethal to render the organisation a *coup de grâce*.[46] The attrition script envisages the gradual wearing down of one's opposition, reducing their financial and military capabilities, their political capital and their resolve. As such, it often ends not in the crushing defeat of the enemy, but in their capitulation, often after negotiation, to at least some of the demands made by the terrorists.[47] Although the script can be effective, particularly on oppositions located in foreign territory, the critical problem for the strategist is whether the means available really are sufficient for making a threat—and maintaining that threat—against a state.

Thus far we have examined six scripts, all of which are predicated on violence. It is worth noting that of these scripts, only two have an element directed towards pursuing the political aims that terrorism is designed to achieve. The remainder deploy violence in an attempt to acquire resources, reflecting the persistent concern of most terrorist organisations that their means are insufficient. One script that similarly seeks to accrue resources, although without the use of violence, is co-operation. This script envisages forming alliances (co-operative relationships between those whose political objectives are analogous but whose strategy for achieving political ends, terrorism and insurgency for example, are different) or coalitions (formed with political actors whose objectives are different, often directly opposing, to those of the terrorist) with third parties.[48] For alliances, the logic is that the combined efforts of two opposition movements will increase the coercive leverage on the regime. For coalitions, by contrast, terrorists have the 'breathing space' to acquire support and may even receive benefits from their coalition partners.

Advantages for the latter come in the form of controlling a rival: particular ways of converting means to ends, violence chief amongst them, are outlawed and punishments ranging from sanctions to the dissolution of the coalition are threatened if the other partner transgresses particular 'red lines'.[49]

When all options have been exhausted or deemed unrealistic, terrorist organisations opt for the final script investigated by this research: de-mobilisation.[50] This script is distinguished from the related processes of de-radicalisation and disengagement; whereas the latter are forced on organisations (chiefly as a consequence of counter-terrorism efforts) de-mobilisation refers to the pursuit of political objectives by other, non-violent means.[51] Indeed, to take this further, terrorist organisations adopt this script when, and only when, they calculate that non-violent means are the best way of maximising their resources in the pursuit of desired political ends. In this sense, the de-mobilisation script is solely the feature of System 2 decision-making, in that it is a deliberative strategic choice made by actors still pursuing political goals rather than a fate pressed on an organisation by the success of counter-terrorism strategies. Under this script, organisations reject violence with the intention of pursuing an alternative strategy, normally involving the creation of a non-violent political movement or a political party. This can be a highly effective way of constructing a narrative which confers legitimacy on desired political ambitions but, like all scripts, it can be difficult to implement. All too often, sections of an organisation are reluctant to follow the strategy and continue with their campaigns of violence, fracturing the hard-won image of legitimacy. Equally, oppositions and rivals tend to be sceptical of the claim to non-violence and continue to tar former terrorist organisations as 'terrorists' rather than 'politicians' or 'activists'.

About this book

It is worth saying, at the outset, that I see this book as falling squarely into the terrorism studies tradition, rather than into the area or Middle East studies canon. In part, that is because my own training and intellectual approach were forged in the terrorism studies (or war studies) space, rather than being a regional specialist. In part, it is because I cannot claim the deep language skills that would be required to be a real regional expert. Although I completed a year of intensive Arabic at the beginning of the research, acquiring the level of fluency required to read lengthy and numerous Arabic publications, in which archaic or religious language is rife, was always going to be an ambitious ask—

though definitely worth trying. But perhaps more importantly than my own skills, I always saw this as a study of terrorism as a strategy, of how and why individuals choose that path, rather than a study of the terrorist groups in three different countries. There are plenty of excellent studies of Egypt, Saudi Arabia and Yemen and, whilst I hope my fieldwork has contributed to our knowledge of these, I recognise the challenges of doing so. That is precisely why I wanted this to be a book about terrorism as a strategy and a choice, about how individuals choose it as a strategy and how they see it working.

With that in mind, the remainder of the book falls into four chapters. The three core chapters are devoted to exploring and testing the idea of strategic scripts through three country studies. Chapter 2 focuses on the violent Islamist groups operating in Egypt from the late 1940s, when the Muslim Brotherhood created its Secret Apparatus, to the early 2000s which saw the demise, for different reasons, of the EIG and the EIJ. Egypt is a crucial study: the Muslim Brotherhood was, as Kepel puts it, 'the prototype' of the contemporary Islamist movement and, as we shall see, laid the strategic foundations for al-Qa'ida;[52] the emergence and expansion of larger violent Islamist groups such as *al-Gama'a al-Islamiyya* (EIG) and *al-Jihad al-Islami al-Masri* (EIJ)—as well as lesser known organisations such as *Takfir wa'l-Hijra* and the Military Academy Group—provides fertile territory for analysing the shifting strategies of violent Islamism.

Chapter 3 focuses on the groups which emerged in Saudi Arabia between 1998 and 2007, that is to say the period in which al-Qa'ida in the Arabian Peninsula (AQAP) emerged, escalated and declined. Saudi's religious significance and position in violent Islamist thought has meant that its violent Islamists are not only lauded, but also examined and emulated by other violent extremists. Chapter 4 focuses on Yemen from the emergence of Aden-Abyan Islamic Army through the merger of AQAP's Saudi and Yemeni to the rise of *Ansar al-Shari'a* and ISIS in in 2012. This is the most contemporary and unexamined of the case studies but perhaps, also the richest as the groups under study created new scripts and new challenges for both regional and international regimes.

The concluding chapter draws together a number of reflections from the case studies. In the first place, it identifies a number of recurring strategic scripts, to which the violent Islamists under study returned time and again: survival, power play, mobilisation, provocation, de-legitimisation, attrition, co-operation and de-mobilisation. These are discussed in greater detail below, but the key point is that, while scripts allow strategists to develop expectations about the outcome of a given action, there is a pervasive disparity between the way in which scripts, as theoretical visions, should unfold and the way in which strategies actually unfold. The final chapter argues that this disparity is a consequence of a bias that has been explored in social psychology called 'narrative delusion'. Although strategic scripts are cognitive structures which enable strategists to envisage likely futures, they are also, in essence, stories about the future, describing how situations evolve and conclude. The problem for strategists is that even credible stories can mislead by smothering the role played by luck, shortening the distance between cause and effect or oversimplifying the impact of human agency. But because scripts are persuasive stories, violent Islamists often remain blind to their inherent fallacies. The research concludes by arguing that, for the violent Islamists under study, narrative fallacies very often render scripts inadequate as well as making some more general observations about strategic decision-making outside the world of violent Islamism.

The three main case studies covered in the middle chapters of the volume are underpinned by two sets of sources. The first sources are a set of interviews, not only with a range of diplomatic and security figures with first-hand knowledge of violent Islamism in the countries under investigation, but also with disengaged members of violent Islamist groups as well as individuals with close ties to those organisations. Originally, I had planned to conduct a period of fieldwork in all three countries but various issues prevented travel to Yemen and Saudi Arabia in 2011. In the case of Yemen, as the security situation grew steadily more unstable, it became clear that I would not have been able to obtain insurance for the fieldwork. Skype and telephone interviews were therefore added into the project as alternatives and a number of interviews were conducted in this way. However, I did have the opportunity to conduct periods of fieldwork in Egypt, although the various regime changes throughout the Arab Spring made this challenging. Numerous interviewees were not happy to sign consent forms or go on tape and thus refused to put the interview on a formal footing. This, sadly, meant that much insightful material was not admissible in the study. Over the course of the study, twenty-three formal interviews were conducted; in total, I estimate that a further fifty informal interviews, often producing fascinating material, were also conducted. Reassuringly, the non-admissible interviews did not yield anything substantially different to those which were formal.

The second set of sources were the publications of the terrorist groups under study, in both English and Arabic. This form of data collection presented its own issues: one key problem with these publications was their availability; online magazines published before 2007/8 were virtually impossible to acquire unless they had become part of the *jihadi* canon. More recent publications, in particular of AQAP in Yemen, therefore dominate the research. Equally, English publications, though fewer in number than those in Arabic, also dominate the research because of the difficulties of translation. However, the greatest problem presented by these publications was around credibility. Whilst violent Islamist authors, particularly those disseminating recruitment material, might portray their organisations as functioning in particular ways or as having particular goals, these can rarely be elevated beyond the status of 'claims' without verification. The problem is that verification is hard to come by: how does one authenticate a claim that, for example, the purpose of a particular act of violence was to provoke a target into overreaction? Bearing this in mind, violent Islamist publications are used in this book only in the analysis of an organisation's strategy and scripts. Here, it was felt, the analysis was on safer ground: violent Islamists have much at stake in disseminating a genuine version of their strategic vision, not least in ensuring that all parts of their organisation are working in unison towards shared goals.

2

EGYPT: TERROR AND REPRESSION

Egypt played a central part in the genesis and development of the violent Islamist movement: it was the environment in which the Muslim Brotherhood would be founded and in which it would toy with *jihad*, both conceptually and practically. It was the birth place of less famous organisations, such as *Takfir wa'l-Hijra* (Excommunication and Flight) and the Military Academy Group, who similarly resorted to terrorist violence as they sought to gain critical mass for their confrontation with the regime. Egypt was also the political landscape in which major organisations such as *Tanzim al-Jihad*, Egyptian Islamic Jihad (EIJ; *al-Jihad al-Islami*) and the Egyptian Islamic Group (EIG; *al-Gama'a al-Islamiyya*) waged campaigns of considerable violence. And it was here that ideologues such as Hasan al-Banna, Sayyid Qutb and Abd al-Salam Farag produced the texts that became widely received and perceived as foundational works which inspired and influenced violent Islamist groups for many years.

In light of its position in the trajectory of Islamism, it is not surprising that a good deal of scholarship has examined Egypt's Islamist movement, nor that much of this material focuses, in particular, on the factors and processes that drove Egyptian Islamist groups to adopt violence. For some, particularly political scientists and area specialists, socio-economic failure, ideological reassessment and western hegemony in post-colonial Egypt were central to the emergence of violence in Egypt.[1] For others, predominantly social movement theorists, regime constriction of avenues of political participation was the dominant factor in the production of Islamist violence.[2]

15

Both sets of approaches provide valuable insights into the social and political dimensions of violent Islamism. As yet, however, there are few studies which examine why violent Islamists selected (and eventually rejected) terrorism as a strategy and those analyses which are in circulation tend to focus mainly on ideological factors.[3] In these studies, the decision to adopt terrorist violence—like the decision to reject it—is the product of shifting interpretations of ideology.[4]

In contrast to those studies which view ideological change as the precursor and driver of strategic change, one of the implications of the approach taken to decision-making in this book is that script formation and strategic decision-making are necessarily preceded by a deliberative process which involves envisaging sequences of events, anticipating outcomes, and weighing up options. In this sense, ideology occupies a relatively insignificant role in selecting appropriate strategies, although it may play a greater part when it comes to persuading others that particular courses of action are suitable and should be adopted. This chapter aims to apply the theory of strategic decision-making, outlined in the previous chapter, to a range of violent Islamist groups in Egypt. The chapter not only explores the way in which violent Islamist movements envisage their strategic scripts unfolding but also examines how these scripts work in practice, focusing on the impact and effects of terrorist violence as well as the responses of the Egyptian regime. In order to analyse the de-mobilisation script in detail, the chapter then proceeds to provide an extended examination of the EIG's non-violence initiative of the late 1990s and the EIJ's rejection of violence in the early 2000s; it investigates the strategic reasons for disengagement which underpinned the renunciation of violence and, in so doing, it seeks to relate it to the corpus of revisionist literature produced by the EIG, in particular. The chapter concludes by suggesting that there is a persistent disparity between Egyptian violent Islamist scripts, as stories about the future, and their strategies, as operationalised scripts.

The Secret Apparatus

The foundation of the Muslim Brotherhood (*al-Ikhwan al-Muslimun*) by Hasan al-Banna in 1928 saw the emergence of a formal Islamist movement in the Middle East. At this stage, the Brotherhood was less a political enterprise and more a social and charitable organisation which sought to create an Islamic society through *da'wa* (preaching or, more literally, call (to God)). By the late 1930s, however, the Brotherhood had transitioned from an essentially religious project with limited influence into a well-financed and increasingly political movement whose large membership straddled the full social spectrum.[5] So rapid was its growth and extensive its influence that King Farouk began to see the Brotherhood as a potential threat and when Hasan al-Banna declared himself a candidate in the 1941 general elections, direct conflict between the Brotherhood and the palace seemed a real possibility.[6]

In the event, both parties decided to co-operate, doubtless because they realised that an inevitable and mutually detrimental confrontation was looming. The deal brokered between Mustafa al-Nahhas, the prime minister, and al-Banna, in the spring of 1942, brought welcome reprieve, as well as benefits, for both parties: al-Banna agreed not to stand for election, taking some of the pressure off the regime, in return for the institution of legal measures against prostitution, restrictions on the sale of alcohol and freedom for the Brotherhood to operate throughout Egypt.[7] The deal did not last long; by the winter months of 1942, the British were increasingly suspicious that the Brotherhood had pro-Nazi tendencies and were threatening Egypt's position of neutrality in the war.[8] These suspicions were probably overinflated, but one British intelligence report from this period described a protest during which Brotherhood members chanted '[we] are all Axis soldiers, advance Rommel, down with Churchill'.[9] For the British ambassador, Sir Miles Lampson, this was a step too far and he ordered al-Nahhas to crack down on the spread of the *Ikhwan* across Egypt. Al-Nahhas duly obeyed, retracting the legal measures against prostitution and alcohol consumption, closed all the Brotherhood offices aside from the headquarters in Cairo and temporarily arrested al-Banna.

In response to the crackdown, which signalled the failure of the coalition, alternative strategic scripts were sought and found. In late 1942, al-Banna, fearing further regime aggression, created the Secret Apparatus (*al-Jihaz al-Sirri*) for the specific purpose of protecting the Society by waging defensive *jihad*. It is clear from an open letter in 1943 that, from the outset, al-Banna envisaged a particular situation in which the Secret Apparatus should be used:

> 'Your message is yet unknown to many people, and when they know it and recognize its purposes, they will meet it with the severest opposition and the cruellest enmity. You will then be obliged to face numerous hardships and obstructions. ... One government after another will obstruct you, and each of them will attempt to hinder your activity and block your progress. All the oppressors will exert every effort to restrain you and to extinguish the light of your message... This will lead you to the stage of trial, wherein you will be

imprisoned, detained and banished; your property will be confiscated, your special activities stopped and your homes searched. ...

My Brothers: you are not a benevolent society, nor a political party, nor a local organization having limited purposes. Rather you are a new soul in the heart of this nation to give it life by means of the Qu'ran... If you are told that you are political, answer that Islam admits no such distinction. If you are accused of being revolutionaries, say 'We are voices for right and for peace in which we dearly believe ... If you rise against us or stand in the path of our message, then we are permitted by God to defend ourselves against your injustice'.[10]

Al-Banna realised that the growth of the Brotherhood and increasing popularity of its message would present the regime with a threat to which it was likely to respond with repression and he accordingly furnished the Brotherhood with the resources (the Secret Apparatus) and the strategy (*jihad*) to protect itself. This defensive *jihad* was not only a way of removing obstacles to the Brotherhood's programme of *da'wa* and re-opening the political and social space that had been constricted by the regime, but also of ensuring the continued existence of the movement.[11] In this sense, al-Banna saw *jihad* as a defensive and reactive strategy which could ensure the continuation of the movement by rebuffing state intervention when it threatened to destroy or substantially weaken the Brotherhood. *Jihad*, under this view, was about doing whatever it took to secure one's own survival.

Although al-Banna first activated the Secret Apparatus in late 1947 in response to the partition of Palestine, it was not until 1948 that it was put into action in Egypt—and when it was, it sparked a cycle of violence. The cycle began in January when a cache of weapons and explosives was discovered by police in the Muqattam Hills outside Cairo; a firefight ensued in which several were killed, the weapons confiscated by police and a number of Secret Apparatus members were temporarily arrested, only to be released after claiming that the weapons were for Palestine.[12] Later that year and reportedly on the orders of al-Banna himself, the Secret Apparatus assassinated Ahmed al-Khazinder Bey, a judge notorious for giving harsh sentences to Brotherhood members.[13] When further caches of arms were found along with papers proving the existence of the hitherto unknown Secret Apparatus in the winter of 1948, the relationship between the Brotherhood and the government disintegrated yet further.[14] On the night of 8 December 1948, the government attempted to put the confrontation to an end by confining all Brotherhood volunteers in Palestine to camp and dissolving the Society; the headquarters in Cairo were surrounded and, with the exception of al-Banna, all present were arrested. The Secret Apparatus responded to this just three weeks later by assassinating Mahmud al-Nuqraishi, the prime minister; six weeks after that, the regime responded in kind as Hasan al-Banna himself was gunned down in the street by the secret police.[15]

By limiting the Brotherhood's ability to disseminate their message through *da'wa*, denying them access to weaponry and dissolving the Society, the regime threatened the movement's continued existence. The Secret Apparatus responded with violence in what was essentially an intuitive reaction to the loss of resources and the threat of extinction; this defensive, impulsive *jihad* was used in an effort to persuade the regime that the actual costs of repression (resulting, for example, in the assassination of high-profile political figures) were greater than the potential benefits (a far smaller, less political Islamist movement). In this sense, al-Banna recognised that, when vulnerable, violence is a useful strategy for ensuring survival; it can force an opposition to keep their distance and allow the strategist to get to a place of comparative safety in reasonable shape and from there, new options may emerge.

There was nothing new about the survival script. In the natural world, animals threatened by predators or rivals display an instinctive fight or flight responses to ensure their survival. Nevertheless, it seems that at least part of the reason that the fight script appealed can be found in the political landscape in which al-Banna and the Brotherhood operated. Here political violence was not only rife but widely perceived to be the best way of achieving an organisation's ambitions.[16] The execution of the British Minister for the Middle East, Lord Moyne, by members of the Stern Gang in 1944, for example, was not met with the embittered contempt one might expect amongst Egyptian Islamist movements, but with grudging respect. As Gamal Abdel Nasser said at the time, 'here were men ready to die for their cause, who hold an example to us'.[17] Indeed, it was an example which groups of diverse ideological persuasions took to heart: nationalist organisations attempted to amplify their political voice through violence; communist groups rose to notoriety in the final years of the Second World War with a series of attempted assassinations; and anti-colonialist groups similarly began to target British soldiers in order to force a British withdrawal.[18] In a landscape of competing ideologies in which violence was the *mode du jour*, it seems reasonable to suggest that al-Banna modelled his script on the way in which others sought to achieve their political ambitions.

Whatever the inspiration behind the script, there were clearly inadequacies in the formulation. Al-Banna had underestimated the level of violence required to fend off the regime and had failed to anticipate the extent of the regime's counter-reprisals in response to the assassination of major political figures. In the event, violence simply provoked the palace into responding in kind and the Secret Apparatus lost further members to counter-reprisals and arrest; the atmosphere of repression deepened; the Secret Apparatus responded with more high-profile assassinations and the government with even more wide-ranging arrests and repression. This is one of the critical problems for embryonic movements when they come into direct confrontation with their regimes and when their survival hinges on the outcome of that confrontation. Essentially, as we shall see, there are two options: movements can fight the regime to force it to leave them alone or they can escape confrontation by going into hiding. Both strands of this fight or flight script have difficulties. By fighting, violent Islamist movements often trigger a cycle of violence which depletes their already limited military, human and financial means both through attacks and regime offensives.[19] By withdrawing, however, there are reputational effects: those in the movement committed to the logic of violence may follow another strategic script of their own or defect to a rival organisation *en masse*; supporters urging the leadership to act in pursuit of political goals are likely to be marginalised and lose faith in the movement and the leadership.

Although the Secret Apparatus' fight strategy failed to reflect the script, the Brotherhood's primary goal—survival—was accomplished nonetheless, though this was the product of political necessity and luck rather than strategic intelligence. After the death of al-Banna, open confrontation between the Brotherhood and the regime dwindled and was replaced by a cautious, if hostile, truce. Despite the disparity between the fight script and the realities of confrontation with the regime, this perceived success meant that al-Banna's strategic vision would be praised, emulated and, as its flaws became apparent, critiqued by violent Islamists in Egypt in years to come.

The Fringes of the Brotherhood

On 23 July 1952, King Farouk was deposed by the Free Officers Movement in a coup which ushered in a period of cordial relations between the newly installed regime and the Brotherhood.[20] Nasser recognised that his position was too precarious to risk direct confrontation with the largest organised religious force in Egypt and, although he sought to limit opposition by abolishing all political groups in January 1953, he made a special exception for the

Ikhwan—even going so far as to offer ministerial posts to the Brothers in an attempt to bring them under his control.[21] As Nasser consolidated his tentative hold on power, the Brotherhood sought to cope with the death of al-Banna who, even after his execution, 'remained, in full measure, the final and unqualified authority in the Society'.[22] Under the fragile leadership of Hasan al-Hudaybi, a man far less able to instil loyalty than al-Banna, elements within the Brotherhood began to form their own ideas about how to achieve the Society's political aims, namely the truly Islamic state governed according to the precepts of *shari'a*.

The 1965 Organisation

The informal coalition between the regime and the Society came to an abrupt end in October 1954, when a member of the Brotherhood attempted to assassinate Nasser. The attempt triggered a typically heavy-handed response from the regime, who summarily executed the movement's leaders and arrested thousands of suspected Brothers.[23] Amongst those arrested was Sayyid Qutb and it was under the harsh conditions of the Tora prison in southern Cairo that he wrote his foundational texts to which contemporary violent Islamists would look for strategic and ideological guidance. In theory, Qutb, like al-Banna, considered violence in the form of *jihad* as a purely defensive strategy implemented to 'repel aggression if it occurs' as a consequence of the 'inevitable confrontation' with the regime.[24] A close analysis of his key work, *Ma'alim fi'l-Tariq* ('Milestones'), for example, reveals that violence is never mentioned *per se* and, as John Calvert has pointed out, 'although Qutb spoke about the inevitability of conflict... nowhere in his writings did he advocate the tactic of the Leninist-style coup that become the hallmark of some radical Islamist groups'.[25]

In practice, however, Qutb did consider more aggressive scripts. In 1965, only a few months after he had been released from the Tora prison, Qutb began to meet with a group of Brothers which had coalesced around the material he had written whilst in prison.[26] The group, which came to be known as the 1965 Organisation, consisted primarily of younger, radical members of the Brotherhood and emerged as a distinct faction beyond the control of al-Hudaybi and the Guidance Council.[27] After Qutb's release from prison, this faction began to formulate alternative scripts and to re-interpret Qutb's works to support these strategic scripts. Although Qutb frequently urged restraint at these meetings, pointing to the ordeals of 1954 and 1949, his own vision of a defensive *jihad* increasingly became one of aggression and other strategic options—such as assassinating Nasser in revenge for his treatment of the Brotherhood in 1954, killing the prime minister and directors of the intelligence services or attacking electricity substations to cause panic and confusion—began to be discussed.[28] Attacks on infrastructure were discarded early on because 'such attacks would weaken Egypt's economy and play to the advantage of Israel, the[ir] implacable enemy'; nevertheless, the attraction of political assassination remained and Qutb asked the organisation to step up the pace of their training.[29]

Qutb's original script was purely defensive—it was designed solely 'to deal immediate defensive, preventative and retaliative blows against the government if it moved to crush the organization'—and thus exactly mirrored al-Banna's fight script.[30] Increasingly, however, Qutb began to see this defensive script in ever more offensive terms; it became a way of bridging the gap between the Brotherhood's meagre means and their ambitious ends by confronting the state and mobilising the by now fragile Islamist movement. In the event, the group was unable to realise any of these visions, defensive or offensive: in late July, Qutb's brother, Muhammad, although completely uninvolved in the 1965 Organisation, or indeed the Brotherhood, was arrested. For Qutb, this was an effort to put personal pressure on him and he reportedly remarked that 'the forces of the state feel the presence of the organization, but they lack meaningful information about it. So they strike hoping to find a thread that will lead them to the organization'.[31] And a thread they found: as information about the 1965 Organisation came to light, the regime response was typically uncompromising. Thousands were detained and police brutality was rife; as John Waterbury puts it, 'the basic rule in those days was that if you were found guilty, you went to prison; if you were found innocent, you went to the concentration camp'.[32] Indeed, in the 1966 trial, mere possession of *Ma'alim fi'l-Tariq* was enough to secure a conviction and the prosecution produced, in the words of Sivan, 'a whole dossier—a veritable *explication de texte*—which... was to serve as a linchpin for the act of accusation and of the prosecutors' speeches'.[33]

In August 1966, Sayyid Qutb and the leadership of the 1965 Organisation were sentenced to death: the loss of the ideologue and the harshness of the crackdown all but destroyed the Brotherhood and in the years that followed it barely functioned. Nevertheless, the failures of the Secret Apparatus and the 1965 Organisation provided valuable lessons from which other Islamist groups would learn. With these examples clearly in mind, these groups recognised the inherent difficulties in trying to achieve political ends from what they would call a 'state of weakness' (*marhalat al-istid'af*). Rather than resorting to impulsive acts of revenge, these organisations began to focus on what became the central problem of violent Islamist movements: how to transition from a state of weakness to a state of power.

Takfir wa'l-Hijra and the Military Academy Group

> Our foremost objective is to change the *jahili* system at its very roots—this system which is fundamentally at variance with Islam and which, with the help of force and oppression is keeping us from living the sort of life which is demanded by our creator. Our first step will be to remove ourselves from the *jahili* society and all its values and concepts.[34]

Thus Sayyid Qutb described his vision for achieving the pure Islamic society in *Milestones*. The problem with this vision was that, once again, there was substantial disagreement in the Islamist movement over strategy. This was manifest in an ideological debate about the meaning of *jahiliyya*. The old guard interpreted the term with reference to its less evocative origins (*juhl*) which best translates as 'foolishness'.[35] They argued that *jahiliyya* referred to human flaws and imperfections which should be remedied through *da'wa* (discourse or preaching). To the younger Islamists on the fringes of the Brotherhood, often labelled neo-Islamists or neo-Brethren, *jahiliyya* was an inherent condition of the un-Islamic state, marked specifically by the absence of *shari'a* and the failure to resort to the Qur'an and *hadith* to inform decisions in all areas of public and private life. The neo-Brethren argued that the only way to achieve the truly Islamic state was withdrawal (*mufasala*) from society.

At the fringes of the Brotherhood, as it fractured into multiple competing cliques in the early 1970s, emerged a group who took withdrawal from the *jahili* state very seriously. The organisation called itself the Society of Muslims, but the media referred to it as *Takfir wa'l-Hijra* (Excommunication and Flight), neatly acknowledging the two stages in their strategic vision. Under the leadership of Shukri Mustafa, who had been imprisoned for six years in the 1965 round-up of the Brotherhood's members, the organisation swelled.[36] Shukri demanded complete withdrawal from *jahili* society in order to establish a pure Islamic counter-society. After the arrest of some of his members in 1973, Shukri put this vision into practice. He excommunicated the regime on grounds of apostasy (*takfir*) and, accompanied by a number of followers, promptly departed from Cairo to camp out in caves in the mountains for several months. Even on their return from the mountains in 1974, the group remained withdrawn from society, sharing a number of furnished flats in Cairo's impoverished suburbs of Shubra and Imbaba.[37]

By October 1976, after avoiding the attention of the authorities with some success and gaining a considerable following in the process, a handful of Shukri's followers had absconded to a rival organisation. He ordered the defectors to be punished, but the reprisals inadvertently caught the attention of the police, who stepped in and arrested dozens of his confederates.[38] While police intervention was damaging, the subsequent media attention was of greater concern: a number of articles were written, probably on the government's instruction, in which the Society was characterised as a group of crazed religious oddballs.[39] It did not take long for the Society to respond: in early 1977, the Society kidnapped Muhammed al-Dhahabi, former minister of *waqf* (religious endowments) in an effort to raise their profile, challenge the propaganda campaign and coerce the government into acceding to their demands (which included releasing their imprisoned Brothers, retracting the 'deceitful stories' in the daily newspapers and delivering 200,000 Egyptian Lira).[40] The government was intransigent and refused. A few days later, Shukri ordered the execution of al-Dhahabi, to which the Government responded as it always had done to Islamist violence—with extreme repression.[41] Within days, the entire leadership and the vast majority of the membership had been arrested and, after a suspiciously rapid trial, five were sentenced to death, Shukri among them.

In the beginning, and despite the fact that they were not under immediate threat from the regime, Shukri's strategic vision was based on the fact that the movement was vulnerable and that greater resources needed to be acquired if they were to resist challenges from the regime. For Shukri, then, the crucial problem for violent Islamists was in transitioning from what he termed the 'state of weakness' (*marhalat al-istid'af*) to a 'phase of power' (*marhalat al-tamakkun*). He explained that:

> power, like everything else, has degrees. This phase begins, in my view, when the circle of oppression and weakness is broken; it then progresses to conquest and expansion. There is no doubt that when the Muslims made the *hegira* from Mecca to Medina, they were already at the first stage of the phase of power since no one could impose anything on them any longer.[42]

The central problem of getting to the 'phase of power' was at the core of Shukri's strategic calculations and drove much of his vision. In this sense, Shukri's Society of Muslims sits in sharp contrast to the Secret Apparatus.

The latter had opted for the fight strand of the survival script in response to state repression, the former, by contrast, chose the 'flight' strand in order to gain sufficient strength to withstand potential regime intervention or to challenge the regime if circumstances allowed. So important was the acquisition of resources that the failures of Secret Apparatus and the 1965 Organisation, which Shukri attributed to their failure to cultivate and expand upon their resources, loomed large in his strategic calculations. 'I accuse these leaders of the Muslim Brethren...', Shukri reportedly said, 'who have led men to their doom, who have delivered them to the executioners, the gallows, the prisons, of high treason. They have ruined men's lives, toying with them irresponsibly'.[43]

For Shukri, throwing away lives in the state of weakness was an act of treason; he recognised that resources were difficult to come by and should be nurtured and shepherded with diligence. Attempting to challenge the regime before 'critical mass' had been acquired, he reasoned, could only bring about the demise of Islamist oppositions. The police intervention of 1976 and subsequent media ridicule, however, changed the situation and Shukri was forced to find an alternative script. It was no longer enough to simply build up resources in an effort to attain the 'phase of power'; he had lost too many people, and too much financial resource already and, more importantly, the media had tarnished Shukri's standing amongst other Islamists. As the situation altered, so Shukri recognised the need for an alternative strategy which could restore the Society's reputation, reassert their Islamist credentials and reacquire some of the resources which had been lost. In this script—the power play script—he essentially envisaged using violence as a way of sending a message that the organisation had sufficient resolve, capacity and ability to threaten the government, satisfy potential supporters and outrank rivals.

At around the same time as the Society of Muslims was shifting strategies, another movement, which became known as the Military Academy Group, was founded on the margins of the Brotherhood by a young man called Salih Siriyya.[44] The two organisations quickly became rivals, not least because both aimed to recruit from a limited number of devout Islamists and jealously guarded their members. The difference between the two organisations was entirely strategic, pivoting on the way in which their similar political goals could be brought about. Where Shukri believed all society to be *jahili* and preached *mufasala kamil* (complete separation), Siriyya and his supporters were convinced that only the regime was *jahili*.[45] As Kepel puts it, 'unlike Shukri, Siriyya created no counter-society and organized no *hijra* to Cairo's furnished flats. His disciples continued to lead normal lives so as not to attract the attention of the authorities'.[46] In April 1974, the group developed an ambitious plot to seize the Military Academy in Heliopolis, raid the armoury and then use the weaponry they plundered to kill Sadat as he drove by in his motorcade. It was too ambitious. The operation was a complete failure; the attackers were spotted by soldiers stationed at the Academy, killed in the ensuing shoot out and in the days that followed, the majority of the organisation were arrested and Siriyya was sentenced to death.[47]

Although Siriyya's Military Academy Group withdrew not to the mountains but into society, they essentially acted upon the same 'flight' strand of the survival script as the Society of Muslims. They sought to avoid detection and, by keeping all members safe from state intervention, to increase their available means and reach critical mass. The 'flight' strategy was remarkably successful in achieving both organisations' short term ambitions—namely to avoid detection and to allow them to get to the next stage without being eliminated in the process. Although they were similar in selecting, if not in implementing, the 'flight' strand, both organisations diverged when they reached the next stage, evaluated their options and followed a new strategic script. *Takfir wa'l-Hijra* adopted the power play script in the face of arrests and a media smear campaign, deploying violence to signal their resolve, demonstrate their operational expertise and to repair reputational damage in an effort to cement their status as an Islamist movement. The Military Academy Group, by contrast, selected the mobilisation script; they saw Sadat as the final obstacle between a *jahili* and an Islamic state. In this sense, violence for the Military Academy Group was not about bringing publicity to the cause but about clearing the way for a popular, but decidedly religious, uprising. Neither strategy worked in practice: the kidnapping of Muhammed al-Dhahabi failed to coerce the regime to concede to Shukri's demands, leaving the organisation's reputation in tatters and its carefully gathered membership dead or dispersed; Siriyya's strategy failed on tactical grounds at the first stage, though it seems highly unlikely that the assassination of Sadat would have toppled the regime and paved the way for the Islamic state.[48]

A large part of the problem for both Shukri and Siriyya was deciding when to change the focus from acquiring resources to pursuing ends or, to put the same problem a different way, how to judge when sufficient resources had been acquired. This 'use it or lose it' dilemma troubles most violent opposition movements: although there is a certain logic to gathering resources, eventually the need to attend to political goals will outweigh the benefits of recruitment, in particular when there is pressure from below to pursue objectives. There are numerous considerations over whether further resources actually can be acquired, whether sufficient resources have been found to proceed to the next stage, if not to long-term political ambitions, whether resources are of a magnitude comparable to both one's political ambitions and those of one's opposition, whether the only way to get further resources is to proceed to the next stage and hope that violence is (to echo Bakunin) the best way to spread principles. With so many factors, the possibilities for self-delusion, absurd optimism and 'bad mathematics' are seemingly endless. Time and again, as we shall see, violent Islamists devoted considerable energy to accruing political support and recruiting new personnel only to lose them by confronting the enemy before sufficient resources had been acquired.

Tanzim al-Jihad

The first half of the 1970s had been more amenable for violent Islamists. Relations between the Islamist movement and the regime had begun to thaw, as large numbers of Islamists were released from jail as part of the presidential pardons in the aftermath of the 1973 war; as part of this more relaxed environment, government funds were even being poured into Islamist student bodies on university campuses (known as the *jama'at Islamiyya* (Islamic Associations)).[49] But the actions of the Military Academy Group and the Society of Muslims in the mid 1970s irrevocably altered Sadat's perception that Islamists could ever be potential allies.

As he attempted to negotiate a peace deal with Israel, he became increasingly reluctant to expend political capital on organisations which fundamentally opposed him and he began the awkward process of unravelling his relationship with the Islamist movement. Despite the fact that the *jama'at* enjoyed a considerable popular following, he focused his efforts on university campuses, retracting the Islamic Associations' funding, re-structuring the General Union of Students and freezing its assets. In confronting the *jama'at*, Sadat achieved his short-term ambitions of limiting Islamist authority in the universities; but it did not take long for the *jama'at* to simply go to ground and, in the process, fragment into myriad cliques and loose coalitions outside the campuses and beyond the control of the regime.[50] As Heikal puts it:

> Consciously or unconsciously, the régime seemed determined to put to the test Marx's dictum that religion is the opium of the people ... [this was] a rough and ready attempt to mask political and social problems beneath the *galabiyeh* and the *chador*. Other strains of fundamentalism were at work elsewhere, unseen and

uncontrolled by the authorities. The régime and its backers were creating a monster, and one day, sooner probably than they expected, it was going to turn and rend them.[51]

One organisation which emerged, inspired by Qutbian ideology and the call to *jihad*, from the dissolution of the *jama'at* was *Tanzim al-Jihad* (The *Jihad* Organisation). The organisation had its roots in a number of Islamist 'clusters' in Cairo and Middle Egypt.[52] The leader of the Cairo branch, main ideologue and author of their central text, *al-Farida al-Gha'iba* (The Neglected Imperative), was an electrician named Abd al-Salam Farag.[53] His work focused on the strategic reasons for the failure of the Military Academy Group and the Society of Muslims and argued that the Islamist movement required a radical reassessment of its strategies if it was to achieve its political goals.[54] The leader of the Middle Egypt branch was Karam al-Zuhdi; having read Farag's work and heard of his reputation, he arranged to meet him in the spring of 1980 to discuss the possibility of co-operation. The two leaders agreed that the Islamist movement desperately needed a strategic re-evaluation if it was to attain its political goals and decided in a second meeting in June 1980 that a formal (if loose) alliance between the two groups could be profitable. To lend the embryonic organisation the religious credibility it would need for recruitment, they co-opted Umar Abd al-Rahman, a Sheikh from Faiyyoum, to provide theological justification for their actions in the form of *fatwa* and to act as a figurehead.[55]

Sadat was perfectly aware that the Islamists were regrouping and had violence in mind, but there was little he could do without isolating non-violent Islamists. Indeed, it was not until 1981 that Sadat was able to confront these radical Islamist clusters. The pretext came after a brutal episode in al-Zawiyya al-Hamra in June 1981. The origins of the tragedy remain unclear, but what is known is that clashes of startling violence took place in the impoverished Cairene suburb of al-Zawiyya al-Hamra between Coptic and Muslim communities in which '[m]en and women were slaughtered; babies were thrown from windows, their bodies crushed on the pavements below; there was looting, killing, arson'.[56] Sadat capitalised on the episode, formally dissolving the *jama'at* and issuing warrants for the arrest of its members. The reprisals were reasonably successful in breaking the remnants of the *jama'at* on the campuses, but they did nothing to challenge the violent Islamist clusters nor the less lethal *jama'at*, many of whom, in the words of a former British diplomat 'dispensed with their *galabiyyat*, shaved their beards and went underground to join more violent associations such as *Tanzim al-Jihad*'.[57]

The events of al-Zawiyya al-Hamra in 1981 and the subsequent repression not only produced increasingly embittered antipathy towards Sadat amongst the Islamist movement, but presented its more radical and violent elements with an opportunity. Khalid al-Islambuli, whose brother Muhammad had been arrested in the round-up, was a lieutenant in the artillery corps and had been placed in charge of an armoured transport vehicle at the anniversary celebration of the 1973 war, which Sadat would be attending. In the wake of his brother's arrest, which left him devastated, he came up with a crude but effective plan for assassinating Sadat which he passed on to Farag: he would replace the men under his command with three accomplices, smuggle in hand grenades and machine guns and kill Sadat as the vehicle passed the presidential box.

In late September 1981, Farag and his deputy, Abbud al-Zumr, met with their opposite number from Middle Egypt, Karam al-Zuhdi, to discuss the attack. Although both Farag and al-Zuhdi agreed that the assassination of Sadat was necessary, there was little agreement about how to proceed after the assassination. For Farag, the plan was an ideal opportunity to kill Sadat, initiate a *coup d'état* in Cairo and establish the Islamic State. For al-Zuhdi, the assassination would leave Egypt ungoverned and create the kind of confusion and panic in which he could overthrow security structures in Asyut, occupy and Islamise the city and from there gather the momentum required for establishing the Islamic Society. By contrast, al-Zumr, an air force intelligence officer with a speciality in security, argued that the government forces, even in the aftermath of the assassination, would be able to regain control unless there was significant popular support—a precondition which was, he argued, absent. In the event, al-Zumr was overruled and the strategic visions of Farag and al-Zuhdi merged: the assassination would be followed by a military offensive against security 'nerve centres' in Asyut; this, in turn, would allow Farag to incite a popular religious revolution which would overthrow the last remaining vestiges of the *jahili* regime.

On 6 October, al-Islambuli and three associates leapt out of their armoured vehicle, erratically hurled hand grenades and opened fire on the president. In full view of the television cameras, al-Islambuli could be heard shouting: 'I am Khaled al-Islambuli. I have killed Pharaoh. I do not fear death'.[58] Although the Asyut operation was meant to follow immediately, the uprising had taken longer to organise than al-Zuhdi had bargained on and it was not until 8 October, on the first day of *Eid al-Adha*, that the operation took place. Several groups of militants broke into the security headquarters, beheading the Christian commander and massacring those inside; at first it seemed the operation was a success as local security forces failed to respond but, the following day, paratroopers were flown in from Cairo and brought the situation under control.

As al-Zumr predicted, the assassination of Sadat changed very little. Although Sadat's death was received with jubilation in both Islamist and non-Islamist circles, not least because he was seen to be dictatorial, eccentric and living 'in a world of his own creation in which he was the continuing star and from which all hostile forces were effectively excluded', it singularly failed to bring about the mass uprising which Farag had envisaged, nor indeed, to paralyse state security structures as al-Zuhdi had predicted.[59] Indeed, Kepel sums up the long-term effects of the assassination as:

> a spectacular success for the movement, coming after two decades of abortive confrontations with the state and triumphant repression. But after 6 October and the brief alarm aroused by Islamist sedition in the city of Asyut on 8 October, that success proved to be no more than spectacle. Sadat was replaced by his vice-president, and there was no structural modification of the state likely to satisfy the Islamist movement. Repression against the movement intensified, and it was condemned to languish. To employ the terminology inspired by Qutb, the movement entered a new 'phase of weakness'.[60]

Although both Farag and al-Zuhdi had their own strategic visions, the opportunity to assassinate Sadat was so enticing to both parts of the alliance that they had to reconsider and reformulate their scripts in cooperation with one another. In the end, neither Farag's nor al-Zuhdi's strategic scripts remained in their original form, rather they were combined and melded to produce a new hybridised script. The assassination undertaken by Farag's group was to be followed by a military offensive against security 'nerve centres' executed by al-Zuhdi's group. These two blows, they anticipated, would send the state reeling in confusion, freeing the population to rise up in a popular religious revolution which would overthrow the last remaining vestiges of the *jahili* regime.[61] In this sense, the strategy that was implemented was the product of two separate scripts which were latticed together in the meeting of September 1981. It is important to take each script separately in order to establish how, individually, both groups envisaged their strategies unfolding and why particular scripts appealed to them before going on to examine how these strategic visions were merged and exploring the effects of this hybridisation.

Essentially, the Cairo group under Farag followed what we might term a 'mobilisation' script: he saw violence in the form of political assassination as a tool for liberating the Egyptian people from the authoritarianism of a *jahili* regime and thus for inciting a popular Islamic insurrection which would overthrow the government and pave the way for the establishment of the Islamic state. This strategic vision was modelled, in large part, on the Iranian Revolution of 1979, whose popular uprising had found its imitators across the Muslim world.[62] In his interrogations, Farag would return time and again to the Iranian Revolution as a successful model for inciting an Islamic revolution and achieving political goals.[63] Abbud al-Zumr, the deputy of the Cairo branch, was equally clear about the influence of the Iranian script. At his trial he said:

> Our plan was based on a popular revolution and the preparation of the rank-and-file was towards that aim... popular revolution will solve the problem of the armed forces and the police because it is impossible for them to turn their guns on the people... The Iranian experience shows that in the event of popular revolution it is very difficult for the armed forces and the police to combat the popular masses who want the application of God's *shari'a*.[64]

In this sense, Farag and al-Zumr envisaged popular uprising as a way of presenting the regime with two choices, both of which were detrimental to the regime and advantageous to the *Tanzim*. State repression of vast portions of the population would not only be morally unacceptable and politically untenable but also serve explicitly to legitimise Islamist claims about regime authoritarianism and impiety. If, on the other hand, the regime chose to weather the storm by not reacting to an Islamic revolution, they would once again implicitly condone and legitimise the Islamist politico-religious philosophy.

The fact that, in formulating this script, Farag focused so heavily on the regime, is significant. Although he sought to emulate the Iranian revolution in his strategic vision, it was largely to avert what he saw as the causes of the strategic failure of other Egyptian violent Islamists, about which he was absolutely clear. As he wrote in *Farida al-Gha'iba*:

> How can nonviolent propaganda [*da'wa*] be widely successful when all means of mass communication today are under the control of the pagan and wicked state and under the control of those who are at war with God's religion...There are, however, those who say that they will emigrate to the desert and then come back and confront the Pharaoh, as Moses did, and then God will make the ground swallow the Pharaoh up together with his army... All these strange ideas only result from having forsaken the only true and religiously allowed road towards establishing an Islamic state. To begin by putting an end to imperialism is not laudatory and not a useful act. It is only a waste of time. We must concentrate on our own Islamic situation: we have to establish God's religion in his own

country first, and to make the Word of God supreme ... There is no doubt that the first battlefield for jihad is the extermination of these infidel leaders and to replace them by [sic] a complete Islamic order. From here we should start.[65]

Farag therefore felt that other groups failed not because of the gulf between their means and their ends, but because they attempted to gain critical mass before confronting the regime; this was, according to him, a fruitless enterprise at best and plain dereliction of duty at worst. Rather, Farag argued, the best way to maximise meagre means was to escalate as soon as possible: this would not only increase the coercive volume of political demands, but provide far greater 'advertisement of the cause' than producing pamphlets or hiding in the mountains. In this sense, Farag essentially attempted to bypass the survival script which had been adopted by groups as they transitioned to violence; based on the outcome of his predecessors in Egypt, he rationalised that there was little point in attempting to gather resources in order to reach the 'phase of power', 'since ultimately it all led to the gallows'; instead, Islamist groups had to confront the enemy if they were to persuade others that they had resolve and expertise and were therefore deserving of popular support.[66]

Al-Zuhdi and the Assyut group, by contrast, wanted to follow an attritional script which fell into two distinct strategic phases. In the first stage, terrorism would be used in the south in order to drive out Coptic influence, reduce the authority of the regime and, ultimately, create an Islamic mini-state. For al-Zuhdi, the Copts represented a genuine threat to the Islamism in Upper Egypt and, therefore had to be the first targets.[67] As Montassir al-Zayyat, a member of the Cairo grouping who would become a lawyer for many violent Islamists, put it, 'we were preparing ourselves for an armed struggle in the desert. Our goal was to resist a possible attack by the Christians who we really believed were stockpiling weapons in their churches'.[68] At his trial, al-Zuhdi echoed this, saying:

> The way I see it, the Christians are concentrated in Minya and Asyut and they take advantage of numbers to hold demonstrations of strength and superiority. They have arms and this is what encourages the Muslim youth to react forcibly against missionary proselytism [da'wa]... [they are] waiting for the day to take them out, as in Lebanon, so they can turn Egypt into a Coptic country whose capital would be Asyut...[69]

It is interesting that al-Zuhdi's analysis of Coptic strategy should so closely mirror his own script. The Copts, so his argument runs, practise a parallel form of da'wa in order to achieve a state of strength from which they will launch an insurgency, capturing the South and creating a Christian state on

Islamic territory. The only way to prevent this, in al-Zuhdi's strategic calculation, was to pre-empt Coptic violence and gain the upper hand by coercing
them to leave the south. Only once the Coptic presence had been removed
could the regime be confronted and expelled.

In the second stage, al-Zuhdi envisaged abandoning terrorism as a strategy
and replacing it with an insurgent war waged from the safe havens of the now
truly Islamic mini-state. This stage was born from parallels abroad. Al-Zuhdi
was conscious that outside Egypt other organisations with consonant ideological visions were successfully making headway for their causes by deploying
attritional insurgent scripts. As the image of the *mujahid*, living off the land
and attacking vastly superior enemies before melting into the distance came
to the fore as a key item of Islamist propaganda, so al-Zuhdi became increasingly convinced of the potential success an insurgency could have in the
Egyptian context. As one lifelong observer of violent Islamism in Egypt noted
to the author, 'don't underestimate the sexiness of the AK47. The image of the
lone Palestinian from the PLO or Fatah wandering through the desert had its
impact on… the *Gama'a*'.[70]

In the end, of course, neither script was implemented in its original form.
With the exception of al-Zuhdi's pre-emptive campaign against the Coptic
communities of the south, both scripts were woven together in their entirety:
Farag's decapitation of the regime and al-Zuhdi's occupation of territory
would simultaneously paralyse state responses and incite an Islamic uprising
which would overthrow the, by now, fragile regime. Indeed, there was nothing fundamentally wrong with the new combined script: none of its internal
elements were inherently in conflict with one another and the various stages
seemed plausible in theory. In practice, however, the script made a number of
unrealistic claims and the strategy was a failure: in particular, Farag's assumption that the assassination of Sadat would initiate a popular uprising was—as
al-Zumr had pointed out in the meeting in 1981—ill-judged and, although
al-Zuhdi's group were able to overthrow security centres in Asyut, they could
not defend themselves against the subsequent military response from Cairo.
In this sense, the hybrid script failed not because it contained elements of
two different scripts which were interwoven, but because these constituent
parts were inherently flawed: Sadat's death was followed by jubilation but not
by a popular insurrection, the regime remained broadly functional and the
security 'nerve centres' far from being paralysed responded to a new situation
rapidly. Despite Farag's careful evaluation of the failures of his predecessors
and the attention he devoted to bypassing these, the 'strategic gap'—the space

between how scripts were envisaged to work and how they actually worked—remained.

The Decline and Fall of the EIG

After the assassination of Sadat, the regime responded as it always had done to Islamist violence—with severe repression. Mubarak reactivated the Emergency Law, first established in 1958 under Nasser, which suspended constitutional protections and members of the *Tanzim al-Jihad* in both Cairo and Middle Egypt were rapidly rounded up.[71] In April 1982, Abd al-Salam Farag, Khaled al-Islambuli and his three accomplices were sentenced to death and the remaining leaders of the *Tanzim* were given life sentences. A second trial of three hundred and two lower-ranking members of the *Tanzim al-Jihad*, amongst them Ayman al-Zawahiri, lasted for over three years at the end of which most were given relatively short sentences which they had already served in the intervening period.[72]

The execution of Farag and the brutal prison experience was central to the development of violent Islamism in Egypt. Structurally, it paved the way for a younger leadership to fill the void created by the loss of Farag. The members of this faction, informally led by the young Ayman al-Zawahiri who had risen to the fore during the trials, became increasingly militant as they witnessed the torture of violent Islamists and experienced it for themselves.[73] During his incarceration, al-Zawahiri described his treatment at the hands of the prison guards in an interview to foreign journalists who were brought to the prison, saying:

> We suffered the severest inhuman treatment. They kicked us, they beat us, they whipped us with electric cables, they shocked us with electricity... And they used the wild dogs... [and] they hung us over the edges of the doors with our hands tied at the back! They arrested the wives, the mothers, the fathers, the sisters and the sons... where is justice?[74]

As the younger members gained respect and authority as a consequence of this treatment, there developed a vigorous—eventually, vituperative—debate over who should lead the *Tanzim al-Jihad* which, ultimately, dissolved the (by now fragile) alliance. The Cairo group argued that Sheikh Umar Abd al-Rahman could not lead a group of the faithful because he was blind; those from Middle Egypt responded that al-Zawahiri could not lead such a group either because he was imprisoned.[75] As hostility grew, so the two groups diverged and became discrete identities with their own formal titles: the Cairo group emerged as the EIJ under the command of Ayman al-Zawahiri; the Middle Egypt group fell under the leadership of al-Zuhdi and became the EIG.

In reality, as we shall see, this was less a debate about leadership and more a question of conflicting strategic visions.[76] Al-Zawahiri, like his strategic mentor Farag, envisaged a mobilisation script which involved assassinating the leaders of the regime followed by the establishment of an Islamic state through a popular Islamic revolution. Al-Zuhdi, by contrast, continued to champion his long-standing attritional script of occupying territory and establishing an Islamic mini-state from which they could conduct their final insurgent confrontation with the regime.[77] These two groups, with their similar titles, the shifting allegiances of their members and their shared experiences in prison and beyond, make for difficult, sometimes incoherent, history. In order to simplify matters, this section falls into two parts. The first part examines the EIG, focusing on the scripts they envisaged and the strategies they implemented in Egypt; the second explores the growth of the EIJ, scrutinising the way in which their strategic scripts were moulded by al-Zawahiri's experience of Afghanistan.

In the mid-1980s, as the war in Afghanistan against the Soviets reached its climax, most members of EIG left Egypt for Peshawar where Abdullah Azzam and Osama bin Laden had established the *Maktab al-Khidamat* (Services Bureau) to sort administrative difficulties for the *mujahideen* and the *Bayt al-Ansar* (House of the Supporters) which provided them with quarters.[78] Although the EIG was nominally run by Karam al-Zuhdi who was the central figure in the organisation's 'historic leadership', he remained in prison and it was Ta'lat Fu'ad Qasim who took over the day-to-day running of the organisation in Peshawar. Meanwhile, Sheikh Umar Abd al-Rahman had re-installed himself in the Faiyyoum Oasis, and, aside from making trips to Afghanistan via Peshawar, occupied his time by issuing a tirade of *fatawa*, devoted largely to attacking the Coptic community and to enforcing Islamic morality in urban centres.[79] Nevertheless, as the Afghan *jihad* wound down and, in February 1989, came to a formal end in the Soviet withdrawal, EIG members returned home to swell the ranks of the organisation on Egyptian territory.

As the Afghan Arabs returned from the *jihad* at the end of the 1980s, there was a noticeable escalation in attacks in Egypt. In the years from 1970 to 1989, approximately a hundred and twenty deaths were recorded in total, but between 1992 and 1997, there was a total of 1,442 casualties in near daily attacks, about ninety per cent of which were the work of the EIG.[80] Kepel usefully describes the EIG's strategic vision at this stage:

[The EIG] envisaged open, widespread recruitment, the control of whole areas of territory seized from the state, and the imposition in those areas of the Islamic order. Militants understood this in moral terms (harrying individuals whose morality was suspect, forcing closures of video shops, hairdressers, liquor stores, cinemas and so on). It also had a doctrinal-juridical aspect (Copts should be coerced into paying the protection tax prescribed by the sharia for non-Muslims living under Islamic domination) and a political-military one (state officials, policemen and so on should be physically attacked at every opportunity).[81]

In this sense, the EIG envisaged, as they had prior to the assassination of Sadat, a decidedly attritional script. Violence, both vigilantist and terrorist, was to be used against the local population in order to coerce them to behave according to Islamic rules and thus to 'Islamise' territory; equally, violence was to be used against the state to erode its resources and, in so doing, to force the regime to retreat thus giving the organisation control over tracts of territory.[82]

Buoyed by the return of veterans of the Afghan *jihad*, the EIG began to escalate their attritional script. Following a rumour that the Christians had developed a special spray which, when applied to veils of Muslim women, would produce the sign of the cross if washed, they resumed their campaign of attacks on the Coptic communities of Upper Egypt.[83] These attacks increased threefold between 1992 and 1994 in comparison with the entire preceding decade and continued until the EIG de-mobilised in 1997.[84] Attacks on critics of Islamist ideology similarly escalated. In October 1990, the EIG executed Rifaat al-Mahgoub, a former academic who became speaker of Egypt's Parliament.[85] On 8 June 1992, they assassinated Farag Foda, a sharp-witted satirist of the Islamist community who had recently written an article which argued that Islamist motivations were less about politics and more about sexual frustration.[86]

In the following years, the EIG continued to target secular intellectuals: threats were made against Nasr Abu Zeid, a university professor who was forcibly divorced from his wife by a special tribunal on the grounds that a Muslim woman could not be married to an apostate; numerous threats were also made against Nobel laureate, Naguib Mahfouz, which culminated in an assassination attempt when he was stabbed by a member of the EIG in October 1994. To these by-now-standard elements of the attrition script, the EIG added attacks against the tourist trade and, by extension, Egypt's financial sector. In 1992, Sheikh Umar Abd al-Rahman, who had now relocated to the US from Sudan, issued a *fatwa* declaring tourism *haram* and 'an enterprise of debauchery that promoted alcoholism'.[87] EIG members duly acted. The campaign began in Upper Egypt, where they attacked a boat on the Nile and later

German tourists in Asyut and in Qena; in 1993, Cairo became the focus with bombings of tourist hotspots, cafés and coach parties. Although these attacks, which continued intermittently until 1997, had negligible long-term impact on tourism, they were at least partially successful in advertising the cause and gaining the attention of the under-privileged youth on the periphery of Egypt's urban centres.[88]

Indeed, the EIG were becoming increasingly popular. Hafez and Wiktorowicz, for example, argue that they had been able to establish "'liberated zones" in some of the towns of Upper Egypt and Greater Cairo. In the Asyut city of Dairut, the Gama'a controlled approximately 150 mosques and in some neighbourhoods, they imposed complete control'.[89] One interview with a former British intelligence official suggested that various parts of Cairo—al-Zawiyya al-Hamra, Boulaq al-Dakrour and Imbaba—were essentially 'Gama'a fiefdoms', which the 'regime left them to run'.[90] My own wanderings through Imbaba and interviews with its inhabitants—even twenty years on—confirmed this: people remembered deliveries of rice and bread, even meat; others remembered hand-outs of clothing and, in the aftermath of the 1992 earthquake, medical supplies and tents marked with '*Islam howa al-hal*' (Islam is the solution).[91] Increasingly, the EIG (and the Islamist movement more broadly) were capitalising on the permissive climate by running political and social systems which the state had failed to implement properly.[92]

By 1992, with their ranks swelled by personnel from the Afghan front and widespread popular support, the EIG escalated their campaign of attrition. They not only increased the rate and lethality of their violence, as we have seen, but focused it on multiple targets: secular intellectuals, the tourist industry and the Coptic community alike. Simultaneously, they began to take control of certain districts in Cairo and the cities of Upper Egypt through social activism, regulating behaviour with the threat and reality of vigilantist violence whilst doling out supplies to improve their image. As Ta'lat Fu'ad Qasim said in an interview with Hisham Mubarak:

> First we are making ongoing preparations for a military coup. The security forces don't know about these because they are preoccupied with skirmishes in the *Sa'id* [Upper Egypt]. Second we are working in the area of mass mobilization. When the Islamic revolution happens there will be mass support to head off foreign intervention.[93]

Although Qasim talks of mobilisation, the EIG's strategic vision fits more comfortably with the description of attrition. Violence was not used in order to destabilise the regime and incite a popular Islamic revolution, as Farag had seen it and as it would be in a 'mobilisation' script, but to remove *jahili* presence by enforcing Islamic behaviour and evicting Copts, tourists, secular Egyptians and government authority from Islamic space. Indeed, it was broadly consonant with traditional scripts of attrition used by insurgents. Robert Taber provides an enlightening account of the insurgent script of attrition:

> Analogically the guerrilla fights the war of the flea, and his military enemy suffers the dog's disadvantages: too much to defend; too small, ubiquitous, and agile an enemy to come to grips with. If the war continues long enough—this is the theory—the dog succumbs to exhaustion and anæmia without ever having found anything on which to close his jaws or to rake with his claws.... the flea, having multiplied to a veritable plague of fleas through long series of small victories, each drawing its drop of blood, each claiming the reward of a few more captured weapons to arm yet a few more partisans, concentrates his forces for a decisive series of powerful blows.[94]

The EIG's script virtually replicates this description. In essence, they envisaged attrition by 'Islamisation': they sought to occupy territory by expelling all influences that were not deemed to be Islamic and nurturing all those which were. This was a painstaking process, driven by a series of small victories—an assassination here, a foothold in a district there—rather than a single confrontation with the opposition. Eventually, they rationalised, they would transition from the 'state of weakness' to the 'phase of power', by gaining territory and ensuring that that territory was occupied solely by 'true' Muslims. Once critical mass had been reached, they could confront the regime directly with force.

In practice, however, the script failed to take account of the fact that if one constantly gnaws at an opposition, carving off minute morsels here and there, then that opposition will, in all likelihood, try to swat the flea before allowing itself to bleed to death. In mid-1992, Mubarak took this option and confronted the EIG, largely, one suspects, in response to the assassination of Farag Foda and execution of Rifaat al-Mahgoub.[95] Primarily, this involved mass arrest of suspects: between 1992 and 1997, more than 47,000 were arrested; in 1992 alone, 9,248 people were detained (an average, Burgat points out, of twenty-five per day) and by 1994, the total number of political prisoners exceeded 24,000.[96] Even in 2000, after the release of some detainees as a result of the Non-Violence Initiative, it was estimated that between 15,000 and 16,000 political prisoners were still in detention. The policy of mass arrests was facilitated by the introduction of Article 86 of Law 97 in 1992 which incorporated elements so generalised that it could 'brand almost anyone it deemed fit as a terrorist'.[97] Article 86a was particularly ill-defined, allowing for a sentence of execution or a life sentence of hard labor for the supplying of groups, gangs or other terrorist formations with weapons, ammunition, explosives, materials, instruments, funds or information that assist them in carrying out their aims.[98]

Arbitrary detention was accompanied by military presence and aggression. In May 1992, 2,000 troops were deployed for several months in the south where they imposed a curfew and established what amounted to martial law in areas where the majority of the population had clearly sided with the EIG.[99] In 1992, Sheikh Gaber, a military commander in EIG, boasted to Reuters that Imbaba had become 'an Islamic Republic' (a name which it still holds, affectionately, today). A month later, 14,000 troops moved in and occupied the quarter for six weeks, removing some 5,000 supporters and militants.[100] Individuals were arbitrarily stopped, detained temporarily and tortured; by the late 1980s, female members of Islamist families were increasingly being included in these round-ups.[101]

By late 1996, the group was beginning to flag. Regime repression had brought about the death, arrest or execution of many of the *mujahideen* who had returned from Peshawar and although the group was far from destroyed, they had lost significant morale and confidence in their script. This is, perhaps, not surprising: in spite of the organisation's best efforts, considerable finance and sizeable membership they had not been able to realise their strategic vision. In 1997, the *Shura* Council of the EIG decided to relinquish violence as a strategy for achieving its ends. While the decision was widely adhered to (it was even briefly supported by Sheikh Abd al-Rahman, from jail in the US), various elements of the organisation resented the ceasefire and five months later, on 17 November 1997, EIG elements, disguised as members of the security forces, massacred fifty-eight civilians and four security guards in the Temple of Hatshepsut in Luxor.

As we shall see, this is the problem with escalation. By pursuing a script with greater vigour in order to increase the coercive volume of one's political demands, one inevitably invites a backlash which endangers one's own survival. Neumann and Smith, who examine the EIG's escalation policy, echo this analysis in their discussion of what they term the 'escalation trap', arguing that 'any belligerent that faces a militarily more potent adversary has to take extreme care not to push the enemy into a corner to a point where it feels sufficiently desperate to escalate the war to a level at which the repression becomes ruthless and total, thus threatening the terrorist group's very existence'.[102] From the perspective of scripts, the escalation trap is a further manifestation of the gulf between strategic vision and strategic action. The EIG's attritional script was carefully formulated and, judging by the fact that EIG members acted according to their assigned roles within scripts rather than pursuing their own personal terrorist visions, carefully communicated throughout the organisation; moreover the escalation was supported by considerable resources and substantial public support.[103] But, despite the fact that the strategy was implemented as intended, inadequacies in the script meant that the EIG failed to bring about any substantive change in the Egyptian political landscape.

The EIJ

If the story of the EIG is one of strategic unity, then the story of the EIJ is one of internal debate, dissent and, ultimately, organisational fracture. In 1986, after completing his prison sentence, al-Zawahiri went to Peshawar via Saudi Arabia; here he joined Sayyid Imam al-Sharif (a.k.a. Dr Fadl),who had been part the *Tanzim al-Jihad* but, by fleeing to Pakistan, had avoided the October 1981 arrests. In the years that followed, al-Zawahiri and Dr Fadl began to reconstitute the EIJ: they released a monthly magazine, *al-Fath* (The Conquest), along with a book by Dr Fadl, *al-Umdah fi Idad al-Uddah* (The Essential Guide for Preparation), and became fully embedded in the community of Afghan Arabs.[104] This was an important period of development for the EIJ during which they were confronted with new strategic visions and had to defend their own: the Afghan theatre, as Linschoten and Kuehn suggest, was a cauldron where '[p]eople met, thoughts and perspectives met, and personalities met. Groups fought out their rivalries, and different thoughts and ideas competed'.[105] By the time the Soviets announced their departure from Afghanistan in 1988, a vigorous debate over the strategic future of violent Islamism, which had already run on for some months, reached its apogee.

Sageman argues that there were essentially two groupings amongst the loose body of expatriate *mujahideen*: Abdullah Azzam, the founder of *Maktab al-Khidamat*, advocated a 'defensive' *jihad* to liberate Muslim lands from their occupiers in central Asia, Kashmir and Palestine; others, however, largely Egyptians and particularly those attached to the EIG, wanted to wage their attritional campaign in their home countries.[106] Al-Zawahiri's own strategic vision between 1989 and 1995 was divided: on the one hand, he seems to have envisaged mobilising the EIJ against Egyptian targets across the Muslim world, and Yemen, Pakistan and Sudan in particular; on the other, he wanted to confront the regime directly in Egypt. As a consequence, the EIJ organically split into two entities: the first 'exiled' element was under the command of al-Zawahiri and consisted of those who were unable to return to Egypt for fear of arrest and persecution and who therefore continued to attack the Egyptian regime abroad as and when they could. It was this group that, with the blessing and logistical help of bin Laden, now in Sudan, attempted to assassinate Mubarak as he visited Addis Ababa in June 1995 for a meeting of the Organisation of African Unity.[107] This group was also responsible for the November 1995 attack on the Egyptian Embassy in Islamabad.

The second element, nominally under al-Zawahiri's control though largely autonomous, consisted of those who had returned to Egypt by 1992 with the intention of confronting the regime directly on Egyptian soil. Things did not start well for this faction, which became known as the 'Vanguards of the Conquest'. In 1992, an EIJ leader was captured with the entire list of EIJ personnel on a computer, allowing the *Mukhabarat* to detain more than eight hundred members.[108] Although the group never really recovered, it did not stop them from three major attacks: the first was in August 1993, when they attempted to assassinate Hasan al-Alfi, then interior minister, in the first use of the suicide bomb in Egypt. The second was in November when the group attacked Atef Sidqi, the prime minister, as he drove past a school. The blast left Sidqi unharmed but killed a schoolgirl. In the public outcry that ensued, the regime responded efficiently, arresting a further two hundred and eighty with connections, predominantly, to the EIJ. This was followed by an attempted attack on an Israeli tourist bus in the Khan al-Khalili, which similarly resulted in the arrest of a hundred and seven suspects.[109]

Al-Zawahiri lost considerable authority in the EIJ in this period, partly as a consequence of these failures and partly because of his growing conviction that the US was a more appropriate target for their attentions. This appears to have occurred to him from as early as 1995 and it rendered his strategic vision chaotic. In a 1995 article entitled 'The Road to Jerusalem is through Cairo', he advocates attacking the Egyptian government both at home and abroad, whilst simultaneously indicating that he would have preferred to attack the US:

> We had to react to the Egyptian government's expansion of its campaign against the fundamentalists of Egypt outside the country. So we decided to target a painful goal for all the parties of this evil alliance. After studying the situation we decided to assign a group to react to this and we assigned their targets, first bombing the American Embassy in Islamabad and if that wasn't easy, then one of the American targets in Islamabad. ... If that didn't work, then the target should be bombing a Western embassy famous for its historic hatred for

Muslims, and if not that, then the Egyptian Embassy. Their extensive and detailed surveillance found that targeting the American Embassy was beyond the abilities of the assigned group, so we decided to study one of the American targets in Islamabad, and we discovered it has few American employees and most of the victims would be Pakistani. We also discovered that targeting the other Western embassies was beyond the abilities of the assigned group, so we settled on targeting the Egyptian embassy in Islamabad, which was not only running a campaign for chasing Arabs in Pakistan but also spying on the Arab Mujahedeen…later, Pakistani security found in the ruins of the embassy evidence revealing the cooperation between India and Egypt in espionage.[110]

As he became closer to bin Laden and his philosophy, al-Zawahiri began, whether intentionally or not, to marginalise elements of the EIJ and, in so doing, to lose control of the organisation. As Scheuer puts it:

> Zawahiri faced stiff opposition from many in the EIJ over his intention to drop the group's historic Egypt-first orientation. Some EIJ leaders… objected to al-Zawahiri's insistence on co-operating with bin Laden, saying that he had caused the EIJ to deviate from its main aim [establishing an Islamic state in Egypt through a military coup] and pushed the organisation into battle with the United States.[111]

In an effort towards reunifying the group, he adopted two scripts in succession. The first was power play. In the face of dissent and the looming prospect of a split in the EIJ, al-Zawahiri sought to stamp his authority on the organisation by ordering attacks on traditional EIJ targets in the form of the government: violence was intended to send a message to members of the EIJ that al-Zawahiri remained committed to attacking the near enemy and that he remained in control of the organisation. That this involved a major escalation demonstrates al-Zawahiri's determination to retain authority: all the intended targets were conspicuously high-profile (the prime minister and the interior minister) and one of the attacks heralded the first use of suicide tactics in Egypt. By escalating, al-Zawahiri sought not only to underscore his own claims to authority, but to demonstrate that the EIJ's commitment to violence exceeded that of its rival, the EIG.[112]

Although al-Zawahiri's power play script was successful in healing the EIJ's rifts in the short-term, government reprisals meant that the EIJ had little in the way of personnel with which to threaten the regime in Egypt. In this sense, he fell, like many before him, into the escalation trap: as the coercive leverage of attacks increased, the regime, already pressurised by the increase in EIG violence, retaliated with mass arrests which saw the detention of over a thousand people in just over a year. With severely limited resources, al-Zawahiri then proceeded to follow a second script, co-operation, by forming alliances. In April of that year, he attempted to establish a formal union between the EIG and the EIJ.[113] The EIG, however, viewed bin Laden and his 'far enemy' philosophy with caution; moreover, the animosity between the EIG and the EIJ which started in Egyptian prisons in 1981 and reached a climax in the Afghan *jihad*, had never been fully resolved.[114] Al-Zawahiri's offer of partnership was rejected and with that rejection, al-Zawahiri began to look for other resources. After a trip to the US to raise funds, al-Zawahiri returned to Afghanistan in mid-1996 to join bin Laden after he was banished from Sudan. In late 1996, al-Zawahiri and bin Laden began to formulate a clear-cut strategy for attacking the US in the region, which culminated in the 1996 'Declaration of War against the Americans Occupying the Land of the Two Holy Places'.[115]

By 1998, only a few months after the EIG announced its intention to relinquish violence, al-Zawahiri and Osama bin Laden signed a document which explicitly stated their intention of attacking the 'far enemy'.[116] This front was, in effect, an alliance of violent Islamist organisations; in addition to bin Laden, the text was signed by al-Zawahiri for EIJ and Rifa'i Taha on behalf of EIG.[117] As he aligned with bin Laden and effectively ostracised much of the rest of the EIJ, al-Zawahiri faced a mutiny within the organisation, whose members were not only suspicious of bin Laden's 'dark past' but wanted to target the Egyptian regime rather than the 'far enemy'.[118] In the face of the upheaval of EIJ, al-Zawahiri threatened to resign and take with him bin Laden's financial support. For most in the EIJ, 'the only choice was to follow Zawahiri or abandon al-Jihad'; in the event, many, including al-Zawahiri's brother Mohammed, took the latter course.[119] Al-Zawahiri had evicted or disempowered the other leaders in a power struggle so unceremoniously that al-Zumr defected to the EIG.[120] Others joined similar groups in Yemen such as that established by Tariq al-Fadhli or simply relinquished their dual membership and devoted themselves to al-Qa'ida.[121] By the end of 1998, to all intents and purposes, the organisation ceased to exist: in a trial towards the end of that year, it was estimated that a core of only about forty militants, who remained only semi-active and based outside Egypt, continued to sustain the organisation's existence.

Strategic Scripts and The Escalation Trap

This period saw two organisations emerge, develop and ultimately escalate their campaigns. The EIG intensified their attrition script by increasing the rate and lethality of their attacks and expanding the targets of their violence. The EIJ escalated in their power play script by deploying violence in new, more extreme forms and by targeting increasingly high-profile political figures. In this sense, escalation, which is not a script in its own right but a way of adapting an existing script, is about convincing others of one's increased resolve and capacity to fight. In terms of allies, escalation is designed to act as a rallying-cry for the cause which convinces doubters and detractors to join the enterprise. In terms of enemies, escalation is designed to force them to conclude that, based on costs and benefits, the confrontation is not 'worth the price in blood and treasure' and the accommodation of terrorist demands is necessary.[122]

But, by escalating, both the EIG and the EIJ risked what Smith and Neumann refer to as the escalation trap: '[i]nsurgents who employ terrorism as their principal means to obtain their objectives need to engage in a systematic analysis of their political and strategic situation... Failure to appreciate the limits inherent in a strategy of terrorism is likely to lead in one direction only, towards the escalation trap'.[123] Stone echoes this observation in his study of al-Qa'ida, noting:

> [I]f a terrorist organization... is to make progress toward its ultimate objectives, it must inflict just sufficient death and destruction to ensure that its enemies are frightened and that potential supporters are rallied to the cause. If it is too timid in this regard, its activities will go largely ignored and its political program unfulfilled. On the other hand, if it causes a very great deal of death and destruction it risks incentivizing a crushing military response.[124]

The implication of all this is that terrorists must make difficult calculations about the scope of violence if escalation is to achieve the maximum levels of coercion possible whilst successfully avoiding repression.[125]

A closer look at the case study, however, suggests that far from being difficult, these were exceedingly easy calculations; it was simply that the answers were unattractive. Decades of violent Islamism had shown that it did not take much in the way of terrorist action for the regime to react with full-scale repression and the EIG and the EIJ could reasonably assume that any attempt to escalate would be handled in a similar fashion. Nevertheless, despite the fact that repression was essentially guaranteed, both organisations proceeded to escalate their scripts: why? The theoretical approach taken in this study suggests that scripts are at the heart of the problem. By hitting the enemy harder and faster than they had previously, so the strategic vision ran, they would be able to weather the storm of the inevitable reprisals while increasing the coercive volume of violence until it was so deafening that the opposition were forced to acquiesce to their demands. In practice, however, both groups were unable to withstand government retaliation: between 1992 and 1993, for example, the state not only established new emergency laws and deployed 30,000 soldiers to Islamist strongholds in a six month period but also detained 27,214 individuals in what was an extraordinary display of repression.[126]

From this analytical perspective the escalation trap does not occur from bad arithmetic and hard sums which aim to eke out maximum coercion for minimum repression. Rather, the escalation trap arises from a fundamentally flawed script which fails to recognise that, when an opposition is left with only two choices—react or concede (or, to return to the image used earlier, swat the flea or allow itself to bleed to death)—retaliation is likely to be desperate, brutal, all-encompassing and thus all the more likely to be life-threatening. In this sense, escalation, as a way of adapting scripts, underplays the opposition's commitment to the *status quo* and, more broadly, its continued existence; it is a product of the 'strategic gap' between terrorist strategic visions and the way those visions unfold when they are implemented.

De-Mobilisation as Strategic Choice

Although full-blooded reprisals and government intransigence in the face of violence meant that neither the EIG nor the EIJ achieved their objectives in the long-term (or indeed, the short-term), repression did not obliterate the organisations in the way it had the 1965 Organisation, *Takfir wa'l-Hijra* and the Military Academy Group. It did, however, mean that both organisations recognised that their scripts had been inadequate or unsuitable and both began to re-assess the situation and to formulate alternative strategies. For both groups, there were potentially two options.[127] The first possibility was to replace the old strategy with a new, potentially more effective, violent strategy: al-Zawahiri and a portion of the EIJ 'exiles', for example, followed bin Laden's script of attacking the 'far enemy'. The second option was to reject violence completely in favour of alternative, non-violent strategies for pursuing political ambitions. In the event, both organisations adopted a non-violent 'de-mobilisation' script in order to pursue their political ends.

The EIG had signalled their increased commitment to violence by escalating their scripts between 1992 and 1997, so the rapid de-mobilisation of this group caused some surprise (and suspicion) in Egypt in the late 1990s. Not surprisingly, it has also elicited much academic interest, normally with a view to examining ways in which the de-mobilisation script might be implanted into other countries in the fight against al-Qa'ida.[128] Broadly speaking, these theories on the EIG's disengagement can be usefully put into one of three camps. For some, it was solely the consequence of negotiation and dedicated post-arrest de-radicalisation efforts on the part of the Egyptian regime.[129] For some, it was a process of ideological revisionism undertaken by the EIG, with the regime playing only a supplementary role as a facilitator.[130] For others, this was a process which started in the EIG leadership but which was nurtured and propagated by negotiation and de-radicalisation strategies used by the regime.[131]

Common to all these studies is the notion that state repression played a part in the EIG's disengagement.[132] Rashwan, for example, argues that 'the severe security strategy shook the ranks and cohesion of the Gama'a, prompting a reconsideration of its acts and concepts'.[133] Ashour echoes this, noting that 'historical leaders have referred to state repression as a cause for revising their behavior and their ideology' because it forced the EIG to 'reassess the costs and benefits of violently confronting the Egyptian regime'.[134] Part of the problem with this is that repression was the standard government response to Islamist violence and that groups like the EIG had experienced similar behaviour since their emergence in the 1970s without showing any sign of demobilising. Indeed, to the contrary, it was precisely because repression brought about the capture and torture of their co-religionists and prevented their participation in the political system that Islamists resorted to violence: a 1992 document produced by the EIG, to take one example, states that violence is a reaction to 'the execution of some of the leaders of the Jama'a and the torture of Jama'a members under arrest'.[135]

There is also general acknowledgment in these studies that 'leadership matters': charismatic leaders who are trusted by the ranks, so the argument goes, are needed if authoritative disengagement messages are to be disseminated to a reluctant membership.[136] Blaydes and Rubin note that 'by allowing the EIG to remain cohesive within the prisons, the regime was able to use the leadership council of the group to disseminate changes to ideology once those ideological transformations had been made'.[137] Ashour takes this much further, arguing that 'the charismatic leadership of an armed Islamic organisation seems to be the decisive factor in the success or failure of any de-radicalisation process'.[138] Whilst this may be true—strategies always have to be communicated throughout an organisation if they are to be followed—it is, perhaps, simplistic. The evidence from the case studies suggests that charismatic leaders have as much difficulty at convincing others to follow their strategic visions as anyone else, or to put it less bluntly, charismatic leaders may be highly respected and trusted whilst still failing to unify an organisation's actions. Al-Zawahiri, for example, presumably fitting the definition of a charismatic leader, failed on several occasions to persuade the EIJ that attacking the 'far enemy' was preferable to attacking the near. Even Hasan al-Banna, who was so respected by the Muslim Brotherhood that even after his execution, he 'remained, in full measure, the final and unqualified authority in the Society', was unable to convince the Secret Apparatus of the advantages of restraint.

The third and final point to note about theories of de-mobilisation is that they emphasise debate as a central factor in disengagement. Stracke notes that the primary reason for the success of the Egyptian 'de-radicalisation' programme was that the authorities facilitated 'the many and long meetings that took place between the leaders of the organization and its members'.[139] El-Said similarly notes that '[a]lthough the government did not initiate the reforms, it nonetheless played an important role in facilitating the *muraja'h* (revision) process among imprisoned leaders and members once it started… [by permitting] dialogue, debate and meetings inside prisons between the leaders, their members, and other secular and political prisoners'.[140] Al-Zayyat suggested '[i]n prison, they were exposed to other ideas and teachings and began accepting different opinions. It had to do with knowledge and experience'.[141] Ashour takes this a little further, arguing that 'external interaction [e.g. between the EIG and other political groups] has mostly affected the historical leadership's behavioural and ideological transformations, whereas internal interaction [e.g. between the leadership and lower ranks] has mostly affected the members'.[142] Once again, there may be an element of truth to this, but it is not clear how this form of debate differs from any other type of discussion over strategy and ideology: bearing in mind that, in the first chapter, it was argued that the considerable gulf between limited resources and political ambitions means that violent Islamists spend a great deal of time debating (and falling out over) their strategy and ideology, it seems unlikely that this near-permanent feature of violent Islamist groups should be a prerequisite for de-radicalisation.

The EIG

It was during a military tribunal in April 1996 that Khaled Ibrahim, part of the EIG's leadership and former commander of Aswan, called for the unilateral cessation of terrorist violence.[143] Just over a year later, on 5 July 1997, Muhammed al-Amin Abdul Alim similarly took the opportunity of using his trial as a publicity tool to announce that six members of the EIG leadership had signed a document which formally rejected violence and stated their intention to pursue peaceful forms of political involvement.[144] Although the document was originally meant to be secret and thus the announcement caught the historic leadership by surprise, they supported the statement and began to publicise their commitment to strategic change by releasing a series of published texts which received broad distribution amongst EIG prisoners and which were further disseminated beyond the prisons in interviews with journalists.[145] These went hand-in-hand with visits to various prisons where violent Islamists would be gathered in the courtyards to listen to lectures from their now non-violent leaders.

Not that the ceasefire was universally popular. EIG elements, particularly those in the South, resented being told what to do by a leadership who had spent more than fifteen years in prison and responded to the Non-Violence Initiative with the attack on the Temple of Hatshepsut in Luxor in November 1997 which left sixty-two dead. Although the EIG leadership later described this as a 'hard stab in the back' and explained that those 'in hiding and operating in remote Upper Egypt areas did not hear about the declaration and carried on with an older order given to them in 1996', the sheer brutality and intensity of the attack (which involved the death of infants and the disembowelling of victims with machetes) marks it out as unique in the history of EIG violence.[146] The message in the massacre was clear: some in the EIG remained committed to the coercive logic of violence and those who thought likewise should join them.

Indeed, in the late 1990s and early 2000s, it seems that much of the EIG were reluctant to follow the de-mobilisation script (although the brief support of Sheikh Umar Abd al-Rahman from jail in the US convinced many of its strategic and religious wisdom). As one EIG middle-ranker put it: 'we would ask individual members to comply, but between us, we still did not agree'.[147] On top of dissent in the middle ranks, more senior leaders simply rejected the 'de-mobilisation' script: Muhammad al-Islambuli refused to support the Non-Violence Initiative as did Rifa'i Taha who not only rebuffed it but demonstrated his continued belief in violence by signing bin Laden's International Islamic Front on behalf of the EIG in 1998—an act which saw him dismissed from the EIG *shura* council. Other violent Islamists outside the EIG lent their voices to the chorus, arguing that they had 'simply surrendered to the government, betraying the cause and hence the entire movement'.[148] Al-Zawahiri, for example, released statements in 1996 and 1997, the latter imploring the EIG not 'to give the regime a chance to buy time [or] to dissuade Muslim youth [from the cause]', as well as devoting portions of his 2001 book, *Knights under the Prophet's Banner* to criticising the EIG's de-mobilisation.

There were essentially three elements to the strategic revision. In the first place, the EIG were clear that violence was simply a means for achieving political goals and, so the argument ran, because violence had failed to achieve those goals, alternative strategies needed to be found. This was couched in both strategic and ideological terms. Hamdi Abd al-Rahman, for example, presented a pragmatic argument:

> We used to engage in jihad without taking any account of the benefit or harms that would be incurred by our actions. Now, however, our understanding has changed: it is the broader aims and objectives that determine the application of the text. So if the text says, e.g. wage war against the Jews, I must first determine... [whether] my interests will be realised by fighting or by not fighting. This is the sound approach.[149]

For Abd al-Rahman, violence, even if prescribed by Islamic texts, could only be used if it would bring about desired goals. This is a fundamentally strategic argument which revolved around examining goals, weighing up options and identifying the most suitable way to achieve those goals. The major revisionist text translated the same idea into the ideological realm, arguing in religio-strategic terms that '*jihad* is neither the goal nor the intent. *Jihad* is the way to raise the banner of religion and God's word. And if *jihad* is unable to achieve that, it is forbidden [*haram*]'.[150] In this sense, *jihad* was a form of 'propaganda of the deed' and if it failed in that respect, it was not only strategically counter-productive but religiously proscribed. From the strategic perspective, then, violence had been unsuccessful in achieving political ambitions and therefore non-violent scripts needed to be pursued. This, however, was coated in an ideological veneer: *jihad* could only be permitted if it brought about political ambitions, and because the EIG's *jihad* had failed to realise interests, violence was not only strategically illogical, but forbidden in Islam.

In the second place, the EIG argued that violence had not only been unsuccessful and therefore forbidden but had actually been counter-productive, succeeding only in uniting their enemies, fracturing Egyptian society and, in so doing, rendering their political ambitions all the more difficult to realise. The EIG's main text, for example, *Initiative for Stopping Violence* (*Mubadarat waqf al-unf*), stated that it was 'obvious that in the fight between Islamic groups and the police, neither one can benefit. The state cannot benefit from the lasting violence. However, the biggest benefactors in the struggle within Egypt are the enemies of Egypt and Islam'.[151] Nageh Ibrahim asked rhetorically 'was it sensible to wage war against the world at large? Was it sensible to increase the number of enemies against Islam?'.[152] Hassan al-Khalifa echoed this, saying:

> When I entered into the confrontation with the state, I was thinking that this confrontation with the system would, through pressure, lead to a solution of the problems of the country and eliminate corruption and free prisoners. But after that, it became clear to me ... that confrontation had caused great harm instead of helping the country; it ruined everything and no good was realised from it.[153]

The argument, in basic terms, was that violence had not only been unsuccessful, but that it had been self-refuting, both because it damaged Egyptian society and because it created a united front of the enemies of the EIG.

The third element was, however, perhaps the most important. The EIG leadership were absolutely explicit that, although their strategy had changed, their political ambitions remained essentially the same. Goerzig agrees, arguing that the EIG 'did not change its ends of confronting the enemies of Islam substantially. What it changed are its means... The EIG reinterpreted *jihad*'.[154] Indeed, Khalid Ibrahim's speech, which marked the beginning of the implementation of de-mobilisation, was just as extreme, ideologically speaking, as other EIG speeches of the early 1990s. 'We should all combat this sedition', he said, 'by turning the blood that was shed through fighting between people of one nation into constructive work that can extend our civilization... let's turn these torn-off limbs into bricks that can build your glory and your fort to protect you from your many enemies, especially Israel'; he went on to call for a year-long ceasefire to prepare for confrontation with Israel on behalf of Egypt.[155] The EIG leadership were equally clear about their new political role when they asked Montassir al-Zayyat to make a statement describing their future role, which similarly makes reference to a potentially devastating threat to Egypt:

1. There should be an outlet for Islamic groups through a political and *da'wa* entity that calls people to Islam and fights external power and their destructive ideas.
2. Islamic groups should be granted all the freedoms and rights to which they are entitled according to the Egyptian constitution. This would eliminate any reason for taking up arms.[156]

Despite EIG (and Goerzig's) claims to the contrary, a careful examination of the quotations above suggests that there is a subtle but significant shift.

Embedded in both quotations is the notion that the EIG aims to unify the Islamic community against an unspecified external force and its destructive ideas. Their major revisionist text elucidates the idea further, describing an *éminence grise* who profits 'at the expense of Egyptian blood', namely, 'Israel, the US and the West'.[157] Although the EIG had never been particularly fond of Israel or the West, much of its vitriol had been reserved for the Egyptian regime. However, after the declaration of the ceasefire, it is noticeable that the government is rarely the object of EIG criticism, let alone venom. This is not surprising—clearly the EIG could no longer be seen to oppose the regime lest their fragile claim to non-violence be compromised—but it did mean that, if their non-violence initiative was to persuade the organisation that this was solely a change in the way that political goals were pursued rather than a change in the goals themselves, the EIG leadership had to search for a new target.

The point about these three elements is that they were designed to communicate strategic change in the most persuasive fashion possible. The skeleton of the argument was straightforward: violence has been unsuccessful and is therefore *haram*; violence has not only been unsuccessful but counter-productive; and yet political goals broadly speaking remain the same and must be pursued in some fashion. In the event, the argument was extremely effective, largely because it was straightforward and because it framed de-mobilisation as both a strategic advantage and religious imperative.[158] The message was adopted, not always eagerly, throughout the organisation and, with the exception of the Luxor attack, the leadership successfully de-mobilised their group, returning to their original non-violent strategies of achieving political ends, namely *da'wa* and *hisba*; in 2011, after the release of most of the historic leadership, the EIG added a further political element to their 'de-mobilisation' script by forming the Building and Development Party (*Hizb al-Banna' wa'l-Tanmia*) and participating in parliamentary elections.[159]

The EIJ

Although the EIJ's decline was, for the most part, a consequence of the organisational fracture described in length in the previous section, it was hastened by the EIG's calls for non-violent strategies. The fact that the EIG's de-mobilisation narrative was so compelling was of considerable concern to al-Zawahiri in particular, who recognised that he was not only losing control over the EIJ, but its main rival was presenting coherent arguments for rejecting violence. Indeed, so concerned was he that he sought to counter the EIG's 'de-mobilisation narrative' by devoting large portions of his 2001 book, *Knights under the Prophet's Banner*, in an effort to portray members of the EIG leadership as little more than government lackeys.[160] Al-Zawahiri's concern was not ill-placed. By late 1997, EIJ regional commanders had begun to follow the example of the EIG by calling on their followers to 'put out the fires of civil strife between the state and some of its citizens'.[161] By 2000, there were growing calls for a non-violence initiative in the style of the EIG and members of the leadership were openly advocating the rejection of violence. Although the process stuttered to a halt in 2005, it was revived in 2007, when Dr Fadl manufactured a credible 'de-mobilisation narrative' in the form of a book, *The Document for Guiding* Jihad *in Egypt and the World*. Here, he used both his prestige and authority to call for the complete disengagement of the group from all military activity.[162] This narrative, produced by one of the foremost Egyptian violent Islamist ideologues, was widely received—by supporters and detractors of non-violence in the EIJ alike—as a valid statement of strategic and religious reasons for disengagement.

Not surprisingly, there were marked similarities between the de-mobilisations of the EIG and the EIJ. Firstly, the process of revision was structured around the publication of revisionist material, namely Dr Fadl's book and prior to that the EIG texts, both of which espoused the benefits of non-violent strategies. Indeed, there were significant similarities in the content of the two texts, particularly over the strategic and religious justifications for rejecting violence. For Dr Fadl, the essential point is, as Hamzawy and Grebowski have argued, that '[if] Jihadists do not possess strength comparable to that of their enemies (whether rulers in Muslim countries who do not rule in accordance with Islam or foreign powers occupying Muslim countries), [then] they are forbidden from acting violently against these powers'.[163]

Secondly, the process was facilitated, once again, through tours of prisons to disseminate their de-mobilisation narrative and to verify and legitimise the strategic shift.[164] Thirdly, the EIJ did not fundamentally restructure their political vision: there was still great antagonism towards 'malignant Zionist hands' and infidel regimes which failed to implement *shari'a*. Mohammed al-Ghazlani, the EIJ *emir* in Giza, for example, said in his trial of 1998 that:

> International Zionism, the most active of the three conspirators against our Muslim and Arab nation, is behind this civil strife in Egypt. There are malignant Zionist hands behind any destruction that happens... The Jews will benefit from civil strife in Egypt because this will assure [sic] that Egyptian officials are too

busy with their internal affairs to notice the Jews conspiracies and expansionist schemes... they want a Mediterranean market in which Zionism controls the whole region... I hope that these efforts [the Non-Violence Initiative] will help unite our nation to face up to the grave dangers besetting us.[165]

However, there was a critical difference between the EIJ and the EIG. The historic leadership of the latter was essentially unified over the decision to reject violence and could therefore formulate a clear and persuasive argument for pursuing that course of action. By contrast, the EIJ was under the authority of a fragmented, dispersed leadership: al-Zawahiri had effectively moved to bin Laden's World Islamic Front, taking the few EIJ members who wanted to target the 'far enemy' with him. Dr Fadl had not been formally involved in the EIJ leadership since 1993, though he was respected as a theoretician and ideologue. Abbud al-Zumr, the deputy *emir* in the days of Abd al-Salam Farag, had washed his hands of EIJ entirely in the mid-1990s as al-Zawahiri marginalised him, and had been co-opted into the *shura* council of the EIG. To make matters worse, by 1998, the EIJ was essentially 'composed of multiple loosely related cells each with its own commander and taking different stances of deradicalisation and offering allegiance to different factional leaders'.[166]

The fact that the EIJ's leadership was fragmented and its membership was divided into a series of disconnected cells meant that a clear narrative could not be formulated or disseminated to the other ranks until 2007.[167] Without a formal de-mobilisation narrative, a unified leadership or coherent structure, de-mobilisation took nearly a decade to be adopted, by which time elements of the EIJ, far from disengaging, had relinquished their membership of the group and joined al-Qa'ida and its various affiliates or formed small clusters of violent Islamists in the Sinai.[168] Nevertheless, for those who did disengage the logic was clear: they recognised that if the EIG—a much larger, more united and more popular movement—had spent years involved in an intense long-term campaign in an attempt to achieve their political ambitions and still failed to coerce the regime into instituting their political demands, then the EIJ—by contrast, smaller, less popular and less unified—would almost certainly fail as well. Confronted with the inevitable failure of strategic violence, these elements found the EIG's and, later, Dr Fadl's de-mobilisation narrative—that non-violent methods were ideologically more appropriate and strategically more likely to achieve political ambitions—highly convincing.

The de-mobilisation script then consists of two stages: the first stage is to formulate a compelling argument that non-violent strategies are (religiously, ideologically, strategically, politically and so on) better than violent strategies.

The second stage is to communicate this to those who need to be de-mobilised. Although this sounds straightforward, like other scripts, it is often deceptively difficult in practice. Compelling arguments have to work on multiple audiences: on the one hand, they must persuade allies to reject violence and on the other, they must convince oppositions that strategic change is genuine and that the organisation no longer presents a threat.

A persuasive argument, however, is useless unless it is communicated effectively. Arguments which are communicated in such a way that they leave room for misunderstanding or misinterpretation are likely not to be followed or at least only followed by some. Formulating and disseminating these arguments, particularly if, like the EIG, an organisation does not blindly follow commands, requires deliberation and diligence. In this sense, de-mobilisation is decidedly a product of System 2 decision-making and is thus a calculated strategic choice. This is an important point, because it distinguishes de-mobilisation (a strategic decision to reject violence which requires persuasive arguments to be communicated successfully to one's terrorist organisation if it is to follow the prescribed course of action) from the related but converse process of 'de-radicalisation' (the strategy employed by governments to persuade terrorist organisations to reject violence or to recast their political goals).

From this perspective, the EIG made a strategic choice to reject violence and to adopt non-violent courses of action in pursuing their political ends. In order to communicate this, they formulated a simple but persuasive argument that violence had been unsuccessful, counter-productive and thus their goals must be pursued by non-violent methods; this was then given an ideological varnish—what Benford and Snow refer to as a 'motivational framing'—to provide 'a compelling account for engaging in collective action and for sustaining their participation.'[169] That the EIG's de-mobilisation narrative was both well-formulated and well-communicated is evident in the fact that it was taken up by some factions in the EIJ. Of course, the compelling arguments were not specifically formulated for the EIJ and thus the script took some years to be pursued formally, but the point is that the de-mobilisation script was sufficiently persuasive to influence the behaviour of others for whom it was not intended. These elements essentially 'borrowed' the EIG's de-mobilisation script. Like the EIG, they retained their political ambitions, they re-used and re-cycled elements of the EIG's arguments not only through meetings with EIG leaders, but in Dr Fadl's revisionist text, and they sought to disseminate this narrative by touring the prisons.

Conclusion

This chapter has argued that Egyptian Islamist groups selected a range of strategic scripts in the pursuit of their political ends. The Secret Apparatus followed the fight strand of the survival script to force the regime to reconsider repression because the costs of confronting the Brotherhood outweighed the benefits. Other organisations which emerged on the fringes of the Brotherhood, such as *Takfir wa'l-Hijra* and the Military Academy Group, recognised that the gulf between means and ends was too great for confronting the regime and opted for the 'flight' strand of the survival script in an effort to increase their resources. In the late 1970s and early 1980s, Abd al-Salam Farag envisaged decapitating the regime and inciting an Islamic revolution in a mobilisation script; by contrast, Karam al-Zuhdi imagined a terrorist war of attrition which would drive out the Coptic community and the regime and thus create a truly Islamic mini-state from which to wage an insurgency. As an opportunity to assassinate Sadat arose, these two strategic visions became hybridised in the embryonic *Tanzim al-Jihad*: the assassination of Sadat was to be followed by the overthrow of state security structures in the south and these two stimuli would fuel an Islamic revolution which would overthrow the remnants of the regime. As the Afghan *jihad* came to an end, the EIG regrouped in Egypt, redeploying the attritional script and subsequently escalating it in the face of regime intransigence. Al-Zawahiri recognised that the strategic fractures emerging in the EIJ were a consequence of his growing desire to attack the 'far enemy' and sought to heal these rifts by deploying extreme forms of violence in an effort to signal his resolve and commitment to violence against the regime in Egypt. And, as the scripts of the EIG and the EIJ failed, both opted for the de-mobilisation script, seeking to pursue their political goals through non-violent means.

These scripts were all born from the need to find ways to attenuate the gap between the relatively meagre means available to violent Islamists and their ambitious political goals. Some scripts—survival, co-operation, power play and de-mobilisation—were used with the aim of getting to the next stage of the confrontation with equal or greater resources than possessed at the outset. Other scripts—mobilisation and attrition—aimed to maximise the resources available by raising the coercive 'volume' of their political demands. Nevertheless, the pervasive problem faced by violent Islamists was that the gap between their means and their ambitious ends was too wide to be bridged. Some violent Islamist groups, the EIG in particular, attempted to deal with this problem by escalating their strategies. By increasing the lethality, intensity and scope of violence, so the logic ran, terrorism would increase coercive leverage, capture greater popular attention and, consequently, force the regime to concede. Other violent Islamists reassessed the situation and, concluding that their existing script was either ineffective or inappropriate, sought alternative, potentially more effective, scripts.

Despite violent Islamist efforts, however, their strategies were essentially ineffective in achieving their long-term aims. Indeed, Thomas Schelling's observation that 'despite the high ratio of damage and grief to the resources required for a terrorist act, terrorism has proved to be a remarkably ineffectual means to accomplishing anything' certainly seems to apply in this case study.[170] As has been suggested, there was a persistent 'strategic gap' between the way in which violent Islamists expected scripts to unfold and the way a situation took shape in practice. This occurred on numerous occasions: the Secret Apparatus' script failed to force the regime to leave it alone, the *Tanzim al-Jihad*'s visions of inciting a popular revolution through the assassination of Sadat failed to initiate mass protests, and the EIG's plan to coerce the regime through an attritional war was met with full-blooded retribution rather than half-hearted concessions.

The disparity between strategic vision and strategic action, at least for Egyptian violent Islamists was not just a consequence of failures in implementing terrorism as a strategy, though doubtless these existed—*Tanzim al-Jihad*'s strategy, for example, might have worked had the Sa'idi grouping been able to attack security centres in the south at the right moment. The greater problem lay in violent Islamist scripts themselves. Specifically, the chapter identified three flaws in their scripts. The first flaw was that scripts generally underplayed the extent of the gap between means and ends with the consequence that goals appeared attainable when in reality they were essentially inaccessible. The best illustration of this was *Takfir wa'l-Hijra* who, after some years of patiently gathering supporters, attempted to coerce the regime to concede to a set of limited, short-term demands by kidnapping Muhammed al-Dhahabi. The regime response was so swift and uncompromising that it effectively obliterated the organisation within months. This provides an indication of a broader problem in terrorist script formation: scripts govern decision-making by providing a set of expectations about the likely outcome of events; if scripts gloss over the tension between means and ends, or, more broadly, are based on erroneous assumption, then they can only make fallacious predictions and force bad decision-making.

The second problem with violent Islamist scripts was that they oversimplified the complex relationship between cause and effect. This was less of a problem when the intended chain of events is relatively short, for example in the survival and de-mobilisation scripts, but it is a significant problem when it is long. In the EIG's attrition script, for example, repeated acts of violence were intended to coerce Coptic communities and security forces to leave particular territories whilst encouraging others to remain until, eventually, specific areas of the south had become sufficiently and properly Islamic that an insurgent war could be implemented from safe havens. The difficulty is that other parties may choose to act in ways for which the script has not taken account (e.g. repression and reprisals) or follow their own, completely different scripts.

The final problem with violent Islamist scripts was that because they are relatively simple structures that described the way in which strategists might expect events to unfold, they were extremely easy to transfer. On a number of occasions in the case study, organisations adopted scripts or portions of scripts which they believed had the potential for success and to adapt, reject or replace those elements which they saw as flawed. To this end, the Secret Apparatus adopted assassination as part of their survival script because they operated in an environment in which assassination was rife; the EIG envisaged an insurgency, drawn to the strategy by the stories of successful insurgencies waged in the desert by the PLO; time and again, Abd al-Salam Farag and Abbud al-Zumr would argue that they sought to emulate the model of the Iranian Revolution precisely because it had so effectively side-stepped state security who were unable to fire on their own people.

The problem with this was not just that violent Islamists emulated the strategic scripts of others without taking account of differences in political, strategic, social, economic (to name a few) contexts. The real problem was that violent Islamists were deriving their scripts from stories told about (and by) other movements in confrontation with their regime. In this sense, Egyptian violent Islamists suffered from what this research refers to as 'narrative delusion'. These groups were convinced of the accuracy and reliability of their scripts because they were derived from compelling accounts of other violent Islamists and their successes (and occasionally failures) in coercing their oppositions. As we shall see in the final concluding chapter, the trouble with stories, to echo Charles Tilly, is that they can be misleading.[171]

3

SAUDI ARABIA: TERROR AND LEGITIMACY

This type of diplomacy [terrorism] is normally written in blood, decorated with corpses, and perfumed with gunpowder. It has a political meaning connected to the nature of the ideological struggle. That is, it is considered the way to send messages to multiple audiences. Therefore, the choice of targets must be made extremely carefully.

Abd al-Aziz al-Muqrin[1]

If the story of violent Islamism in Egypt is one of a long campaign of violence which moved gradually towards its apex in the early 1990s and rapidly dwindled, then the story of violent Islamism in Saudi Arabia is one of a short campaign which flared, sputtered and died in quick succession. But during its ephemeral existence, al-Qa'ida in the Arabian Peninsula (AQAP), in its Saudi phase, explored their strategic options in great detail.[2] They calculated that, if terrorism was to be both means- and ends-focused—in the sense that it was designed both to lure in new recruits and mobilise support as well as to pursue political objectives by coercing near and 'far enemies'— then the objects of violence needed to be chosen with due care. The dilemma, recognised by both bin Laden and AQAP leaders, was that the population were not likely to bestow their political blessing on an organisation which attacked them. These leaders spent much energy attempting to solve this 'targeting dilemma' and, in response, essentially produced two scripts: attrition and provocation.

It is this singular focus on means and ends, targets and audiences which provides fertile territory in which to examine how AQAP made decisions about its strategies. Specifically, this chapter explores how the Saudi violent Islamist movement's scripts were constructed, how its strategists envisaged these scripts reaching their desired outcomes and how their strategies unfolded in practice. In order to answer these questions, this chapter begins by focusing on the way in which the attitudes of both bin Laden and Saudi Arabia's non-violent Islamist movement towards the regime changed throughout the 1990s and how these changes significantly influenced his strategic vision for the peninsula. The second part of this chapter examines the emergence of two contrasting strategic visions in the networks of Yusuf al-Uyayri and Abd al-Rahim al-Nashiri and examines how these two visions were derived from scripts whose assumptions were flawed. The third section focuses on the 'campaign of violence' used by AQAP between 2003 and 2005 under the leadership of Abd al-Aziz al-Muqrin and explores the structure and flaws in his three-stage script. The fourth part of the chapter examines the Saudi regime's strategic responses to Islamist violence, focusing in particular on the search for legitimacy. The chapter concludes by examining a number of assumptions in the scripts formulated by the violent Islamists and examines how these assumptions were translated into failed strategy, producing the 'strategic gap'.

Bin Laden and the al-Sahwa Movement

Throughout the 1980s, bin Laden was absolutely clear that violent Islamists should avoid attacking the House of Saud in word or in deed.[3] Part of this derived from the fact that he saw himself, in the words of journalist Steve Coll, as 'an international Islamic guerrilla leader who worked in the service of his king—someone so loyal to the family of al-Saud that he even tried to think ahead on their behalf'.[4] Iraq's invasion of Kuwait changed everything: as a loyal subject, bin Laden promised the regime 100,000 *mujahideen* to expel Iraqi forces from Kuwait.[5] His offer, however, was rejected and with the rejection of that offer, he gradually turned against the ruling family.[6] For bin Laden it was not simply that his services had been passed over for the military power of the US, it was that he had 'exposed the infidel's great role in the Arabian Peninsula and depth of the religious institutions' hypocrisy'.[7] His speeches went from mild critique to vociferous opposition and his relationship with the ruling family declined as they increasingly felt that he had changed from 'a calm, peaceful and gentle man interested in helping Muslims into a person who believed that he would be able to amass and command an army to liberate Kuwait'.[8]

Whilst bin Laden's opinion of the regime was gradually metamorphosing from the cordial to the vituperative, a similar shift was taking place amongst the non-violent Saudi Islamist movement, known as *al-Sahwa al-Islamiyya* (The Islamic Awakening), who were displaying increasing animosity towards the ruling family.[9] The origins of this change, like bin Laden's, were in US presence on Saudi soil: as Gwenn Okruhlik points out, 'with the stationing of U.S. troops during and after the Gulf war, Wahhabism was transformed into a Salafi movement that was now explicitly political. The private became public; the spiritual became political... [and] individuals became organised'.[10] The defining moment in non-violent Islamist dissent towards the ruling family came in 1991, when a 'Letter of Demands' (*Khitab al-Matalib*) was sent to King Fahd signed by four hundred scholars, judges and academics.[11] Another longer and more strident letter called the 'Memorandum of Advice' (*Mudhakirat al-Nasiha*) was sent in 1992, accusing the House of Saud of corruption, nepotism and a failure to implement *shari'a* in the running of the Kingdom.[12] The most important aspect of these letters was not only that they were public displays of dissent but that for the first time, in the words of Roel Meijer, that:

> the theme of *takfir*, the proclamation of unbelief of one's opponent, was used as a means of de-legitimising the ruling family of Sa'ud. The second theme, which was to become part and parcel of oppositional rhetoric, was the condemnation of the United States as the embodiment of evil, decadence and the spearhead of the Western, Christian 'war on Islam'.[13]

The Saudi ruling family reacted in much the same way as the Egyptian regime did in the face of Islamist dissent and opposition: with repression.[14] In the face of an increasingly popular and oppositional *Sahwa* movement, the regime reiterated its intolerance of public criticism, saying that opposition should be 'confined to giving advice for the sake of God... [if] someone has things to say, then he can always come to those in charge and speak to them in any region in any place'.[15] This overt demarcation of the boundaries of acceptability was enforced by further repression of those in the non-violent Islamist movement who transgressed established limits: for example, those who had signed the 1991 and 1992 letters demanding the 'Islamisation' of the Saudi social and political arena were silenced, arrested or imprisoned (in some cases, all three). Respected clerics such as Salman al-Awda and Safar al-Hawali, who could claim a significant following in *al-Sahwa*, were banned from preaching on a number of occasions before eventually being imprisoned and losing their jobs at King Fahd University.[16]

As the political arena became increasingly restrictive and repressive, Saudi Islamists began to leave the Kingdom. Members of the Committee for Defence of Legitimate Rights (CDLR) (*Lajnat al-Difá' 'an al-Huquq al-Shar'iyya*), a self-styled human rights organisation that supported further implementation of *sharí'a* through 'democratic' means, relocated their organisation to London where they raised the tempo of their dissent for the Saudi regime and in 1994, another organisation, the Advice and Reform Committee (ARC), was established in London by Khaled al-Fawaz on bin Laden's recommendation.[17] The relocation of prominent Islamist dissidents abroad coincided with further repression in Saudi Arabia. In 1994, those who had signed both letters and still remained in the Kingdom were arrested and the regime reiterated its view that dissent and public criticism were beyond the limits of acceptable behaviour.[18]

On the one hand, the arrests of the early 1990s effectively brought an end to what Lacroix refers to as 'the golden age' of peaceful Islamist opposition in Saudi Arabia.[19] But, on the other, as the non-violent movement failed 'to change the government through vocal opposition by refuting both Al Sa'ud's monopoly on Islam and the ruling family's ensuing claim to legitimacy', so other, now violent, strategies came to the fore.[20] On 13 November 1995, a bomb exploded outside the Office of the Program Manager of the Saudi Arabian National Guard killing five Americans, two Indians and injuring a further sixty.[21] Although different groups laid claim to the attack, their stated logic in communiqués and press statements was identical: violence would continue until American forces left Saudi Arabia.[22] The attack was a major blow to the ruling family. Not since 1979, when, in addition to disturbances amongst the Shi'ites in the Eastern Province, Juhayman al-Utaybi, leader of a Messianic sect calling itself *Ahl al-Hadith* (Family of the Hadith), laid siege to the Grand Mosque in Mecca for two weeks, had Saudi Arabia witnessed violent opposition.[23] Nor was the ruling family given long to recover from this affront to their authority: a few months later, on 25 June 1996, a huge car bomb was detonated outside the Khobar Towers, a building which housed US military personnel from the 4404th Airlift Wing, killing nineteen American soldiers and wounding more than four hundred people. The car bomb was of a different order of magnitude to the 1995 attack; the blast blew away the entire front of the building and the explosion was loud enough to be heard in Bahrain.[24] Once again, the evidence suggests that bin Laden had no part to play in the affair, but in his *'fatwa'* of August 1996 he overtly approved of both attacks on the 'far enemy'.[25]

During this period of growing Islamist opposition in Saudi Arabia, bin Laden had been in Sudan trying to consolidate his own strategic vision. It was during the years of 'exile' that bin Laden's contempt for the Saudi regime became even more entrenched and vituperative. In a document entitled 'Declaration 17', for example, released shortly after he had been stripped of his Saudi citizenship in April 1994, he wrote that the regime had departed 'from the requirements of "no god but God" and its necessities, which are the difference between unbelief and faith'.[26] This was, in effect, an excommunication of the Saudi ruling family and it signalled an end to the increasingly frosty relationship between the two.[27] It also coincided with a shift in his strategic vision: whilst some violent Islamists continued to prefer the traditional *jihad* in which they defended fellow Muslims abroad, bin Laden was, like al-Zawahiri, beginning to favour the socio-revolutionary approach which advocated the overthrow of the authoritarian regimes of the Middle East through insurgency.[28]

Bin Laden's socio-revolutionary period was short-lived; by the mid-1990s, as the *al-Sahwa* rebellion was crushed, his strategic vision had undergone a further shift—one which dispensed with the near enemy and focused instead on the 'far'.[29] The symbiotic relationship between the ruling family and the *ulema* (religious scholars), so his argument ran, provided both with legitimacy and authority and attacking either party would be a public relations disaster which would cripple his emerging violent Islamist movement. As Abu Mus'ab al-Suri wrote:

> There were two methods to confront the Saudi royal family. Either by confronting the Sauds, thereby necessitating confrontation with the Islamic clerics to unveil their hypocrisy in order to overthrow the Sauds' legitimacy. This is a losing battle in the eyes of the people due to the size and influence of the religious establishment. Or a safer route, which is to attack the American presence [in Saudi Arabia].[30]

Bin Laden therefore searched for, and found, a different script. This script, which would form the basis of scripts adopted by elements of Saudi Arabia's violent Islamist movement, was essentially composed of three phases: first, to provoke the regime into an over-reaction, second and consequently to de-legitimise the regime and third (and consequently again) to mobilise the people. The first and second stages were derived from what bin Laden perceived to be other successful operations against the US during which, in the face of difficult choices, they had withdrawn from conflict zones and de-legitimised themselves in the process. In his *Declaration of Jihad against the Americans Occupying the Land of the Two Holy Sanctuaries*, for example, he writes:

A few days ago, the news agencies communicated a declaration issued by the American secretary of defense, a crusader and an occupier, in which he said he had learned only one lesson from the bombings in Riyadh and Khobar: not to retreat before the cowardly terrorists... Where was this supposed bravery in Beirut, after the attack of 1403 [1983], which turned your 241 Marines into scattered fragments and torn limbs? Where was this bravery in Aden which you fled only twenty-four hours after the two attacks had taken place?

He calculated that, by attacking the US, whom he held responsible for the corruption of Saudi Arabia's political and religious elite, he could similarly coerce the US into considering a withdrawal, as it had in Beirut and Aden. Even if violence failed to bring about the departure of US forces, it would force the regime to make impossible choices about whom to defend: their own citizens or a vital strategic ally. By attacking the US, Abu Mus'ab al-Suri wrote:

> ... the Sauds will be forced to defend them, which means they will lose their legitimacy in the eyes of Muslims. This will lead the religious establishment to defend [the Americans] which in turn will make them lose their legitimacy. Then the battle will be on clearer grounds in the eyes of the people. Therefore he [bin Laden] was convinced of the necessity of focusing his effort on fighting *Jihad* against America... He then started to call upon those around him to the idea of fighting the war against the 'Head of the Snake', as he would call it, rather than against 'its many tails' (i.e. the authoritarian governments of the Middle East).[31]

In comparison to Egyptian violent Islamist scripts, which were relatively rigid in the government responses they attempted to elicit, bin Laden's vision accounted for several possible scenarios: in the first place, violence was intended to coerce the US to withdraw from the Kingdom; if this did not occur, then violence still would force the Saudi regime to make difficult choices. If the ruling family defended the US in Saudi Arabia, so the logic ran, they would lose legitimacy, particularly if that defence was perceived to be an over-reaction. If they did not protect their allies, the US would be forced to leave the Kingdom and the Saudi regime would have weakened its own position by losing US support, thus allowing al-Qa'ida to foist further demands on a fragile government.

The al-Uyayri and al-Nashiri Networks

Despite the fact that the arrival of US troops in the Kingdom in 1990 drove the changes in bin Laden's strategic vision and in Saudi's *al-Sahwa* movement, this did not bring about a parallel change in the broader violent Islamist movement and initially he struggled to persuade other violent Islamists to adopt his strategy.[32] Many of the former 'Arab Afghans', the Egyptians in particular, still saw *jihad* as a socio-revolutionary enterprise which had to be directed against the dictatorial regimes of the Arab world, rather than against the expansionist authority of the US. Others, by contrast, saw *jihad* in more insurgent terms as a way of retaking Islamic territories by establishing a front and fighting an occupying enemy; for this element in the violent Islamist movement, other fronts (namely those in Bosnia and Chechnya) were more appropriate recipients of their services.

Much the same was true in Saudi Arabia, where bin Laden's strategic vision was slow to take hold in the embryonic violent Islamist community. Indeed, it was not until June 1998, three years after the fall of the *al-Sahwa* movement, that bin Laden's vision of establishing a new *jihadi* front, predicated both on the 'provoke–de-legitimise–mobilise' script and on the principle of attacking the 'far enemy' in Saudi Arabia, began to gather pace. The key figure in driving forward the recruitment push was Yusuf al-Uyayri. Inspired and active in the *al-Sahwa* movement, he had left Saudi in 1991 for the training camps of Afghanistan, attending al-Faruq camp before being appointed as bin Laden's personal bodyguard.[33] Having followed bin Laden to Sudan, he then returned to the Kingdom in late 1993, where he proceeded to forge yet closer links with *al-Sahwa* and, in particular, with Salman al-Awda, one of the 'Sheikhs of Awakening'.[34] By 1996, al-Uyayri had become such a prominent figure in the Islamist scene that he was arrested on the mere assumption of involvement in the attack on the Khobar Towers. While he was in prison, the regime began to co-opt Islamist sheikhs back into the political arena in an effort to mitigate the threat of *al-Sahwa*; for al-Uyayri, the sheikhs' decision to cosy up to the regime was little more than a betrayal of Islamist objectives and it signalled an end to his relationship with the non-violent Islamist movement.[35]

After his release from prison in June 1998, al-Uyayri took on the task, probably on the orders of bin Laden, of recruiting both leaders and lower ranks for the organisation that would become al-Qa'ida in the Arabian Peninsula.[36] Al-Uyayri approached this task in a unique way: he not only explored his links with disaffected Saudi youth who had returned with him from Afghanistan, but also resorted to the internet, frequenting discussion forums and websites, as well as producing propaganda magazines.[37] In July 2000, al-Uyayri departed for Afghanistan; the trip, during which he is alleged to have met senior Taliban officials including Mullah Omar, cemented the change in his political vision.[38] On his return from Afghanistan, his written material began to focus increasingly on the Afghan front and the expansionism of the US, rather than on Chechnya, Bosnia or even Saudi Arabia.[39] In a book he released in 2003, for example, he rails against the US and Israel which he perceived, in the words of Michael Scott Doran, as 'a global anti-Islamic movement—"Zio-Crusaderism"—that seeks the destruction of true Islam and dominion over the Middle East. Zio-Crusaderism's most effective weapon is democracy, because popular sovereignty separates religion from the state and thereby disembowels Islam'.[40] As the US began to occupy al-Uyayri's attention so his written material moved towards a broad but heady mix of the local and the global. As Roel Meijer puts it:

> by combining a broad ideology of the clash of civilisations with locally-specific political, economic and cultural issues... Uyairi in his political writings constructed a much more intellectually satisfying and convincing—albeit horrifying—template, that is both relevant to local issues and resonates with the broader theme of global justice, than that of bin Laden.[41]

From mid-2000 onwards, al-Uyayri was recruiting for the Afghan front whilst painstakingly raising funds for the domestic challenge which had been deferred. The attacks of 9/11, and the subsequent US-led invasion, brought things to a head. Even before 'Operation Anaconda' in March 2002, which effectively decimated al-Qa'ida's Arab Afghan presence in Afghanistan, low- and middle-ranking al-Qa'ida members, Saudis in particular, had begun to pressure the leadership to allow them return home to fight the regime.[42] The vociferousness of the US invasion finally forced a strategic reappraisal in the leadership who valued Saudi Arabia as a key area for recruitment and fundraising, but began to acknowledge the need to address their political ambitions in the Kingdom and to maintain pressure on the US after 9/11.[43] In the end, a sizeable number of Saudi *mujahideen* returned to the Kingdom in early 2002 with bin Laden's personal permission, chief amongst whom was Abd al-Rahim al-Nashiri who had played the central role in the attack on the USS Cole.[44]

At this stage, al-Qa'ida's organisational structure on the peninsula was loosely-connected and nebulous, but rather than reinforcing this network, the arrival of veterans from Afghanistan exacerbated strategic divisions in the movement. Al-Uyayri and al-Nashiri neatly represent both sides of this schism. Al-Uyayri wanted to pursue the provocation and mobilisation script advocated by bin Laden, but equally recognised that the military resources available were not, in early 2002 at any rate, sufficient for bringing about political ends. He therefore advocated a slow approach of establishing a covert organisation designed to attack US presence in the Gulf.[45] In effect, this was to follow the 'flight' strand of the survival script; rather like the Military Academy Group, al-Uyayri withdrew into society and proceeded to recruit, gather weapons and train his personnel. For al-Nashiri and others (including al-Zawahiri), however, this was the perfect time to initiate the move to violence because momentum needed to be maintained after 9/11—not to mention the fact that there were rumours that the regime would order the US to pull its troops out of Saudi Arabia.[46] Al-Nashiri favoured an attritional script broadly based on the socio-revolutionary approach which involved repeated attacks on US and Saudi targets in order to force the US out of the Kingdom. Despite the fact that al-Uyayri and al-Nashiri were working under the broad mantle of al-Qa'ida, the two 'organisations' proceeded to pursue their own scripts regardless of the other. Al-Uyayri, while acquiring materiel on a massive scale, began to form his recruits into loose but independent 'clusters' of violent Islamists across the country and in late 2002, he consolidated these into operational cells under the command of a broader umbrella organisation.[47] Al-Nashiri, meanwhile, initiated his campaign across the Arabian Peninsula.

For Thomas Hegghammer, this two-pronged approach was a deliberate manoeuvre, a two-track strategy formulated by bin Laden and al-Qa'ida's core.[48] This is probably to ascribe too centralised a command and control structure to al-Qa'ida. Although bin Laden might have had broad oversight—in terms of financing nascent ideas or signing off on the use of violence in particular locations—he was not involved in significant decisions about operational affairs. Indeed, it is precisely because al-Qa'ida pursued what Abu Jandal, bin Laden's former bodyguard, described as a doctrine of 'centralisation of decision and decentralisation of execution' that bin Laden was not party to the minutiae of attacks.[49] While al-Uyayri had received authorisation for his plan and was probably acting according to orders, al-Nashiri was more autonomous; indeed, in his interrogations in Guantánamo he said that 'he spoke openly with UBL [bin Laden] and, if he thought UBL was wrong, he would tell him so. [He said] if UBL wanted him to participate in an operation, it would be incumbent upon UBL to convince detainee the operation was important to their cause'.[50] The point is that whilst the organisations were acting towards al-Qa'ida's ambitions, they were not acting according to a grand master strategy developed by bin Laden, but to all intents and purposes formulating their scripts autonomously.

In the event, Saudi Arabia witnessed two different strategic stages, one after the other: whilst al-Uyayri followed the survival script, setting his strategic vision in motion by recruiting and establishing independent cells, al-Nashiri pursued his attritional script. The extent of al-Nashiri's plans surprised both Saudi and US intelligence—as Bruce Riedel, a former CIA operative, put it, 'there had long been suspicions of a significant al Qaeda presence, but no one even imagined what was really there'.[51] In early 2002, al-Nashiri had left Pakistan where he had been devising training programmes with Khaled Sheikh Mohammed and travelled to the Arabian Peninsula, visiting Saudi Arabia, Oman, Bahrain and the UAE; it was during this trip that he attempted to further his existing plans for an attack on the Straits of Hormuz as well as to crash an aeroplane into US Navy ships in Port Rashid. In addition to planning those attacks, he also masterminded the attack on the M/V Limburg (based on his previous experience in organising the attacks on the USS Cole and USS The Sullivans) as well as planning strikes on the US and UK embassies in Sana'a and establishing a cell to carry out attacks on UK submarines in the Straits of Gibraltar.[52] Inside the Kingdom, he allegedly planned attacks on the Ra's Tanura Petroleum Facility, the Interior and Defence Ministries and the Tabuk air base.[53] Al-Nashiri's expansive but unrealised plans for a campaign of violence on the Arabian Peninsula—so expansive that it is inconceivable that he personally oversaw the intricate planning of each—eventually brought him to the notice of both the Saudis and the US and in October 2002, he was arrested in the UAE.[54]

By the beginning of 2003, al-Uyayri had completed his recruitment drive and had engaged about fifty fully paid-up operational members (in addition to a number of hangers-on), whom he intended to organise into five distinct cells in the Kingdom.[55] After al-Nashiri's capture in the UAE, pressure mounted on al-Uyayri to set his plans in motion but he remained adamant in his conviction that the *jihad* in the Kingdom had to be built up slowly in order to avoid detection by Saudi intelligence; he wanted the time to produce a resilient, organised network capable of launching a momentous attack on Saudi soil.[56] Once again, however, for bin Laden and al-Zawahiri, attacks on US targets, whether momentous or minute, were strategically sufficient: they would force the US to leave and, bereft of US support, the Saudi regime would falter and fall. Despite his misgivings, al-Uyayri pressed ahead with the campaign, but the network was under-prepared and the decision to escalate premature. Indeed, it is an indication of the network's under-preparedness that at this stage it still had not coalesced under a unified name. The campaign started on 12 May 2003, when several car bombs were detonated outside housing compounds in East Riyadh frequented by westerners, killing thirty-four and wounding more than two hundred.[57] The attack cajoled the Saudi government into a full-blown crackdown and by November, at least a hundred members of al-Uyayri's network had been arrested and twenty-six had died, including al-Uyayri himself.

The arrival of al-Nashiri in late 2001 brought two contrasting strategic visions to the Saudi theatre. Interestingly, it was not that al-Uyayri and al-Nashiri differed on strategic matters—both recognised the coercive force of terrorism—it was that they differed over the best way of deploying terrorism to reach their political goals. In this sense, the disagreement was essentially over their scripts. Al-Uyayri wanted to attack the US and provoke the ruling family into one of two choices: an over-reaction which would lead both to their de-legitimisation and, in the long-term, the mobilisation of the general population; or an under-reaction which would anger the US and leave the Saudis weakened politically and militarily. Thus the 2003 attacks on the housing compounds in East Riyadh, which were occupied by westerners, were an attempt to coerce the 'far enemy' into pressurising the near enemy to make choices about whom to defend—the US or its own people. Al-Nashiri, by contrast, was so convinced of the weakness of both the US and the regime that he constructed an attritional script; he planned multiple attacks, seeking to exhaust both oppositions through repeated terrorist violence, reducing their military and financial resources and political will in an attempt to coerce the US to withdraw from the Arabian Peninsula and the regime to concede to al-Qa'ida's demands.

The second area of disparity was about the 'phase of strength' (to return to the language of the Egyptians) and whether it had been reached. Al-Uyayri calculated that there was simply too vast a gulf between violent Islamist means and their political ambitions for the latter to be attainable: significant resources would be required to initiate a long-term campaign of terrorist violence against the US and, in so doing, to present the ruling family with difficult choices over their relationship with the Americans. Not surprisingly, bearing this in mind, he adopted a survival script which involved discrete, non-violent recruitment in an attempt to cross the threshold from the 'state of weakness' to the 'state of strength' without drawing the attention of the authorities. From as early as 2000, he had begun to recruit through personal contacts in the Arab Afghan community as well as online where he wrote in forums and released propaganda. Al-Nashiri, by contrast, based his vision on a completely different calculation: in his view, 9/11 had irreparably damaged US-Saudi relations, leaving both weak and ripe for coercion, and he argued that the campaign needed to be initiated without delay in order to take advantage of the situation.

In practice, however, there was a significant strategic gap between these visions and the way that they unfolded in practice. On this occasion, both scripts failed not so much in their implementation as in the assumptions which underpinned the cause-effect structure of their strategic logic. To put it another way, it was not that attacks were a tactical failure, but that the scripts obscured the fact that Saudi violent Islamist cells were too weak, under-populated and under-resourced to weather the storm of the regime's response. This, as was noted in the previous chapter, is part of the problem with scripts. Because they are stories—in the sense that they describe a chain of events which occur as a consequence of (political) actors playing parts in a certain situations—they are subject, like all narratives, to biases, emphases and outright fabrications. Embedded in bin Laden's script and passed through into both al-Uyayri's and al-Nashiri's scripts was the assertion that even very meagre means can be translated into great political effects if the strategy is right. This assumption was derived, at least in part, from the analogies bin Laden drew with strategically successful attacks which forced the US to withdraw from Beirut and Aden. The problem was that when it came to making decisions about whether to implement the script—despite al-Uyayri's warning that resources were insufficient—the script provided unreliable information about the resources required for coercing the opposition with the consequence that both al-Nashiri and al-Uyayri, in particular, escalated prematurely. Their embryonic organisations were not able to withstand Saudi responses and their strategies failed to achieve their long-term and short-term aspirations.

The Search for Legitimacy

Whilst the loss of recruits to government reprisals was a major setback for the organisation, the situation was not without its silver lining. In the following months, the organisation had time to regroup and restructure under the leadership of Abd al-Aziz al-Muqrin who devoted considerable time to creating a formidable media presence, chiefly in the publication of *Muaskar al-Battar* and *Sawt al-Jihad*.[58] It was a decidedly strategic move: the depth and sophistication of their media campaign was successful in camouflaging the group's lack of operational capability whilst simultaneously encouraging new recruits to join the movement.[59]

Slowly, they began to reorganise around their propaganda output and by November al-Muqrin felt that they had consolidated sufficiently for a further attack. On 8 November 2003, a cell calling itself the 'Truth Brigades' drove a police van into the Muhayya residential compound in Riyadh, which housed mainly non-Saudi Arabs, killing seventeen and wounding more than a hundred and twenty. The attack was a 'public-relations disaster' for the resurgent organisation: not only were the majority of those killed Muslims (five of them children), but the attack took place during Ramadan.[60] One AQAP ideologue, Luways Atiyat Allah, even concluded that 'the Saudi government was able to turn the attack ... into a media success by claiming that Muslims were killed, thus inciting some against the *mujahidin*'.[61] As one journalist noted in the aftermath, 'killing Muslims shattered the illusion that somehow the violence, however misguided, was vaguely connected to the idea of pushing reform'.[62] This was echoed by an interviewee who simply noted that 'to all intents and purposes, it [the Muhayya attack] broke the organisation beyond repair'.

The failure of the Muhayya attack and the group's dwindling resources brought about another reappraisal in targeting policy and script. In mid-November, the group formally took the name of 'al-Qa'ida on the Arabian Peninsula' in an attempt, presumably, both to provide a discrete entity around which a membership could coalesce and to distance themselves from the Muhayya disaster. As an assertion of identity, 'AQAP' not only carried the legitimising power of al-Qa'ida branding, but also disseminated an alternative strategic vision—one which was directed at Saudi security forces rather than civilians or the US and was thus tailored to AQAP's need to create and maintain public support. In December 2003, AQAP began to enact this alternative strategic vision: on two separate occasions they attempted attacks on senior Interior Ministry officials, as well as leaving a car bomb near the headquarters of the Saudi *Mabahith* (Intelligence Services) which was intercepted by police. Hand-in-hand with the rebrand went a change in targets as the group increasingly turned its attentions towards Saudi security targets. Strategically, the rationale was that the government's retaliation had all but disabled the group previously and that attacking security targets would reduce the opposition's access to military means and provide the organisation with the room to manoeuvre.

Although the script did not involve the targeting of civilians, attacks on Saudi security services remained difficult to justify. Violence against their co-religionists, whether security personnel or not, was simply inconsistent with a key element of their narrative—that they acted in the best interests of Muslims. In order to prevent loss of public support, AQAP created a 'ghost' organisation called *al-Haramain* Brigades to take responsibility for attacks against fellow Muslims and to shift the socio-revolutionary element of their strategy on to other parties. For Hegghammer the rationale was clear:

> The *Haramain* Brigades was a fictitious entity invented to prevent the QAP from being associated with the 'dirty work' of attacking Saudi policemen. This shows that the QAP feared being perceived as socio-revolutionaries, realising no doubt that attacks on Saudis would undermine whatever public support was left for the campaign. The name [A]QAP had to be reserved for the declared 'Westerners first' strategy.[63]

The theoretical approach employed in this research allows us to take this further. The creation of a fictitious entity was a product of the strategic conundrum which pervades violent Islamist movements: on the one hand, public sympathy and support is essential for a group's survival and success; but if one is to coerce the near enemy, in particular if one intends to use terrorism to engage in that process of coercion, then it is often necessary to induce physical damage and/or a psychological reaction in precisely those constituencies whose support one needs. AQAP sought to bypass this problem, not very successfully, by creating a front organisation to act on their behalf without any association being drawn between the two.

By 2004, AQAP was rapidly becoming dysfunctional: the organisation seemed incapable of adopting and sticking to a single strategy for achieving its aims, choosing a set of targets appropriate to their strategy, or mobilising substantial support among the Saudi population. Indeed, it was only their new leader, Abd al-Aziz al-Muqrin, who kept the organisation going. Under his leadership, the group renewed hostilities again and on 21 April, a car bomb was detonated outside Police Headquarters in central Riyadh, killing six. Again, the casualties were Muslim and the attack was widely seen to be counter-productive for AQAP. In much the same way as they had in December 2003, AQAP distanced themselves from the violence, and the attack was claimed by the *al-Haramain* Brigades.[64] AQAP became increasingly dysfunctional as it struggled to come to terms with whom it should target with violence. Further attacks were conducted against security targets in the Kingdom, as policemen were targeted on five occasions in April 2004.[65]

By the end of April, this targeting policy was dropped and it was westerners in Saudi Arabia who were extensively targeted throughout the summer. On 1 May, AQAP militants burst into the offices of a company in Yanbu, killing five employees of western complexion; later that month, four militants went on a killing spree in a mall in Khobar, targeting random westerners and killing twenty-two in total. Towards the end of May, a German man was killed as he left a bank and in June, Simon Cumbers was killed and Frank Gardner critically injured while filming a documentary on AQAP. The campaign reached its apex, however on 12 June 2004 when Paul Johnson, an American contractor for Lockheed Martin, was kidnapped and, six days later, beheaded.[66]

Under extreme US pressure to react, the Saudi counter-terrorism effort was precise and uncompromising: the discovery of a number of computers and documents allowed the Saudi authorities to track down al-Muqrin who was killed on 18 June; a month later, the group's headquarters were raided by police and further arrests were carried out. Indeed, so complete was the action against the organisation that, in the eyes of the Saudi intelligence officials, it had run out of steam. This was something of a miscalculation: further assassinations of westerners occurred in August and September, followed by an attack on the US Consulate in Jidda in December, which left six dead; yet another attack was planned for 29 December, when two car bombs, one near the Interior Ministry and another near a National Guard training area blew up before they reached their intended targets. Not long after, AQAP ceased to release its major publications—as the organisation had announced itself as a resurgent threat by publishing *Sawt al-Jihad*, so, for many observers, its death was marked by its absence.[67]

The campaign of violence shifted as al-Muqrin tried to find a solution to the persistent problem of how to deploy violence which would mobilise popular support whilst simultaneously pursuing political ends. He recognised that political oppositions seeking to induce sympathy from and recruit within a constituency repeatedly addressed only in the language of violence were likely to lose legitimacy. As al-Muqrin struggled with this conundrum, the campaign under his leadership shifted on a number of occasions; for the purposes of this analysis, it essentially fell into three stages which neatly demonstrate the struggle with this inherent problem for terrorist strategists. The first stage, in which the local population were targeted, was a near-complete disaster: the attacks on the Muhayya compound left Muslims dead and fomented anger in the population. This failure brought the second stage as AQAP moved to attacking security targets between December 2003 and May 2004. Once again, the targeting doctrine produced a public outcry as the regime argued that those who had been killed were not simply policemen but Muslims and countrymen. AQAP sought to avoid a further stain on their character by deflecting the blame onto a 'front' organisation, the *Haramain* Brigades. The third stage, beginning in May 2004, dispensed with targeting Muslims and proceed to focus violence on westerners in the Kingdom.

Although the targeting doctrine shifted, al-Muqrin was clear about his strategic vision. In his text, *A Practical Guide for Guerrilla War*, he describes three phases. The first was 'strategic defence' in which violence was 'fierce and frantic' and deployed from 'mobile bases' in order to 'smash the prestige of the regime and to clarify the picture for the members of the *Ummah* to the effect that the enemy is incapable of stopping military strikes by the *mujahidin*, in other words, to encourage people to oppose the enemy'.[68] The second phase, 'relative strategic balance', involves establishing 'conventional forces able to extend security and replace the regime in the liberated areas... [which are] able to stand up to the regime's conventional forces. At this point, the *mujahidin*'s power will grow by leaps and bounds'.[69] In the third and 'decisive stage', al-Muqrin envisages 'finishing off' the enemy by attacking 'smaller cities and exploiting in the media their successes and victories in order to raise the morale of the mujahideen'.[70] From this perspective, al-Muqrin envisaged a script of attrition in which terrorist violence would de-legitimise the regime and subsequently 'mobilise' the population; as recruitment grew, the attrition script was to be re-used as an insurgency, further increasing recruitment until, in the final stage, sufficient resources had been acquired to 'annihilate' the enemy in a conventional war.

In practice, of course, there was a cavernous 'strategic gap' between the vision and practical implementation of the script. Indeed, this gap was so wide that al-Muqrin never had the opportunity to enter the second and third phases of his strategic vision. The primary problem was not just that AQAP was unable to survive the inevitable repression (on which al-Muqrin has little to say, other than noting that the regime would embark on 'fierce, violent, intense, unrelenting campaigns intended to put an end to the power of the *mujahidin*') but that it was unable to de-legitimise the regime or gain the support of local populations under the threat or reality of terrorist violence. In this sense, there was a fundamental flaw in al-Muqrin's script: it was predicated on the assumption that sufficient means were available to weather the storm of regime repression or at least that those resources lost would be replaced by a population rapidly mobilising as they recognised the illegitimacy of the regime. In practice, however, the regime did not respond simply with repression, but with 'softer' counter-extremism strategies and a façade of reform in an effort to lay claim to the legitimacy that AQAP sought to question. It is worthwhile examining these responses in greater detail to examine why al-Muqrin's script failed.

The Struggle for Legitimacy

> War means war. It does not mean a boy scout camp. War does not mean softness, but brutality... it is a war against terrorists and aggressors, with whom there can be no compromise. We should stop blaming others. What ails us lies within our own ranks ... If we confront it with hesitancy, thinking of the deviants wishfully as misled young Muslims, and that the solution is to call upon them to return to the path of righteousness, hoping they will come to their senses, then we will lose this war.[71]

The primary reaction to the campaigns of violence in Saudi Arabia by the regime was serious repression. As Prince Bandar al-Saud, then ambassador to the United States, wrote in an article, the strategy essentially involved arresting all those with links, however tenuous, with violent Islamism. In 2005, Cordesman and Obaid quoted Prince Turki al-Faisal as stating that Saudi police and intelligence had arrested over six hundred individuals and questioned more than 2,000 in its attempt to limit al-Qaʻida's operational capacity in the Kingdom, and this number has doubtless risen in the intervening years: in November 2007, the Saudis arrested two hundred and eight individuals who comprised six cells and were planning multiple co-ordinated attacks; this mass arrest was followed by another round of a hundred and twenty-two individuals who were recruiting Saudis for Iraq and Afghanistan.[72] 2008 saw still further arrests: in the first six months of the year, more than seven hundred suspects had been arrested and detained on suspicion not only of terrorist activity in the Kingdom, specifically plotting to assassinate religious and security figures, but also of involvement in fighting in Iraq.[73] A Human Rights Watch report released in March 2008 estimated that, even after a number of amnesties, the Saudis still held between 1,500 and 2,000 detainees on suspicion of involvement in terrorist activity.[74]

Hand-in-hand with mass arrests went a shoot-to-kill policy. Between May and November 2003, for example, a number of senior al-Qaʻida leaders in Saudi Arabia were killed in gun fights with the police. Yusuf al-Uyayri was killed after a car chase, Turki al-Dandani was killed when the police laid siege to a safehouse, Ahmed al-Dukhayyil, who was al-Uyayri's right-hand man, was killed after a shootout at a farm, and Sultan al-Qahtani was killed during a gun battle at a hospital in Jizan.[75] Indeed, of all the members on the 'List of 19', which was released by the Minister of the Interior on 7 May 2003 and contained the photographs of the most wanted men in Saudi Arabia, five were killed just a few days later in the compound bombings in Riyadh, six were killed in 2003 and a further three in 2004; only two were arrested.[76] Similarly, at least half of the 'List of 26', which was released in early December 2003, were killed in the eighteen months that followed.

Although annihilation in the form of mass arrests and executions can be effective in crushing an Islamist opposition by depriving them of the means they so value, it carries with it a real potential to compromise one's own legitimacy, particularly where those detained are perceived by the general public to be innocent. The regime partially countered this problem by underscoring the disasters which al-Qa'ida created in an effort to de-legitimise the group as fully as possible. Newspaper editorials condemned violence, front page spreads showed wounded Arab children and once-violent Islamists appeared on television denouncing al-Qa'ida as predatory recruiters who had used deceit and cunning to lure naïve young men into the *jihadi* fold.[77] This was extremely successful—as Hegghammer suggests, 'the genius of the Saudi information strategy was that it portrayed the militants as revolutionaries, thereby exploiting the taboo of domestic rebellion in Saudi political culture to delegitimise the militants in the population'.[78] At the same time, the regime created the *al-Sakinnah* (Tranquillity) programme in which security officials logged on to radical chatrooms and forums in order to challenge the radical opinions of those present—often referring them to a number of other websites containing *fatawa* reiterating the regime's legitimacy as well as enforcing the proscription of rebellion against the ruler.[79]

Whilst the regime reacted to violent Islamism with repression and by delegitimising its opposition, it simultaneously attempted to secure its own legitimacy. This took two forms. In the first place, it involved acquiescing, at least partially, to demands for reform which would permit 'a pluralistic atmosphere that paves the way... towards the acceptance of the different' such as an independent judiciary, legislative measures to fight corruption, and an end to discrimination against the Shi'ite community.[80] A critical moment in this was in the creation of a series of National Dialogue sessions in 2002 to be held in June and December 2003 and June 2004. These focused on a range of topics, but for the purposes of this research it was the second session, entitled 'Extremism and Moderation: a Comprehensive View', which was the most important. The outcome of the dialogue was a series of eighteen recommendations which were presented to Crown Prince Abdullah. In particular, there were demands for elections of the Consultative Council, separating the legislative and judicial bodies, permitting the institution of trade unions and broadening freedom of expression.[81] This position was, at least rhetorically, supported by the regime; in *al-Sharq al-Awsat*, Prince Turki al-Faisal, then ambassador to the UK, wrote an article stating that 'reforming the kingdom is not a choice, it is a necessity... we have become more open and keen on reform after the attacks of September 11 while the US has become more closed'.[82] These reforms did bring about some political freedom: newspapers became more critical of the government (but never of the ruling family), municipal elections were held in 2005 and a National Organisation for Human Rights was approved and established.

In practice, however, while with one hand the ruling family gave at least the façade of greater participatory political space and instituted reform, they took away political expression with the other. A closer examination of the reforms suggests that this was not surprising: only 4.8 per cent of the population voted in municipal elections which Mai Yamani describes as 'partial, heavily managed, and of no consequence'; journalists who transgressed established 'red lines' were censored and threatened; and, the National Organisation for Human Rights was widely perceived as a paper tiger, unable to deal with the pressing concerns of political detention and freedom of expression.[83] This extended beyond the suppression of dissenting political voices into the core of the state's symbiotic and legitimising relationship with the *ulema*. In early 2004, the ruling family dismissed a hundred and sixty imams and forty-four Friday preachers and suspended a further five hundred and seventeen imams and ninety Friday preachers (not to mention seven hundred and fifty muezzins) for 'incompetence'.[84] Charitable organisations were also subject to the clampdown: restrictions were placed on donations at mosques and the al-Haramain Islamic Foundation, which had suspected links to militants, was replaced with a Saudi Commission for Relief and Charity Work Abroad, whose finances were more transparent.[85]

Alongside reform, the regime sought legitimacy by establishing a de-radicalisation programme, designed to rehabilitate 'misguided' Muslims and reintegrate them into society. The 'Counselling Programme', as it has become known, was launched in the aftermath of the attacks of November 2003.[86] The origins of the programme lie not only in Saudi social mores, which lay emphasis on the role of the family and the authority of the *ulema*, but in similar strategies adopted in Yemen and, to a lesser extent, in Egypt.[87] The programme was organised and run by an Advisory Committee divided into a further four subcommittees: Religious Subcommittee, the Psychological and Social Subcommittee, the Security Subcommittee, and the Media Subcommittee.[88] Participants would attend the programme, according to most sources, for six-week long courses catering for up to twenty violent Islamists; at the end of the period, those cleared for release into Saudi society were provided with appropriate employment, housing, funds and, according to some, the opportunity to marry.[89] By and large, those cleared for release were marginal participants in violent Islamism, 'terrorist sympathizers and support personnel, and at the most, individuals caught with *jihadi* propaganda or who have provided logistical assistance.'[90]

The Saudis hailed the programme as a resounding achievement; initially, they claimed a hundred per cent success rate on the grounds that no participants had returned to their former ways. The emergence of al-Qa'ida in Yemen videos in January 2009, however, in which two former Guantánamo inmates and participants in the Counselling Programme appeared, put paid to this optimistic assessment.[91] Boucek cites data from an interview with Prince Mohammed bin Nayif in which he stated that about 3,000 prisoners had participated in the programme of whom 1,500 recanted their views and were released; a further 1,000 had attended the programme but were still detained; further data suggests that only thirty-five individuals who had attended the programme had been arrested for 'security-related' offences at a recidivism rate of between one and two per cent. Marisa Porges, like Boucek, notes that the standard figure of success rate is between eighty and ninety per cent and that this includes those detainees who refused to participate in the programme.[92]

The multiple efforts of the regime to limit and counter AQAP were largely successful. They were ruthless in repeatedly and relentlessly removing the resources available to leaders such as al-Uyayri and al-Muqrin and restricting their ability to use violence against any targets.[93] The logic was straightforward: the counter-terrorist strategy was 'targeted, varied and measured'; it sought, simultaneously, to deprive the movement of key personnel by arresting or killing them.[94] The 'non-kinetic' strategies, by contrast, were an attempt to control AQAP rather than deter or coerce it. Rather than focusing purely on capturing or killing personnel, the regime calculated that violent Islamists had already acquired resources and attempted to disable or reclaim those resources before they could be used (or, if de-radicalisation took place in prison, re-used).

Although the Saudi counter-terrorism campaign must receive at least some of the credit for the demise of al-Qa'ida in the Kingdom, at least in terms of removing the means available to violent Islamists, it is important to note that the real success was in garnering legitimacy for themselves and appropriating it from the opposition. In this sense, the regime had to toe—and did with some success—the fine line between instituting reforms and repression: on the one hand, liberalisation of the political system had the potential to dilute its own hold on power whilst weakening the violent Islamist claim to popular support in the Saudi population; on the other hand, repression was a tried and tested tool for crushing violent Islamist oppositions but carried the risk of losing the regime the legitimacy it enjoyed. The need to toe this line resulted in a 'schizophrenic' attitude not only to reform (as Mai Yamani has argued) but also to violent Islamists who were repressed on the one hand whilst being confronted with 'softer' counter-extremism and de-radicalisation initiatives on the other. In practice, this meant that the regime had to react not just with repression, but with strategies intended to retain and reclaim their legitimacy in the eyes of the population whilst simultaneously framing terrorist violence in the worst possible terms. In essence, this was a battle not only for tangible resources in the form of personnel and materiel, but for the far more elusive and intangible resource of legitimacy.

Conclusion

This chapter began by outlining two key strategic shifts in bin Laden's strategic vision. The first was triggered by the arrival of US troops in Saudi Arabia and saw bin Laden, like the *al-Sahwa* movement, become increasingly opposed to the House of Saud whom he condemned as hypocrites and apostates. For a short time, he envisaged waging a socio-revolutionary war against the regime; during the Sudan years, however, his strategic vision underwent a second shift as he recognised that the ruling family could lay claim to significant authority as a consequence of their symbiotic and legitimising relationship with the *ulema*. Rather than seeking to attack the regime, bin Laden's strategic vision therefore shifted towards the US, whose presence in the Arabian Peninsula he credited with the corruption of Islamic territory. As bin Laden's strategic vision shifted, so he discarded the attritional script which had been used in Afghanistan and adopted a new script, provocation and de-legitimisation in which violence used against US forces would coerce them to leave, or failing that, would thrust difficult choices on the Saudi regime and in so doing, de-legitimise them in the eyes of the population.

On returning to the Kingdom from Afghanistan, al-Uyayri began, like bin Laden, to move away from attacking the regime and towards executing terrorist attacks against the US. For al-Uyayri, however, the resources were simply not available to threaten the regime and he adopted a survival script, recruiting and arming in secret. The arrival of al-Nashiri saw a second strategic vision actively pursued in the Kingdom, as he implemented his attrition script with great intensity and breadth against both the 'far enemy' and the near across the Arabian Peninsula. Following al-Nashiri's capture in 2002, bin Laden and the al-Qa'ida core put significant pressure on al-Uyayri to initiate his campaign which was essentially modelled on bin Laden's own provocation and de-legitimisation script. This he did, only to be killed in police reprisals days after the first attack in the campaign. The leadership was then taken on by al-Muqrin who combined elements of al-Uyayri's and al-Nashiri's script to form a three stage strategic vision: attrition, de-legitimisation and mobilisation.

Amongst these complex shifting patterns of scripts and strategies, one factor remained relatively stable. All these scripts were based on the assumption that means, however meagre, could be translated into political ends, however large, if the formula was correct. There were a number of problems with this, the first of which was, as Saudi violent Islamists found out, that whilst limited resources might be translated into short-term successes, such as forcing difficult decisions onto the regime or gaining publicity, they are often too weak to sustain losses in the inevitable backlash. As has been repeatedly argued in this research, because there is a vast gulf between what is available and what is desired politically, significant resources—financial, military and human—are needed to initiate and crucially to maintain a campaign of sufficient force to garner the coercive traction required for long-term, ambitious political ends. In practice for AQAP, these resources were simply insufficient to stave off the mass arrests and shoot-outs with security forces, creating a disparity between the way in which strategic visions were intended to work and the way they developed in practice.

The second problem with bin Laden's script and, because they inherited their scripts at least in part from bin Laden, those of al-Uyayri and al-Muqrin, was that the assumption that meagre means could be translated into long-term effects was derived from analogies with other opposition groups who had successfully forced a US withdrawal in Aden and Beirut. These analogies were essentially flawed. In the first place, they were based, at least in part, on false stories. As we shall see in the following chapter, the attacks in Aden had not actually produced a US withdrawal: US Marines had been staying in Aden on their way to Somalia and departed from Yemen as planned and on schedule. Second and more importantly, these analogies smothered the considerable differences between violent Islamists in Saudi Arabia and the perpetrators of attacks in Yemen and Lebanon. Hizb'ullah, for example, could lay claim to far greater political support and legitimacy than AQAP, and the Aden-Abyan

Islamic Army, likely responsible for the attacks on the Gold Mohur and Mövenpick hotels, had an implicit coalition with the Yemeni regime. Once again, these flaws led to a significant disparity between the way that violent Islamists in Saudi Arabia envisaged their strategy unfolding and the way it worked in practice.

The third problem with these scripts was that they relied on the regime responding in certain ways to violence and on other parties reacting in specific ways to these responses. Indeed, their basic structural logic was that violence would produce an over-reaction (or under-reaction) which would, in turn, de-legitimise the regime and mobilise the people. The difficulty was that this cause-effect structure was highly suspect. Whilst the coercive violence of terrorism was able to produce short-term objectives in the form of a reaction, it also allowed the regime to calculate these reactions with care in order to avoid de-legitimisation. This is part of the broader problem with scripts: as sequences of events, they invariably imply causality when it is in question, or over-simplify the causal relationship between those events. When it comes to making decisions, this has repercussions: strategic visions are often structured on these cause-effect relationships when they are faulty or absent and, when implemented in practice, strategic visions—as in Saudi Arabia—fail to emerge as planned.

4

YEMEN: COALITIONS OF TERROR

The Yemeni context shows an Islamist movements at its most convoluted and intricate: it was (and is) characterised by a shifting web of characters, clusters of individuals, identities and allegiances which often exist only fleetingly as elements of the movement rise to notoriety only to recede without a trace. However, like the violent Islamist groups we have already seen developing in Egypt and Saudi Arabia, the groups that emerged in Yemen similarly struggled with the classic dilemma faced by their ideological cousins in those countries: they also had too few resources, too grandiose ambitions, and few options to bridge the two. But, unlike Saudi Arabia and Egypt, Yemeni violent Islamists were operating in a country where the regime was far weaker, far more reliant on juggling relationships between numerous factions, and far less able to resort to mass repression.

Yemen's own turbulent history is, perhaps, somewhat responsible for the astonishing lack of scholarship exploring the country. Although it has one of the most developed Islamist scenes anywhere—it has been fully functioning for at least the last seven decades—it is largely unexamined. In part, one suspects, this is because the violent Islamist scene in Yemen throws into sharp relief many of the challenges of researching violent Islamism. Scholarship on Yemen is, apart from a handful of committed researchers, scant. Prior to the attempted attack of the now notoriously dubbed 'Underpants Bomber', Umar Farouk Abdulmutallab, academic studies, by and large, only mentioned al-Qa'ida's presence in the country in passing.[1] Information that actually comes out of Yemen is patchy and unreliable. Moreover, accurate information con-

cerning the identities of groups, their inter-relations and the roles of key players can be difficult to access and is often available only 'second-hand' through
the media. Even the most visible actions of violent Islamist groups—their
attacks—can be frustratingly hard to piece together with certainty: information is hard to come by and difficult to verify; 'events', in the words of Paul
Dresch and Bernard Haykel, 'must be combed for clues'.[2]

Despite the challenges of researching in and on Yemen, what does seem
to be clear is that the 1960s were foundational for the Yemeni Islamist
movement. Two major upheavals in the Yemeni political system took place
that were formative in shaping the violent Islamist groups that emerged. The
first upheaval took place in North Yemen on the 26 September 1962, when
a Free Officers movement, financially supported by Egypt, surrounded the
residence of Imam Muhammed al-Badr, newly-crowned after the recent
death of his father, and shelled it.[3] Although al-Badr escaped, announce-
ments on the radio declared him dead and proclaimed the foundation of the
Yemen Arab Republic (YAR). Despite the coup, there remained vociferous
local support for the deposed Imam; tensions mounted between the 'royalists' and the 'republicans' and, by 1963, the YAR had descended into a civil
war in which Saudi Arabia supported the royalists and Egypt supported the
republicans. Although a truce between Saudi Arabia and Egypt was eventually called in 1965, tensions between the royalists and republicans remained
in full measure.

The second upheaval followed hot on the heels of the first in South Yemen.
In late 1967, a growing Marxist movement, backed again by Egypt, moved 'to
burn down the oil refineries' of the 'agent Sultans' and to destroy the 'base of
colonialism' in Aden.[4] As the revolution gathered pace, it first drove out the
British and then brought about the fall of the sultans who went into exile. By
1967, foreign presence had largely left the southern tip of the Arabian
Peninsula and with their departure, Yemen turned in on itself. Socialist and
Marxist activists from the south converged on Sana'a to defend the republicans from the growing body of royalists who had encircled the city. In effect,
a stalemate ensued and Sana'a was besieged for seventy days: in this period the
republican army 'expanded hugely from hundreds to thousands' while the
royalists were running short of supplies and in the end, they were forced to
retreat to the mountainous regions north of Sana'a, lifting the siege and giving
the republicans an effective victory.[5]

In practice, the 1967 Civil War changed the political situation very little.
Yemen remained divided between north and south along the colonially-con-

structed (and long-ignored) Anglo-Ottoman line: Aden became capital of the south, and strengthened its ties with the Soviets, Cubans and Chinese whilst working its way on to the US list of state sponsors of terrorism for allowing Palestinian groups to train there.[6] Sana'a was announced as the capital of the north and from here the republicans continued their fight against the royalists. In 1990, a merger was hastily agreed between the northern Yemen Arab Republic and southern People's Democratic Republic of Yemen, but enduring inequalities and tensions between the north and the south continued to pervade Yemeni politics.

Coalitions in Yemen's violent Islamist movement

It was against this backdrop of civil war, unification and enduring inequalities between the north and south that discrete identities began to emerge in Yemen's violent Islamist movement. At least part of the driving force behind this was bin Laden who saw Yemen as an ideal theatre where he might relocate the *jihad*.[7] As early as 1989, he had begun to consider the potential advantages to be had in opening a front in South Yemen, broadly replicating the paradigm of the Afghan *jihad*. The similarities between the two were obvious: these were tribal societies on Islamic territory which had been oppressed by a communist regime and there was added appeal in the fact that a growing mass of militants who had proved themselves on the *jihadi* frontline in Afghanistan were now returning to Yemen. The al-Qa'ida strategist, Abu Mus'ab al-Suri, summarised Yemen's prestigious position in bin Laden's vision:

> Since the unification, the project of Sheikh Osama became to try *jihad* on the whole of Yemen. The conflict about the Constitution of the Unified Yemen and the differences between Islamists and secularists [on this issue provided] an opportunity to declare *jihad* on Ali Abdullah Saleh and the newly born government of unified Yemen. Sheikh Osama moved to exploit that opportunity.[8]

Yemen's unification of 1990 made her an even more attractive candidate for the *jihad* because, in bin Laden's calculations, it had left the regime weak, riven with internal splits and ripe for the ouster. Abu Walid al-Masri, an Egyptian journalist close to bin Laden, wrote:

> He talked frankly about the need to liberate South Yemen from communist rule, the Afghan way. All his moves and preparations were within that framework. To him, the Afghanistan arena was just one for training or preparing the decisive confrontation on the land of Yemen. He wished to Islamize the cause internationally after the Afghan example, so as to have a massive Muslim presence in

Yemen similar to the one in Afghanistan. It is for this purpose that he established the al Qaeda organisation to internationalise *jihad*. He meant specifically the internationalisation of *jihad* in Yemen.[9]

Bin Laden's first move was to exploit the power of the prominent ideologues—chiefly, Abd al-Majeed al-Zindani and Muqbil al-Wadi'i of the newly-formed Islamist *Islah* party.[10] He recognised the influence that they held over the attitudes and actions of broad constituencies within the Yemeni population and their ability to incite those constituencies to join the *jihad*. Despite the fact that he made repeated overtures, he failed to make headway because the regime had pre-empted him by co-opting Islamist ideologues into the political arena as part of the GPC-*Islah* coalition. As al-Suri put it, 'he spent a great deal of money on this project but they turned him down because Saleh gave them prestigious jobs and granted them money and power', later recalling that 'we lost a golden opportunity'.[11] In the strategic calculations of leading non-violent Islamists, increased political power and the opportunity to engage in legitimate political discourse provided a better chance of achieving their ambitions than did bin Laden's global *jihad* and they adamantly rejected his advances.[12]

With this avenue sealed off, bin Laden's second move was to provide 'seed' money to the violent Islamist 'clusters' which consisted of Yemeni and non-Yemeni *mujahideen* who had returned from Afghanistan in the mid- and late-1980s and which had started to coalesce in the early 1990s.[13] At this stage, bin Laden's primary objective was almost certainly to replicate the insurgency from the *jihad* in Afghanistan. As such, his financial input was broadly comparable to investing in a 'start-up' company whose ethos and world-view was akin to that of its financial backers: it was an opportunity to see whether the Afghan strategy was repeatable in other theatres and whether it could be expanded upon or adapted.[14] This stage was rather more successful, not least because bin Laden had a personal relationship with key leaders which he could exploit. His plan was also helped by the fact that, unbeknownst to him, these militias were already on the rise thanks to the unofficial backing of the predominantly northern government who still viewed the southern communists with suspicion and wanted to limit their involvement in the political arena.

One particularly high-profile returnee with whom both bin Laden and Ali Abdullah Saleh formed an alliance, was Tariq al-Fadhli. His father, Nasir bin Abdullah al-Fadhli, was a sultan, a tribal leader and the pre-eminent land owner in Abyan Governorate before the Marxist takeover of 1967 pushed him into exile. In 1985, after spending much of his life in Saudi Arabia and

England, Tariq al-Fadhli left Riyadh for Peshawar before going on to Afghanistan in 1986, where he is said to have met bin Laden.[15] The unification was the impetus for al-Fadhli's return in the early 1990s, but his welcome in the still largely socialist south was far from warm and, with funds from bin Laden and the unofficial support of the regime, he began to assemble an informal alliance of returnees from the Afghan fronts which the media called *Jama'at al-Jihad* (The Jihad Group; YIG).[16] By 1991, al-Fadhli's militia were actively engaged in low-level conflict with the Marxists and had opened a camp for the Afghan Arabs in the mountainous area of Jibal al-Maraqsh, north of Ja'ar and Zinjibar and to the north-west of Aden.[17]

Not that al-Fadhli's was the only Islamist cluster with which Ali Abdullah Saleh formed a coalition in order to confront the south. Under the logic of 'my enemy's enemy is my friend', Saleh forged temporary partnerships with a variety of violent Islamists in order to wage covert, deniable attacks on members of the Yemeni Socialist Party and southerners more generally. This policy of 'outsourcing' was supported by members of the political and religious elite: Abd al-Majeed al-Zindani, for example, one of Yemen's fieriest and most prominent Islamists, provided legitimacy in the form of vituperative ideological criticism of the Yemeni Socialist Party (YSP), and Ali Mohsen al-Ahmar, a leading general and brother-in-law of Tariq al-Fadhli, is alleged to have provided materiel.[18] In that it would exist beyond the Civil War, the most significant of these clusters was the Aden-Abyan Islamic Army (AAIA) which formed around the figure of Abu Hassan in 1990 or 1991.[19] Abu Hassan was a Yemeni who had gone to Afghanistan to support the *jihad* and, while there, formed a close relationship with Abu Hamza al-Misri, the London-based cleric of Finsbury Park Mosque, who would play a formative role in the organisation as its semi-official spokesman and 'public relations consultant', releasing statements and ideological support from London.

The years between 1990 and 1993 were a bloody time for Yemen's southern political elite as these Islamist clusters executed more than a hundred and fifty socialist figures and carried out further attempts on senior YSP leaders and their families.[20] Although assassination had been a standard, if sporadic, feature of the political landscape for much of Yemen's modern history, the rise of violent Islamism in Yemen also produced the first attack on the 'far enemy' in December 1992, when two bombs exploded outside the Mövenpick and the Gold Mohur hotels in Aden. It was a crude and rudimentary attempt at best. The intended targets—US Marines who had been staying at the hotels on their way to Somalia for Operation Restore Hope—had been moved to different hotels the week before and the casualties were limited. Indeed, the only political effect of the attacks was to sour the relationship between the regime and the Islamists and to force the former to take action against the latter in order to keep the US on their side.[21]

By the end of 1993, as elections gave considerable power to the *Islah*-GPC and weakened the socialists, the southern leadership 'moved to protect itself', and by 1994, 'there were clear signs... that the south was preparing for secession and the north for war'.[22] The near-inevitable conflict came on 27 April 1994, and, as it reached its height in May, relationships between states were re-structured and new alliances were both formed and broken. At first, the US, still lingering in the Cold War mentality of fighting communism, supported the north in order to counter the communist south. The Saudis, still furious that Sana'a had vacillated over Saddam Hussein's invasion of Kuwait and calculating that the threat of a communist south was less concerning than the threat of a united Yemen whose impoverished population could exploit the porous border, provided financial (and, allegedly, military) support to the south.[23] The US, eager to keep the Saudis on side, reneged on their original offers and reduced their materiel support for Saleh's northern regime. The regime stated that Saudi financial support of the south was 'filthy money—the same money that once tried to abort the revolution and now tries to abort unity' and instead sought help from the Russians, who provided military aid, ironically, to quell the southern uprising that, until recently, they had supported.[24] In this shifting web of state allegiances, it was the non-state actors—the Islamist militias—that tipped the balance in favour of the north. The 'clusters' which had provided military support to the regime as part of their informal coalition were reinforced by bin Laden (who, like the US, viewed the communists as an enemy) and were used by General Ali Mohsen al-Ahmar as an organised and significant force.[25] In the event, the southerners' bid for secession was defeated and in the process they lost yet further power in the new, unified Yemen, such that Fred Halliday commented bleakly, 'the space for democratic discussion in the country has been closed; the power of the YSP has been broken, its former leadership is in disarray in exile, and a new, pliant but powerless replacement YSP leadership has been established in Sana'a'.[26]

The problem for President Saleh was what to do with the Islamists, who had proved themselves a potent force, after the Civil War. They had demonstrated their penchant for violence, but could not be allowed to attack the south further for fear that they might incite another bid for secession. In the end, he resorted to his traditional strategy and incorporated them into his extensive patronage network. Al-Fadhli was co-opted into the political system, serving as an adviser to the president until his defection to the Southern Secessionist Movement, *al-Hirak*, in 2011; others, like the AAIA, entered into a less formal 'non-aggression pact' with the regime.[27] There were mutual advantages to these coalitions: on the one hand, the regime acquired a certain level of control over violent Islamists who potentially posed a threat to security and unity and on the other, the AIAA and similar clusters could acquire resources without fear of regime reprisals.

It was in the autumn of 1998 that Abu Hassan felt that the AAIA had acquired enough political and military materiel to break its 'non-aggression pact' with the regime and to raise the stakes.[28] Relations with Abu Hamza and his Supporters of Shari'a group had continued to improve in the intervening period, giving the AAIA an international dimension and aura of power. A number of would-be British militants, including Abu Hamza's son and godson, went to Yemen in preparation for an attack in December and Abu Hamza became an unofficial public relations officer, releasing communiqués from London. The first of these sent a warning to the US to remove its military presence in Yemen and the second talked of US military presence in the port of Aden as a trigger which would cause Muslims to 'explode in the faces of the United Snakes of America' (as Abu Hamza called the US).[29] Abu Hamza's statements were shown to be more than blistering rhetoric when, on 23 December 1998, the Yemeni police stopped and searched a car, finding a cache of arms and explosives and arrested the occupants who had British and French passports. Five days later, on 28 December, the AAIA retaliated by kidnapping sixteen western tourists in Abyan and demanding, *inter alia*, the release of those arrested in December.[30] The Yemeni regime responded with a rescue mission which resulted in the capture of Abu Hassan and seven of his accomplices—a significant blow to the AAIA, which receded into the background for months to come.[31]

In the early years, violent Islamists sought to co-operate with one another and, in so doing, to build coalitions and relationships to ensure their longer-term survival.[32] Indeed, it is worth noting that all the violent Islamist groups operating in this period—from bin Laden to al-Fadhli—recognised that, simply put, their problem was that their meagre resources were insufficient to achieve their political ends, and sought to address this issue through alliances or, in the case of their links to the regime, coalitions. The strategic logic of both was straightforward: it was a system through which their resources could be combined and increased and goals rendered more attainable.

Bin Laden first sought to increase his authority in Yemen by forming alliances with leading Islamist ideologues; as that tack failed, he moved to acquire military, rather than political, support in the shape of former *mujahideen* from the Afghan front. The point is underscored by the al-Qa'ida strategist, Abu Mus'ab al-Suri, who noted bin Laden's preoccupation both with Yemen and the acquisition of resources:

> While the Afghan *jihad* was under way, bin Laden was focusing on recruiting for the *jihad* in the Arab Peninsula, in Yemen. Osama's main passion was the *jihad* in South Yemen. He worked tirelessly to garner the support to stage a *jihad* against the 'infidel' government there.[33]

Under the informal terms of the alliance, then, bin Laden provided Tariq al-Fadhli and other Islamist 'clusters' with much-needed financial support and himself gained military resources on the ground. In the same vein, Abu Hassan was conscious that his organisation was ideologically thin on the ground and sought to reignite his relationship with Abu Hamza, who was by then in the UK, to lend religious credibility wrapped up in an aura of internationalism.

Whilst the alliances were successful in providing violent Islamist groups with financial resources and/or ideological legitimacy, the coalitions with the Yemeni regime were more precarious. For Saleh, these coalitions enabled him to control militant Islamist groups by providing an outlet for their violence that was beneficial to his broader political aims and he thus welcomed violent Islamists into Yemen provided that they targeted the socialist south, going so far as to permit foreign fighters from the Afghan *jihad* to settle in Yemen.[34] For violent Islamists, the advantage of coalition was in the freedom to build up resources in personnel and materiel; provided they confined themselves to attacking the southerners, so the strategic logic ran, they would be rewarded both financially and with the 'breathing space' to recruit and train new members. In the aftermath of the civil war, coalitions between the regime and violent Islamists degraded, not least because Saleh could not afford another war with the south and ordered violent Islamists to lay down their weapons and enter the political system.

The problem with coalitions between authoritarian regimes and violent Islamists is that whilst political inclusion, as Jillian Schwedler has argued, under the right conditions can be a moderating force on 'extremist' groups (as it was with al-Zindani and al-Wadi'i), when inclusion does not bring about moderation and the gambit fails, it simply provides an organisation with the legitimacy and political space in which to recruit, raise funds and transition from the 'state of weakness' to the 'state of power'.[35] But when groups violate the unwritten rules of the patronage system by transgressing what April Longley Alley refers to as 'red lines', retribution is often dealt out.[36] In the case of the AAIA, this took the form of an aggressive military response which deprived the group of its leader and left it floundering. This is the problem with coalitions which involve violent Islamists: not only are their political objectives in direct conflict with those of their patron but they are so deeply committed to these objectives that violence is never far away. At some point, the desire to pursue ambitions outweighs the benefits of co-operation and the coalition will disintegrate.

In addition to co-operation, there was widespread use of political assassination and, to a lesser extent, terrorism. The former essentially fulfilled the terms of the coalition with the regime. The execution of the attack on the two hotels in Aden was the first use of strategic terrorism in Yemen and, bearing in mind bin Laden's strongly suspected support, must be seen as an early manifestation of the scripts which would be adopted by bin Laden's burgeoning violent Islamist movement, particularly, as we have seen, in Saudi Arabia. Two particular characteristics are familiar. In the first place, the attack was against the 'far enemy'—the US—rather than socialists in the south or the regime. In the second, this isolated terrorist incident fits neatly into the provocation and de-legitimisation script. The aim was to produce a response from the regime which coerced it into making a choice between the US and its own population.

In the event, the script was based on false premises which were, once again, manifest in the strategic gap; in 1992, there was little love lost between the US and the Yemeni regime after the latter had opposed military intervention by non-Arab states and abstained on Security Council resolutions in 1990 and 1991 during the Kuwait crisis; the US, in response, had pulled funding, removed all its aid workers and maintained a skeleton diplomatic presence. The problem was that the Yemeni regime had nothing to lose politically if its response was underwhelming and American political presence in Yemen was so limited that the US had nothing with which to bargain. The regime's only response was to arrest Tariq al-Fadhli briefly, only to release him a few months later so that he could resume his attacks on the southern socialists. In the event, it was the regime's half-hearted response, thinly-veiling its own need for violent Islamists to counter the increasingly restless southern elite, which would lead to the growth of the violent Islamist movement during and after the Civil War.

A Nascent al-Qa'ida in Yemen

After the disintegration of their patron-client relationship with the regime, the AAIA had suffered severe setbacks. Abu Hassan was captured along with key personnel in the rescue attempt on hostages in 1998 and his replacement, Hetam bin Farid, was little more than a *de facto* figurehead who lacked the charisma of Abu Hassan.[37] Abu Hamza released new statements throughout the summer of 1998 in an effort to regalvanise the floundering movement, stating that 'when you find no ears to listen, then military action is permissible by Islam', but he had little impact in inciting violence.[38] Bereft of a leader and regime support, the AAIA seemed to have been put down. Indeed, for much of the period between 1998 and 2000, Yemen, with the exception of sporadic attacks on westerners and southerners which had long been a feature of the political landscape, had a brief respite from violence.

It is important not to overestimate the structure and size of Yemen's al-Qa'ida movement in this period, whose breadth was limited to a few 'heavy-weights' bolstered by an al-Qa'ida logistics network operating in Yemen.[39] This loosely formed logistics network was essential for major attacks but was also seemingly incapable of conducting a major attack on their own and confined to running relatively minor operations in the form of attacking oil facilities and diplomatic figures. Bearing in mind Yemen's position in bin Laden's strategic and political vision, why did the organisation have so limited an in-country presence? The first reason was that there was a noticeable shift in bin Laden's position towards Yemen; whilst it still figured amongst his priorities, it was increasingly supplanted by Saudi Arabia, where he had been keen to establish an organisation but had been unable to recruit significant forces within the country until the release of al-Uyayri.[40] The second reason was that Yemen had become more hostile operating territory. Throughout the 1990s and into the new millennium, the US had cut off all but diplomatic ties to Yemen following the regime's political support for Iraq during the first Gulf War and subsequent warm relations with Saddam Hussein until his capture.[41] This provided ideal conditions in which al-Qa'ida could incubate, plot and execute their strategic visions.

Equally, it is important not to view what this research refers to as 'clusters' like the AAIA in terms of 'subsidiaries', 'franchises' or 'wings' of al-Qa'ida. This is to misunderstand the nature of violent Islamist movements: in a shifting landscape of fluid identities, clusters like the AAIA tend to exist only partially; 'members', if they can really be called that, often had fleeting allegiances to more than one 'group', and were only partially invested in broader ideologies, interested more in resolving local grievances rather than in instituting broad political change.[42] It is into precisely this category that the AAIA, particularly after 1998, falls. Ideologically, they probably identified with elements of al-Qa'ida's philosophy and may even have lent a helping hand in logistics, but essentially the movement was motivated by personal grievances; where these intersected with those of al-Qa'ida, there was room for co-operation. Particular leaders, like Abu Hassan and Tariq al-Fadhli, could acquire 'participants' from the broader Islamist movement and were able to deploy low-level violence in the pursuit of political aims, but in the face of sturdy government opposition, tended simply to adopt the 'flight' strand of the survival script and immerse themselves in the Yemeni non-violent Islamist movement, re-emerging only to execute particular attacks or to aid others.

The most successful and ambitious attack in this period was against the USS Cole: it was a well-planned operation, which had been honed after the relative failure of the attack on the USS The Sullivans, and if the *modus operandi* itself was brutally simple, the coordination of multiple parties and logistics was complex. The attack was originally claimed by a group calling itself the Aden-Abyan Islamic Army (probably identical with the AAIA); almost simultaneously, two other groups, the *Jaish Muhammed* (Muhammed's Army) and the Islamic Deterrence Force, both of whom were previously unknown, also took credit. Aside from the fact they claimed the attacks, however, there is no evidence to suggest that any of these groups was responsible.[43] Indeed, the primary role in terms of preparation was played by Abd al-Rahman al-Nashiri who planned the attack on bin Laden's authorisation. In this, he was supported by al-Qa'ida's minor, but important presence in Yemen in the form of Abu Ali al-Harithi, Fahd al-Quso and Jamal al-Badawi. These facilitators organised the logistics for the attacks on the USS Cole and USS The Sullivans by tapping into the broader Islamist movement while the bulk of the leadership remained in Saudi Arabia.[44]

In the aftermath of the attacks on the USS Cole and USS The Sullivans, not to mention the attacks of 9/11 and the initiation of the Global War on Terror, the US dramatically increased aid and counter-terrorism partnership with Yemen.[45] By 2002, the US was providing training to Yemeni law enforcement agencies and using drones to target high-profile violent Islamists who had had a part to play in the attack on the USS Cole. Indeed, it was in 2002 that a drone strike removed the threat of al-Harithi and five of his followers in the first targeted killing which included a US citizen. The death of al-Harithi delivered the loose logistics network a *coup de grâce* and al-Qa'ida's presence in

Yemen was, for the time being, ended. As the Saudi front increasingly became the focus for violent Islamists on the Arabian Peninsula and beyond, so Yemen enjoyed a respite from major attacks. As yet, no formal al-Qaʻida organisation had been established in Yemen; rather it was AQAP, whose primary base of operations was Saudi Arabia, that sought to attack the 'far enemy' in Yemen.

This period essentially saw two scripts used by inter-related yet distinct violent Islamist movements. The first was the 'flight' strand of the survival script. Violent Islamist clusters like the AAIA receded into the broader non-violent movement, emerging when particular operations required assistance or when local concerns became so fraught that violence was deemed a remedy. In practice, the 'flight' script was, as it had been in Egypt, remarkably success-ful at ensuring a movement's continued survival. The problem for govern-ments faced with a broad social movement rather than a discrete terrorist organisation is that it is extremely difficult to eradicate them entirely. American diplomatic cables, for example, refer to the ongoing presence of the AAIA from 2003 until as late as 2009, and demonstrate concern over the role of Abd al-Nabi, the AAIA's leader from 2000 onwards, on a further two occa-sions.[46] While a broader violent Islamist movement may be kept at bay, deterred by the onslaught of Government counter-terrorism campaigns, there is always the risk that these will re-emerge in the future, as indeed, Yemen's would in support of al-Qaʻida in 2010.

The other script, which was examined in some detail in the previous chap-ter, was al-Nashiri's attritional script used against the US and designed to wear down their resources and morale in an effort to coerce them to withdraw from the Arabian Peninsula. This, in contrast to 'flight', was far less successful. Rather than coercing the US to withdraw, the attack drew American attention onto Yemen with the consequence that bin Laden began to direct his finances and authority elsewhere, and the few resources that Yemeni violent Islamists did have were targeted and removed by a rejuvenated US-Yemeni counter-terrorism campaign. The last vestiges of al-Qaʻida disappeared into the broader violent Islamist movement having 'read the message loud and clear': acts of terrorism in Yemen would receive ruthless responses in the form of drone strikes or long-term imprisonment.[47] It was also in this period that the Yemeni regime established a formal de-radicalisation program which dried up the steady flow of those who were released from prison returning to violence. Although Yemeni support of (and innovation in) its counter-terrorism pro-gramme was welcomed in Washington, the threat of terrorism still lingered. The broader violent Islamist movement had not been completely eradicated but had simply receded into the background, Yemeni prisons held a number of respected militants whose experience in Afghanistan made them a potent force and it was these two groups that would come together in 2006 and beyond to form the backbone of a significant threat to both Yemeni and western security.

The Rise of al-Qaʿida in Yemen

After three years of relative calm from early 2003 until early 2006, the Yemeni regime felt that their efforts in defeating al-Qaʿida had earned them the right to financial and political backing from abroad. By contrast, the international community felt that Yemen had received all the support it deserved bearing in mind its ever-worsening record on human rights and corruption. In late 2005, President Saleh returned from a disastrous trip to the US, during which Condoleezza Rice had told him in no uncertain terms that the US would not view him as a legitimate candidate for the presidential elections if he did not address the ubiquitous problem of corruption.[48] She also gave him notice that the World Bank would cut its programme from $420 million to $280 million, and a $20 million grant from the Millennium Challenge Corporation would also be completely axed.[49] Back in Yemen, the analysis amongst members of the regime, perhaps understandably, was that 'without an al-Qaʿida problem, Yemen was just one more poor country in a world of beggars'.[50]

It was on 3 February 2006, only weeks after the trip and the day after the decision to cut bilateral aid had been formally announced, that twenty-three prisoners escaped from a high-security facility outside Sanaʿa, sowing the seeds of a resurgent AQAP. That they dug a tunnel from their cells in the basement of a Political Security Organisation (PSO) office into the ladies' toilets of a neighbouring mosque has been widely interpreted as evidence for high-level collusion—an interpretation that is still denied by the regime—though, bearing in mind the timing of the escape, looms as a likely possibility.[51] The biographies of the escapees, most of whom had lengthy *jihadi* credentials, are revealing. Of chief concern to the US was Jamal al-Badawi, who was widely seen to be a principal player in the attack on the USS Cole and a previous escapee, having bunked out of jail April 2003.

It seems US worries about al-Badawi were not reflected amongst Yemen's securocrats for when in October 2007 Badawi handed himself in, pledging not to undertake further violence, the regime released him after a matter of days. The release infuriated the US, who promptly refused to sign a

Millennium Challenge Corporation deal which had been recently re-negoti-ated. In a diplomatic cable, the US Ambassador, Stephen Seche, wrote that

> the MCC signing ceremony would be indefinitely postponed because the release of convicted terrorist al-Badawi was so offensive that the U.S. Government was not able to sign a historically symbolic agreement with ROYG [Republic of Yemen Government]...until this situation is resolved and al-Badawi returned to prison... al-Badawi's release might even create obstacles to other avenues of bilateral cooperation.[52]

Despite the status the US attributed to al-Badawi, there were others who, with the benefit of hindsight, presented a greater threat. The most prominent was Nasir al-Wuhayshi, who would become the leader of *Tanzim Qa'idat al-Jihad fi Ard al-Yemen* (The al-Qa'ida Organisation for *Jihad* in the Land of Yemen) in late 2006.[53] He had been bin Laden's personal secretary in Afghanistan before he fled into Iran in 2001 where he was arrested and subsequently extradited to Yemen in 2003.[54] Another prominent figure was Fawaz al-Rabayi'i, who, only months after his escape, organised suicide attacks in Ma'rib before being killed in a shoot-out in October 2006.[55] Qasim al-Raymi also rose to prominence in AQAP as military commander: he had previously been involved in a foiled plot to attack five foreign embassies in Sana'a, and after his escape he organised an attack on western tourists in Ma'rib which killed eight Spaniards.[56] It did not take long for elements of Yemen's violent Islamist movement that had so suddenly receded a few years earlier to coalesce around al-Wuhayshi and to emerge as a real threat.[57] In mid-2006, they were still without a formal name or leader, but they began to make minor, if clumsy, attempts against the regime. The primary focus was the oil industry and, by extension, the economic interests of the state through its financial relationship with the West.

Although the group consisted almost entirely of Yemenis and local targets occupied their attention, it was the arrival of a number of Saudis who gave the movement greater prestige and alternative strategic visions.[58] Two Saudis really drove the change. They were part of a larger group of detainees who were returned to the Kingdom from Guantánamo Bay in late 2007, called 'Batch 10'; they attended the rehabilitation programme only for five of them to steal across the border with Yemen after their release.[59] The first was Mohammed al-Awfi.[60] According to his Guantánamo file, he went to Karachi in 2001 and was then helped by *Jama'at Tablighi* to go a small village in Afghanistan to work with refugees. On his return to Quetta, he was stopped at a checkpoint on the border, arrested for illegal entry and eventually deported to Guantánamo Bay. After attending the rehabilitation programme in Riyadh for a few weeks, he crossed the border into Yemen and spent approximately fourteen months involved in the now burgeoning al-Qaʻida movement before re-admitting himself to the Counselling Programme.[61] The second and probably more important figure is Saʻid al-Shihri, another Saudi who left for Afghanistan in November 2001. He arrived in Lahore and went on to Quetta before travelling on to Spin Boldak, a town on the border of Pakistan and Afghanistan. Shortly after arriving, he was injured in a drone strike, which knocked him unconscious; on his release from the Saudi Red Crescent hospital in Quetta, he was transferred to US custody and transported to Guantánamo Bay. He was returned to Saudi Arabia as part of Batch 10 in November 2007 and attended the rehabilitation programme, after which he too slipped across the border to Yemen.[62]

By late 2007 or early 2008, the two Saudis had been drawn into a nascent al-Qaʻida in Yemen; they joined the leadership, displaying the status of their incarceration at Guantánamo and the prestige of their part in the Afghan *jihad*. At this stage, al-Qaʻida in Yemen consisted of the leadership council and a military wing called *Kataʼib Jund al-Yemen* (Soldier's Battalion of Yemen) which was itself made up of numerous subdivisions (the most prominent being Khalid bin al-Walid Brigade and the al-Muthni bin al-Harith al-Shibani Brigade).[63] Despite this, it is important not to overstate the level of structure in the movement. There were, for example, no identifiable mid-level managers, no regional commanders, facilitators, financiers or full-time militants under the command of al-Wuhayshi. In fact, ʻal-Qaʻida in Yemen' was, at most, a loosely connected alliance of would-be leaders and eager militants: it had ʻparticipants' rather than full-time members, a flat structure, and operated according to the al-Qaʻida principle of ʻcentralization of decision and decentralization of execution'.

The arrival of the Saudi elements coincided with, if not caused, a number of fundamental changes in the nascent organisation. In the immediate aftermath of the prison escape, al-Wuhayshi's al-Qaʻida movement had directed violence against two principal targets: local security targets and the oil industry. But, with the influx of Saudis, this rapidly expanded to include centrally-organised attacks overtly against the ʻfar enemy'; in 2008, tourists were attacked on a number of occasions and diplomatic personnel became a prime focus of violence.[64] Hand in hand with the two sets of targets went two primary strategies of violence: political assassination and terrorism. Political assassination was exclusively used against local security targets. In March

2007, Ali Mahmoud Qasaylah, the chief criminal investigator in Ma'rib, was assassinated and a few months later in June, five police officers, similarly on patrol in Ma'rib, were killed by small arms fire.[65] Terrorism, by contrast, was retained for attacks on the 'far enemy', for example the September 2006 attempted attacks on oil facilities in the Hadhramout and in more developed operations against the US Embassy in September 2008.[66] In this sense, al-Qa'ida in Yemen broadly pursued a script of attrition in an effort to erode the regime's military and financial resources as well as its political will, whilst simultaneously mobilising disaffected elements of Yemeni society. Hand-in-hand with the arrival of the Saudis went a change in targeting to include the diplomatic and touristic presence of the 'far enemy' in additional to the security and financial targets of the near.

As al-Qa'ida in Yemen grew more strategically diverse, there was a growing recognition that the organisation also needed to rationalise violence and disseminate that rationalisation to the local population in order to increase political support and aid recruitment. Starting with basic communiqués and statements in late 2007, this soon built up into a formal magazine, *Sada al-Malahim* (Echoes of Battles), which was published roughly every other month from January 2008 onwards. This was spurred on by the arrival of the Saudi contingent and with the escalation of violence came a noticeable increase in al-Qa'ida in Yemen's propaganda output. On the one hand, the primary purpose of this material was to recruit: it was an attempt to disseminate a world-view in the form of stated political objectives and a rationalisation of violence to interested parties in Yemen, the Arabian Peninsula and beyond and, in so doing, to attract new members who had broadly comparable philosophies and interests.

But *Sada al-Malahim* was more than just a collection of ideological statements concerning political objectives and describing the purpose of violence in an attempt to attract would-be *mujahideen*; it was primarily a tool for mobilising other Islamists in the pursuit of al-Qa'ida's objectives. A close reading of *Sada al-Malahim* suggests that there are two processes at play.[67] The first was to describe strategic visions. Abu Hummam al-Qahtani, for example, describes the logic of terrorism against the oil industry in the attrition script:

> If the enemy's interests in the Arabian Peninsula were devastated, his access to our petroleum interrupted, and the oil refineries put out of order, this would cause the enemy [the US] to collapse—and they won't merely be forced to withdraw from Iraq and Afghanistan, but would actually face a total collapse. If [our

enemy] were to be struck hard in various places, then he would scatter, turn around, and flee forlornly from the land of the Muslims, with his tail between his legs...[68]

In effect, this was to provide stories about the way in which AQAP envisaged events unfolding. The logic here was straightforward: by attacking the main artery which sustains US interests in the Arabian Peninsula—oil—then the US will be forced to withdraw from Islamic territory.

The second stage was to turn these stories from event-based accounts into compelling, persuasive narratives by providing them with what Benford and Snow refer to as frames, which rationalised violence by diagnosing a problem, providing a solution and mobilising supporters.[69] For AQAP, this essentially took the form of identifying local grievances and situating these grievances in both a local and global narrative that laid responsibility for political challenges, social under-development and economic hardship on both the Yemeni regime and foreign governments (Saudi Arabia and the US in particular). By far the most common grievance, with which large portions of the Yemeni population were in agreement, concerned the oil sector and the government's naked profiteering from the industry. One *jihadi* author diagnoses the problem as follows:

> I think that its [the Yemeni government's] intention is to bring the Muslim to a level in which he would not be able to think about anything other than his daily dish of food ... It has failed in the distribution of the fortunes, especially the oil, although all of the oil or most of it is at the hands of the American master, this band [e.g. the Yemeni regime] has morsels that might provide some of the country's needs, but due to the greed and the avidity of this band for these morsels, there was nothing left for neither the country nor the people.[70]

By constructing scripts and providing these scripts with compelling narratives in the form of frames, *Sada al-Malahim* can be seen as more than just the ideological outpourings of another al-Qa'ida front. It was a strategy for increasing and mobilising resources: it articulated a specific script and cloaked this attritional script in political grievances which spanned large sections of the local population. As Sarah Phillips suggests:

> AQAP's narrative displays an awareness that the group's survival depends on its ability to appeal to ordinary Yemenis and to tailor its arguments to the grievances of a Yemeni audience. AQAP has positioned itself as a conductor for entrenched grievances, of which there are many, and which are inextricably linked to the regime's exclusionary approach to the creation and distribution of wealth.[71]

This mobilisation script was taken a stage further by the announcement, on 23 January 2009, of the establishment of al-Qa'ida in the Arabian Peninsula under the leadership of Nasir al-Wuhayshi. The video was carefully stage-managed. First to speak was Sa'id al-Shihri, the deputy commander, who began by reiterating 'to our leaders and elders, Sheikh Osama bin Laden and Sheikh Dr. Ayman al-Zawahiri—may Allah protect them—that we are still fulfilling our promise and Jihad'.[72] Dressed in black and sitting beside an AK47, one of his dominant themes was the injustice of incarceration—both his own in Guantánamo Bay, and that of his compatriots 'who are zealous for their faith and who now number over 18,000 in prison ... and who are subject to imprisonment and torture by the investigators who are corrupt in both their religion and morality'.[73] Sitting next to al-Shihri, clothed in brilliant white and second to speak, is the leader Nasir al-Wuhayshi. His near-Apollonian contribution centres on providing religious justification for violence and his strategic vision. Third is Qasim al-Raymi, the military commander, who delivers a vituperative attack on Israel and the West, going so far as to criticise Hassan Nasrallah, leader of Hizbollah, for having the military means to attack Tel Aviv but failing to use them. The fourth and final speaker is Mohammed al-Awfi, the field commander, whose delivery echoes that of al-Shihri; he focuses on the detention centres and rehabilitation initiatives, warning of the use of psychiatrists who 'persuade us to stray from Islam ... using every tool and method'.[74]

The video was constructed to convey one key point: that this was an alliance between the 'Saudi' AQAP and an emergent 'Yemeni' AQAP and, in conveying that point, to present an aura of invincibility—despite the ruthless efforts of Saudi counter-terrorism forces and US interventionism in the Arabian Peninsula, so the narrative runs, AQAP continues to exist.[75] It was a compelling narrative, woven through with allusion, symbolism and high-blown rhetoric. But, in reality, it was a fundamentally fallacious one replete with unalloyed spin. AQAP had been ruthlessly dismembered by Saudi intelligence and the implication that significant figures in AQAP 'mark one' were involved in AQAP 'mark two' simply has no support in the evidence: neither al-Awfi nor al-Shihri had played any part in AQAP's movement in Saudi Arabia—by the time that the movement had reached its apogee, they had already been transferred to Guantánamo Bay.[76] Similarly, any Yemeni links to AQAP 'mark one', like Abu Ali al-Harithi and Jamal al-Badawi, had been destroyed by the Yemeni-US counter-terrorism partnership between 2002 and 2005. And yet despite the evidence, the video has continued to dominate analysis of AQAP and the episode is routinely referred to as the 'merger' despite the fact that there was no organisation with which Yemen's al-Qa'ida movement could merge.[77]

This, like *Sada al-Malahim*, should not be seen as an exposition of ideology in yet another al-Qa'ida video, but as another tool for mobilising would-be militants. It was an overt statement that a formal al-Qa'ida organisation had been established in Yemen with identifiable political ambitions and a clear strategic vision—all of which was wrapped in a legitimising frame of a griev-ance-based ideology. More broadly, these two mobilisation tools were designed not only to mobilise followers, both in Yemen and abroad, but to channel the behaviour of those recruits. This was vital for a dispersed, a-hier-archical movement like AQAP which had 'adherents' rather than operatives. Because these adherents would, in all likelihood, act semi-autonomously with little or no communication with the leadership, strategic scripts needed to be identified and communicated carefully to all players if attacks were to be in harmony with the broader aims and priorities of the movement. The ability to communicate these scripts clearly and to define boundaries within which its loose, semi-autonomous membership should act was, as we shall see, one of AQAP's great successes.

'To Inflict a Thousand Tiny Cuts'[78]

Between early 2009 and late 2012, AQAP grew substantially.[79] Whilst this presented an opportunity for strategic expansion, one of AQAP's noticeable features was that it kept its strategic vision clearly defined and ensured that its membership operated within the boundaries it had set. Indeed, rather than adopting new forms of strategic violence, AQAP essentially retained its prefer-ence for terrorism, although its alliance with *Ansar al-Shari'a* in late 2010 effectively provided it with a semi-autonomous insurgent wing. AQAP also remained committed to its attrition and mobilisation script but, in contrast to its single-minded strategic focus, it sought to adapt and develop both ele-ments of the script. In order to examine the way in which the scripts were modified, it is necessary to examine these elements in isolation.

After the so-called 'merger' of January 2009, AQAP continued to pursue its attritional script by attacking the 'far enemy' on home soil, targeting the foreign diplomatic and touristic presence in Yemen. In March, a teenage sui-cide bomber, posing for a photo with tourists in Shibam, the 'Manhattan of the Desert', blew himself up killing five South Koreans.[80] Three days later,

AQAP attacked a diplomatic convoy carrying South Korean investigators and relatives of the tourists killed, to the airport, but no casualties were sustained.[81] This remained a standard aspect of AQAP's strategy. On 26 April 2010, a suicide bomber wearing the khaki-brown clothes of Yemeni high school children, blew himself up as the British ambassador was driving past, wounding three.[82] Six months later, a rocket-propelled grenade was fired at the British deputy ambassador. In December 2010, while four US embassy staff were eating at a popular restaurant, their car was blown up outside. AQAP also continued its now relatively long-standing campaign of terrorism against local targets. The oil industry remained attractive for AQAP because these attacks could be couched in the language of local grievances, southern secessionism, and had the potential to appeal to different constituencies outside the traditional Islamist core.

By August 2009, however, the attrition script had been reformulated and began to be implemented against the 'far enemy' abroad. Abdullah al-Asiri, who had left Saudi Arabia for Yemen in late 2007, made contact with Saudi intelligence, saying that he wanted to turn himself in to the rehabilitation programme. The deputy Minister of the Interior, Prince Mohammed bin Nayef, welcomed the opportunity and al-Asiri was invited to Jiddah. On entering the Prince's compound, he asked that the standard search be waived as a demonstration of good faith.[83] The Prince honoured the request, in turn asking him to verify his status as a member of AQAP by introducing him via telephone to another potential AQAP defector. Al-Asiri then called his contact, and after a few moments of conversation, al-Asiri passed the phone on to the Prince before promptly detonating the explosives that had been sewn in to his underwear.[84] Despite the fact that the ploy worked, his body limited the extent and direction of the blast and bin Nayef survived with relatively minor wounds.[85] As further information came to light in the aftermath of the attack, it emerged that Abdullah was the younger brother of Ibrahim al-Asiri, AQAP's notorious if elusive bomb-maker who had himself been arrested at some point in the 2000s for trying to enter Iraq. In *Sada al-Malahim* he said that prison was a foundational experience which made him 'see the depths of [Saudi] servitude to the Crusaders and their hatred for the true worshippers of God, from the way they interrogated me'; like so many others, particularly Saudis, who joined AQAP in late 2007 and beyond, arrest and imprisonment seem to have driven them towards the cause rather than away from it.

The preoccupation with Saudi Arabia was not merely a personal grievance of the al-Asiris but began to pervade the organisation more generally. In

October of the same year, three men were stopped at a Saudi checkpoint on the border with Yemen. Two of the three men were dressed as women and, as a female guard went up to check their papers, they opened fire.[86] A brief firefight ensued in which the two passengers—Ra'id al-Harbi and Yusuf al-Shihri, another member of Batch 10 and brother-in-law of Sa'id al-Shihri—were killed.[87] When the car was searched, a number of light weapons were found, as well as two ready-made suicide vests and the materials to make at least another two. Although the Saudi regime had attracted some of AQAP's ire since early 2008, neatly coinciding with the arrival of the Saudi faction, it was after the 'merger' that this view became increasingly entrenched. In the tenth edition of *Sada al-Malahim*, the author of one article asserts that 'the government of Ali Abdullah Saleh is on the verge of collapsing and fleeing from Yemen... our impending battle is with the Saudi regime, which opened the Arabian Peninsula for the Americans, making it a base from which the Christian legions launched to demolish our Muslim brothers in Iraq and Afghanistan'.[88] As one report puts it, 'by 2010, calls to attack the Saudi royal family and overthrow the Kingdom's government were easily the most common objective articulated by [the] four prominent Saudi members of AQAP'.[89]

By December 2009, however, targeted killings of the Saudi political elite had been exchanged for indiscriminate attacks on western civilians abroad. Umar Farouk Abdulmutallab arrived in Yemen in the spring of 2009. He had studied engineering at University College London and graduated in 2008, before briefly going on to Dubai to study management. Although Abdulmutallab had had strong views before his departure for Dubai, they seem to have become increasingly entrenched while he was there and after a few months, he dropped out of the course and went on to Yemen to study Arabic in Sana'a. It was here that he connected with members of AQAP, having written 'explaining why he wanted to join the *jihad*' to Anwar al-Awlaqi and by November 2009, he was in a safehouse in Shabwa being briefed on his forthcoming operation.[90] A month later, he travelled to Nigeria, stopping off in Ethiopia *en route*. He then flew from Lagos to Amsterdam, where he boarded his next flight, Northwest Airlines 253 to Detroit.[91] During the flight, he attempted to set light to a primitive fuse, and in so doing was spotted by passengers who restrained him. Similarly, in October 2010, following a tip-off from Saudi intelligence, two printer cartridges containing PETN, by now AQAP's explosive of choice, were found on cargo planes in England and in Dubai; the cartridges had been stashed in packages sent from Yemen to Jewish organisations in Chicago, but were designed to explode in mid-flight. That these devices resembled that of Abdulmutallab, and had been coordinated in terms of addresses, delivery and timed explosion are all indicative of a centralised plot, planned, sanctioned, funded and executed by core members of AQAP.[92]

Although the influx of Saudis had a part to play in the globalisation of AQAP's views, directing it in particular against the Saudi regime, there were others that came to the group which made it genuinely global. Most famous amongst these was Anwar al-Awlaqi, the now notorious Yemeni ideologue who had US citizenship. Al-Awlaqi rose through the ranks of AQAP relatively quickly. After leaving the US in 2002 and moving to the UK where he spent two years as an itinerant lecturer, he returned to Yemen in 2004 and took up a position at Iman University, the intellectual stronghold of Abd al-Majid al-Zindani; in August 2006, he was arrested for the kidnap of a Shi'ite teenager and a plot to kidnap a US diplomatic official only to be released in 2008. Once again, his prison experience seems to have driven him closer to al-Qa'ida's philosophy and by the time of the 'merger', he had become ideologically committed to that philosophy. Although he had no military expertise or experience of the Afghan *jihad*, within a matter of a year or so, he had acquired a reputation in the US as the most dangerous member of AQAP, even over the elusive Ibrahim al-Asiri and the leader Nasir al-Wuhayshi.

His reputation in the US as a genuine threat to homeland security was largely predicated on his earlier history: while he was an Imam in California in the 1990s he had links to Nawaf al-Hazmi and Khalid al-Mihdhar, both of whom turned out to be 9/11 hijackers; a few sources mention training camps, but there is no verifiable evidence to suggest this is true.[93] Others have pointed out that al-Awlaqi was connected as vice-president of a Yemeni charity, the Charitable Society for Social Welfare, to a low-level facilitator who paid for bin Laden's satellite phone; media articles have also pointed out that al-Zindani, the fiery Islamist ideologue, also played a role in the organisation.[94] There is further evidence that 'in January 2000, an Egyptian member of [Omar Abdul] Rahman's Islamic Group visited Awlaki's mosque, where he met with the young preacher'; this seems rather difficult to believe bearing in mind that Rahman had been in prison since 1992 and his organisation effectively disbanded since 1997.[95] Indeed, all the publicly available evidence suggests that throughout the 1990s and into the early 2000s, al-Awlaqi was a law-abiding Islamist functioning as a fairly typical participant in a social movement, rather than a budding terrorist.

If al-Awlaqi's early position in the broad spectrum of Islamism is a topic for mild debate, then his role in AQAP from the merger onwards is a source of deep contestation. For some, he was the 'Head of Foreign Operations', tasked with running a small cell structurally adjacent to the organisation. His portfolio, for them, comprised attacking the 'far enemy' beyond Yemen; in the view of these analysts, the cell consisted of about ten individuals, including an expert bomb-maker like Ibrahim al-Asiri.[96] For other analysts, however, he was little more than an ideologue divorced from the operational side—a source of concern for his ability to appeal to self-starters and hangers-on in the West and to incite them to grassroots *jihad* abroad.[97] Very rarely, he is viewed as a peripheral figure whose appeal and charisma was limited to English speaking audiences. Evidence for al-Awlaqi's 'Head of Foreign Operations' role is, like that concerning his role in the violent Islamist movement in the US, extremely thin. Hegghammer suggests:

> in the latest issue of the group's English-language magazine *Inspire*, an article signed 'Head of Foreign Operations' takes credit for the recent parcel bomb plot and outlines in great detail the planning and thinking behind it. The article is almost certainly written by Awlaki. We know this because the article references obscure figures from the history of Muslim Spain, a pet subject of Awlaki's, and because it mentions Charles Dickens' *Great Expectations*, a book he reviewed on his blog in 2008.[98]

This does not quite cover all the angles: it is not entirely clear why al-Awlaqi, who had been far from coy about attaching his name to videos and publications before, did not simply sign off with his own name and why, when he had no military expertise, was he promoted so rapidly into such a decidedly operational role?[99] Indeed, when Nasir al-Wuhayshi wrote to bin Laden asking that al-Awlaqi be instated as leader of AQAP in his stead, bin Laden's response indicates that he had severe reservations because of al-Awlaqi's lack of military experience:

> inform him [Nasir al-Wuhayshi], on my behalf in a private message to him, to remain in his position where he is qualified and capable of running the matter in Yemen ... Additionally, the presence of some of the characteristics by [sic] our brother Anwar al-'Awlaqi is a good thing, in order to serve *jihad*, and how excellent would it be if he gives us a chance to be introduced to him more... ask brother Basir to send us the resume, in detail and lengthy, of brother Anwar al-'Awlaqi, as well as the facts he relied on when recommending him [as leader], while informing him that his recommendation is considered. However, we would like to be reassured more. For example, we here become reassured of the people when they go to the line and get examined there.[100]

For bin Laden, *jihadi* authority and status was a product of time spent 'at the front' and therefore a prerequisite for any senior figure in al-Qa'ida. He recognised all too well that al-Awlaqi had little to offer the organisation in terms of operations. Essentially, he saw him as little more than a useful ideologue who could appeal to different constituencies in English and raise the organisation's profile. As time went on, al-Awlaqi was increasingly considered—not by AQAP or al-Qa'ida Core, but by the West and the US in particular—as a major figure in AQAP and potent threat to security. He rapidly acquired descriptions as 'one of the principal *jihadi* luminaries for would-be homegrown terrorists... his fluency with English, his unabashed advocacy of *jihad* and *mujahideen* organizations, and his Web-savvy approach are a powerful combination'.[101] Intelligence officials began to describe him as 'Public Enemy number 1' and 'Terrorist No. 1, in terms of the threat against us'; indeed, Michael Leiter, head of the US National Counterterrorism Center, went as far as to say that al-Awlaqi 'understood American psychology in a way that led him to try attacks that ... would be particularly terrorizing'.[102]

Whatever the truth behind these characterisations, the crucial point is that, as a target of the Americans and major feature of the discourse on countering al-Qa'ida, al-Awlaqi not only imparted greater kudos to the organisation, but also acquired status and authority in global *jihadi* circles for himself.[103] As his standing and reputation grew, he increasingly became the first point of contact for a number of would-be western militants. It was here that AQAP recognised the opportunity that al-Awlaqi presented, not as an operational planner responsible for the centralised attacks, but as someone capable of organising a different kind of *jihad*—one which had little central planning or support, but which could exert considerable coercive force on their primary oppositions. This 'grassroots' *jihad* was in effect an extension of the attrition script but it relied on inspiring violent Islamists abroad to invent their own *jihadi* enterprises away from Yemen, based on material provided in *Sada al-Malahim* and its English-language magazine edited by Samir Khan, *Inspire*. By galvanising hangers-on, 'wannabes' and homegrown initiates whilst simultaneously providing broad tactical and strategic parameters within which they could act, so the rationale went, the attritional strategy (of which the US was the primary target) could be pursued on multiple fronts

In effect, al-Awlaqi became the first point of call for those interested in self-starter or grassroots *jihad*. Indeed, al-Awlaqi's contact with violent Islamists in the US is telling. By the summer of 2008, al-Awlaqi was in e-mail contact with Barry Bujol, an American citizen, who sought advice on how to wage *jihad* and how to start up an untraceable website, to which he responded by sending a document he had written entitled '44 Ways to Support Jihad'.[104] Al-Awlaqi was also in touch with Zachary Chesser, later arrested in the US for inciting violence against the makers of *South Park* whose two hundredth episode depicted the Prophet Muhammad. One of his most notable exchanges, however, was with Nidal Malik Hassan, a major in the US Army who had previously attended the Dar al-Hijrah mosque in Virginia when Anwar al-Awlaqi was imam there. He sought guidance on the role and legitimacy of violence via e-mail and, in one of these communications, he tells al-Awlaqi:

> There are many soldiers in the us armed forces that have converted to Islam while in the service... Some appear to have internal conflicts and have even killed or tried to kill other us soldiers in the name of Islam i.e. Hasan Akbar, etc... Can you make some general comments about Muslims in the u.s. military.Would you consider someone like Hasan Akbar or other soldiers that have committed such acts with the goal of helping Muslims/Islam [...] fighting Jihad and if they did die would you consider them shaheeds [martyrs].[105]

In November 2009, a few weeks after the exchange, Hassan opened fire at the Fort Hood Army Base where he worked, killing thirteen people, twelve of them soldiers.[106] Although al-Awlaqi replied only three times to Hassan's numerous e-mails and never advocated violence, in time he would adopt a more strategic role in e-mail exchanges by advising would-be militants to take particular courses of action. The dialogue between al-Awlaqi and another grassroots *mujahideen*, Rajib Karim, reveals precisely this growing interest in strategy. Rajib Karim had spent time in Dhaka with his brother Tehzeeb, raising funds for *Jamaat ul-Mujahideen Bangladesh*. In September 2007, Rajib came to the UK and gained employment as a graduate IT trainee at British Airways (BA). The original idea was to attack BA computer systems electronically in order to cause chaos and significant financial damage. On 29 January 2010, Rajib Karim replied to al-Awlaqi, saying:

> I have knowledge about the key people in BA [British Airways] starting from the top management and the key people in BA IT department. I also have knowledge about key IT hardware locations, which if targeted can bring huge disruption to flights and cause BA a major financial loss ... but this would be at the risk of exposing myself as I will have to do that with my own login ID...[107]

In al-Awlaqi's eyes, the attack on infrastructure was insufficient as, indeed, was the UK as a target. For al-Awlaqi it had to be a significant attack on the US:

Our highest priority is the US. Anything there, even if on a smaller scale compared to what we may do in the UK, would be our choice. So the question is: with the people you have, is it possible to get a package or a person with a package on board a flight heading to the US? If that is not possible, then what ideas do you have that could be set up for the UK? ...[108]

In the end, the attack was intercepted and on 25 February, Karim was arrested. However, the attempted attack does demonstrate the growing authority of al-Awlaqi and his influence over foreign recruits.

This scenario was very much in the 'self-starter' mould, in which interested parties made contact with al-Awlaqi, presented their idea for *jihadi* activity which would then be adapted for the organisation's particular script and then approved. A grassroots *jihad* therefore emerged as al-Awlaqi grew in *jihadi* stature and the leadership recognised the advantages of bringing him formally into the group. The portfolio required little understanding of tactics (indeed, some of the tactics outlined in *Inspire*, such as attaching lawn mower blades to cars, border on the ludicrous) or of foreign security procedures. Rather like *Sada al-Malahim*, al-Awlaqi's 'strategy of a thousand cuts', removed many of the barriers to joining the *jihad*. There was no need to travel abroad, nor, with the publication of *Inspire*, to speak Arabic; moreover, the operational advantages—that private *jihadi* enterprise was difficult for foreign intelligence agencies to identify and intercept—meant that potential grassroots activists had to worry less about being caught. Indeed, so effective was this lowering of psychological barriers that Faisal Shahzad, who attempted to detonate a car bomb in Times Square, declared at his trial, 'Brace yourselves, because the war with Muslims has just begun. Consider me only a first droplet of the blood...'[109]

In the two years after the 'merger', then, AQAP adapted its attritional script. From attacks on Yemeni territory against both the near and 'far enemy', the organisation expanded to include centralised and de-centralised acts of terror against Saudi Arabia, the US and the West more generally. Hand-in-hand with this escalation came the emergence of another strategy in the form of an alliance with the loosely insurgent organisation, *Ansar al-Shari'a*. The exact relationship between *Ansar al-Shari'a* and AQAP remains a topic of contention. For some, *Ansar al-Shari'a* and AQAP are identifying terms which are used interchangeably on the ground and they argue that the insurgent wing of AQAP, *Ansar al-Shari'a* has little autonomy over its operations and is broadly tasked with the occupation of territory and recruitment of local militants into the cause.[110] For others, in contrast, it is a separate organisation, characterised by an autonomous leadership which plans and executes operations without authorisation from AQAP leadership.[111]

AQAP essentially used violence—terrorist and insurgent—in an attempt to wear down its oppositions, both in Yemen and beyond. Attrition works, as we saw in chapter 1, by depriving the opposition of its means: the persistent assassination of security personnel, so the logic runs, reduces an opposition's ability to pursue the perpetrators; campaigns of violence against political figures or the general population can reduce the political will to challenge the culprits; insurgencies can wear down governments by stretching their financial resources; repeated acts of terror, centralised and de-centralised, against the West can coerce it to re-think its (financial, military and diplomatic) relationship with the local government. Attritional scripts are an attempt to reduce the gap between one's own means and those of one's opposition, where means are cast in the broadest possible terms to include not just military supplies, human personnel and financial resources, but political will and popular support for the conflict.

In implementing this attritional script, AQAP used violence against the regime on numerous occasions, maintaining a long-term policy of assassinating senior military and intelligence figures, as well as executing surprise attacks on checkpoints and police patrols and attacking political figures. Although none of these attacks was meant, in and of itself, to bring about the fall of the regime, together AQAP saw them as a way of eroding the regime's access to military personnel (senior members in particular) and financial reserves in addition to reducing political and popular will for the fight. Violence used against the 'far enemy' was similarly viewed in attritional terms. Repeated attempts against both the western diplomatic and touristic presence in Yemen was part of a long-standing attempt to wear down the commitment of the West to remain *in situ*. Attacks against the aviation industry were, by AQAP's own admission, less an attempt to reduce the opposition's military resources and more an attempt to reduce their financial capabilities; as a long but enlightening quote from the special edition of *Inspire* released after the cargo plot had been intercepted:

> Two Nokia mobiles, $150 each, two HP printers, $300 each, plus shipping, transportation and other miscellaneous expenses add up to a total bill of $4,200. That is all what [sic] Operation Hemorrhage cost us. In terms of time it took us three months to plan and execute the operation from beginning to end. On the other hand this supposedly 'foiled plot', as some of our enemies would like to call, will without a doubt cost America and other Western countries billions of dollars in new security measures. That is what we call leverage.... From the start our objective was economic. Bringing down a cargo plane would only kill a pilot and co-pilot. It is true that blowing up the planes in the sky would add to the

element of fear and shock but that would have been an additional advantage to the operation and not a determining factor of its success.[112]

By the same token, the grassroots *jihad* developed and expanded upon the attrition script. In effect, the 'strategy of a thousand cuts' sought to increase the number of attacks, whilst necessarily reducing their lethality, in order to erode the resources and resolve of the US. 'Any Muslim', declares Abu Mus'ab al-Suri in *Inspire*, 'who wants to participate in *jihad* and the Resistance, can participate in this battle against America or anywhere, which is perhaps hundreds of times more effective than what he is able to do if he arrived at the open area of confrontation'.[113] Persistent but minor acts of terrorism, so the logic went, would exhaust the enemy and force them to withdraw. Indeed, AQAP were quite clear about how the grassroots *jihad* would function: 'This strategy of attacking the enemy with smaller, but more frequent operations is... the strategy of a thousand cuts. The aim is to bleed the enemy to death'.[114] The result was an attritional strategy which sought not to annihilate the enemy with a single *coup de grâce*, but to weaken him with a thousand tiny cuts until, in the words of Robert Taber, he 'becomes too weakened—in military terms, over-extended; in political terms, too unpopular; in economic terms, too expensive—to defend himself'.[115]

The grassroots strategy however, relied on mobilising would-be and wannabe militants to adopt violence on AQAP's behalf, and here the central role was played by AQAP's propaganda output. By mid-2010, AQAP was releasing a number of magazines in English, Arabic and even Urdu. The expansion of the media arm is probably related in part to the contribution of al-Awlaqi, but more importantly, it was Samir Khan, the editor of *Inspire*, whose arrival initiated the group's increasingly prolific (and prolix) media output. The magazine followed the traditional schema established by *Sada al-Malahim* of establishing scripts and cloaking the script in a frame which provided religious justifications for violence; much of its material was merely translation of other articles, particularly those by Abu Mus'ab al-Suri and bin Laden, and any new material was probably written by Samir Khan and al-Awlaqi. But later editions of the magazine began to extend the emphasis in line with al-Awlaqi's portfolio of inciting *jihad* abroad rather than attracting new recruits from the West into Yemen. In the second edition, an article entitled 'Tips for Our Brothers in the United Snakes of America' made a series of recommendations to the would-be militant. Yahya Ibrahim, who wrote the article, begins by advising potential recruits to fight *jihad* on US soil. In part, this is about avoiding detection: 'if you are clean, stay clean. Avoid contact with jihadi-minded individuals. Do not visit jihadi websites. Do not keep in your possession any suspicious materials'; indeed, Ibrahim advises acquiring published material by going to respected, non-Islamic organisations which publish *jihadi* material like SITE or MEMRI.[116]

But, whilst attrition of the 'far enemy's' morale and will could force them to withdraw, AQAP was quite clear that it would be insufficient for bringing about political objectives in the form of establishing an Islamic state in Yemen. The occupation of territory and attrition of the near enemy required a full-blown insurgency. AQAP clearly viewed the grassroots *jihad* against the 'far enemy' as the first stage of attrition—forcing a withdrawal of the West—to be open to the path for the second stage of attrition—forcing the withdrawal and collapse of the near enemy. As a translation from Abu Mus'ab al-Suri's work, *The Global Islamic Resistance Call*, quoted at length in *Inspire*, makes absolutely clear:

> The *jihad* of [the] individual is fundamental for exhausting the enemy and causing him to collapse and withdraw. [By contrast] the Open Front Jihad is fundamental for seizing control over land in order to liberate it, and establish Islamic law, with the help of Allah. The Individual Terrorism *Jihad* ... paves the way for the other kind (Open Front Jihad), aids and supports it. Without confrontation in the field and seizure of land, however, a state will not emerge for us. And this is the strategic goal for the Resistance project.[117]

Bearing this strategic vision in mind, then, it is not surprising that AQAP formed an alliance with *Ansar al-Shari'a* whose primary strategy was insurgency; indeed, *Ansar al-Shari'a* was highly effective in their attempts to erode the military resources of the Yemeni regime; in June 2011, they occupied the major towns of Zinjibar and Rada'a and succeeded in holding on to them, despite the deployment of significant government forces against them.

As we saw in the theoretical chapter, attrition is predominantly focused on achieving ends. Because it often involves eroding public confidence and morale, the general population is often negatively affected: innocent civilians caught in the conflict between the government and *Ansar al-Shari'a*, for example, are unlikely to show deep support for either party. It is precisely because attrition seeks to achieve ends rather than acquire means that it is often supported, as we saw with the EIG, by non-violent scripts which seek legitimacy. In this, once again, AQAP is notably traditional. In the search for legitimacy, AQAP instigated a broader 'nation-building' strategy. In 2011, they began to provide basic utilities (water, electricity), dispense medical supplies, mend roads and even establish courts in those towns occupied by *Ansar al-Shari'a* in what is clearly an effort to build popular support for the organisation and in so doing, to mitigate the negative effects of their script of attrition.

Essentially, then, this period of violent Islamism in Yemen can be viewed in terms of two scriptual stages: in the first phase, AQAP pursued an attritional script in which they envisaged reducing the opposition's resources and, in so doing, increasing the coercive capacity of their own means. To this end, AQAP used centralised violence against the both the near and 'far enemy' in Yemen and beyond in an effort to force a withdrawal of western presence and to weaken the regime. This 'terrorist' attritional script was expanded when AQAP formed an alliance with *Ansar al-Shari'a* through which they pursued an insurgency against the regime. Here, the goal was to acquire portions of territory as a base of operations from which to implement substantial military attacks against the regime, gradually wearing down its financial reserves and political will for the fight.

The second scriptual phase, which ran concurrently with the first, was to mobilise supporters through propaganda; this material, as has been argued, was not a passive statement of ideology and political ambitions, but an active device which delineated strategic visions and wrapped these visions in a legitimising, motivational frame in an effort to recruit and garner resources. In late 2009, AQAP improvised upon this mobilisation script by deploying their written materials in an effort to incite minor but persistent acts of individual *jihad* abroad and, in so doing, sought to coerce the 'far enemy', specifically the US, into withdrawing from Yemen, thus substantially weakening the Yemeni regime's ability to respond. This propaganda material is now the major channel through which the grassroots *jihad* is advocated and administered and, as such, is a method for gaining resources in the form of fringe militants and, with the strategic parameters that it explicitly outlines, deploying those fringes in the attempt to achieve political ends.

Responding to Terrorism in Yemen

As we saw in the Egypt case study, the problem with attrition is that oppositions rarely allow themselves to be exhausted without some kind of a fight. In the case of Yemen, the regime responded to Islamist violence with repression on the one hand and pre-emption and prevention on the other. In part, this response was the product of a finely balanced political system in which tribal loyalties and patronage networks required delicate handling of detractors, even where violence was involved. On the other hand, it was a consequence of the regime's weak financial resources and limited control of swathes of its own territory, which not only severely hampered its ability to challenge violent Islamist opposition, but also led other wealthier states in the Gulf and the West to provide significant quantities of aid, counter-terrorism assistance and, in the case of the US, to initiate a campaign of drone strikes on Yemeni territory.

Although repression was not the only response of the Yemeni regime, it formed a major strand of their effort to counter violent Islamism. Essentially, an attempt to crush the opposition by depriving it of all or most of its means, repression normally consists of several elements, all of which were present in Yemeni counter-terrorism strategy: mass arrest of Islamists, both violent and moderate; brutality and torture towards suspects; detention without trial; (extraordinary) rendition; and, less frequently, military responses against training camps and operational bases.

The primary and most visible of these elements was mass arrest. Perhaps surprisingly, I could find no evidence of any arrests of Islamists for ideological reasons before the attack on the USS Cole, with the exception of Abu Hassan and members of the AAIA who were convicted of forming an armed group and kidnapping Westerners. It was only in the aftermath of the attack on the USS Cole that the regime moved against violent (and non-violent) Islamists on Yemeni territory: thirty-five Islamists were arrested in December 2000, thirteen a month later and in June 2001, another fifteen were arrested.[118] The first mass arrest of Islamists in Yemen in which individuals were picked up on the basis of their ideology, rather than their involvement in any criminal offence, however, took place in the immediate aftermath of 9/11; an Amnesty International report noted that by the end of 2001, 'the exact number of people arrested in the wake of 11 September who remained in detention was not known; the government acknowledged 21 arrests while press reports indicated up to 500 were detained'.[119] In 2003, another Amnesty International report agreed with this analysis, stating:

> Prior to the 11 September events the government maintained that while it was not perfect, any arbitrary arrest taking place in the country was not the result of government policy. After 11 September, the government's message to Amnesty International has been articulated as the 'fight against terrorism' to preserve the security of the country which necessitates action by the arresting authorities beyond the confines of the law.[120]

This was backed up by political statements in September 2001, when Yemen was 'placed under a *de facto* state of emergency', and the prime minister announced that the regime had 'decided that investigations must be carried out into anyone who had any connection... [with] Afghanistan'.[121] Thereafter, mass arrests continued to be a central strand of Yemeni counter-terrorism strategy from 2002 until at least 2005. Indeed, as Sheikh Abdullah al-Ahmar, the speaker of the Yemeni parliament and leader of *Islah*, said, 'hundreds if not thousands of people [have] been unfairly detained in Yemen since 11 September 2001'.[122]

The mass arrest of Islamists was almost always accompanied by allegations of torture and brutality. Human rights observers, both western and Yemeni, have long noted that torture is rife in Yemeni detention facilities and a special inquiry set up by the Yemeni Parliament noted in 2002 that 'Some detainees... said they were beaten with electric batons, handcuffed and shackled, and sub-jected to insults and verbal abuse. Others said they were threatened with the imprisonment of their female relatives if they did not confess'.[123] Similarly, Yemenis repatriated from Guantánamo Bay were all immediately detained by the Political Security Organisation often without access to their families or legal counsel for several months. One returnee from Guantánamo Bay told Human Rights Watch that he 'was tortured for five days, from nine in the morning until dawn. The cell was dark. They beat me with shoes. There were insults, bad words and threats to do bad things to my female relatives and to imprison my father'.[124]

Although Yemen's human rights record, particularly in terms of profligate arrests, detention without trial and torture—not to mention its virtually non-existent legislative framework for dealing with threats to national security—makes for grim reading, it is worth noting that Yemen's record towards violent Islamists was less damning than that of others. Widespread arrests between the early 2000s and 2012 were common, but stood as a tiny proportion of Egypt's which between 1992 and 1997 totalled more than 47,000; indeed, mass arrests of violent Islamists are dwarfed by the Yemeni regime's far more extensive detention of and brutality towards thousands of southern Yemenis protesting against the regime.[125] To be clear, this is not because Yemen's human rights record is better, but its patronage system requires the regime to seek different ways to bargain and compromise.

Indeed, one suspects that is why mass arrests were avoided, and why the Yemeni regime so eagerly targeted the leadership of opposition groups. It meant handling a smaller number of people, and less in the way of bargaining with multiple factions and tribes. The basic premise of the campaign—at the outset—was to remove opposition leadership, the strategic and/or ideological driving force, and leave the middle and lower ranks bereft of the architects of violence. As Daniel Byman notes:

> Bomb makers, terrorism trainers, forgers, recruiters, and terrorist leaders are scarce; they need many months, if not years, to gain enough expertise to be effective. When these individuals are arrested or killed, their organizations are disrupted. The groups may still be able to attract recruits, but lacking expertise, these new recruits will not pose the same kind of threat.[126]

In the case of Yemen's violent Islamist movement, the regime sought to 'decapitate' Islamist groups by both arrest and targeted killing. The first leader to be arrested was Tariq al-Fadhli in the aftermath of the 1992 attacks on hotels in Aden. As suggested earlier, his arrest was little more than a face-saving gesture to the US and he was released only months later to bolster the regime's forces in the civil war with the south. The arrest and subsequent execution of Abu Hassan, al-Fadhli's opposite number in the AAIA, by contrast, left the organisation leaderless and it effectively receded into the broader Islamist movement for the foreseeable future. Equally, the arrest of key al-Qa'ida figures, Jamal al-Badawi and Fahd al-Quso, in combination with the drone strike on Abu Ali al-Harithi in 2002, dealt bin Laden's small but important presence in Yemen a *coup de grâce*.

Of course, as the US engaged in Yemen more and more, in an effort to support the regime in countering violent Islamist groups, drone strikes also became an increasingly prominent and contentious feature of the counter-terrorism effort in Yemen. 2012 witnessed such a dramatic intensification in airstrikes that, by early September, there was an average of nearly one every week—up from fewer than one a month in 2011 and one every six months in 2009.[127] In 2012 alone, airstrikes were responsible for the death of 193 people, thirty-five of whom were civilians and the remainder alleged members of AQAP or its subsidiaries.[128] Despite this increase, close analysis of the history of drone strikes in Yemen reveals that they have limited effect on the movements targeted. The elimination of both Anwar al-Awlaqi and Samir Khan in September 2011, for example, produced something of a hiatus in AQAP's propaganda output, but by May 2012, Yahya Ibrahim had taken over the role as editor of *Inspire* and immediately released two new editions.[129] Indeed, in the latter of these, he made specific comment on the death of his predecessors, saying that *Inspire*:

> is here to stay because it was not found [sic] to end with the end of its founders. Rather, with their end, it would only become deep-rooted and its objectives would become clearer. This magazine was set up to fulfill [sic] two objectives.

The first one is to call for and inspire to jihad [sic] in the English speaking world and second one is to deliver to every inspired Muslim anywhere around the world the operational know-how of carrying out attacks from within the West. *Inspire* is and will be an effective tool regardless of who is in charge of it, as long as it aims at fulfilling those mentioned objectives. Hence, we are still spreading the word and we are still publishing America's worst nightmare.[130]

Further attempts by the US to decapitate AQAP were unsuccessful: the elimination, in May 2012, of Fahd al-Quso, who played a major role in the attack on the USS Cole, had a negligible impact on the organisation. Much the same can be said about the drone strike which killed Sa'id al-Shihri in September 2012.

Indeed, the only targeted killing I could find which had any long-term impact on violent Islamist groups in Yemen was that of Abu Ali al-Harithi in 2002. His al-Qa'ida presence in Yemen, as we have seen, possessed unique features which made it particularly susceptible to 'decapitation'. Al-Harithi headed up only a very small al-Qa'ida presence which was predominantly preoccupied with facilitating and organising al-Nashiri's *jihad* in Yemen. This limited presence meant that the drone strike was a one-off incident in contrast with the much larger campaign of drone strikes against targets related (often tenuously) to AQAP. In turn, this meant that it was far easier to retain public support for the Yemeni and US governments. A second and related point to note is that Abu Ali's organisation was essentially hierarchical. Abu Ali occupied the leadership role, supported by other figures such as Fahd al-Quso and Jamal al-Badawi; beneath them were the fringe elements tasked by the leadership with minor responsibilities. Once Abu Ali had been eliminated and his two deputies arrested, al-Qa'ida's presence in Yemen was limited to those fringe elements who had no experience or expertise in waging a campaign of violence.

This episode neatly illustrates the way in which successful decapitation works: the elimination of a single leader, primarily responsible for driving an organisation forward, can leave lower ranks unable to organise themselves and unsure of how to proceed. But, in the case of larger organisations and movements like AQAP, there are significant difficulties. The first problem for the strategy, particularly US strategy in Yemen, was that drone strikes tended to fall into the trap of mission creep: the campaign was no longer about decapitating AQAP, but about ridding Yemen of all AQAP personnel, whether key players or marginal participants. Of the thirty-three confirmed US strikes against AQAP in 2012, less than a third could be described as targeting key members of the leadership or those with specialist skills (e.g. bomb makers and recruiters). To put it more contentiously, of the one hundred and ninety-three deaths through drone strikes, only five of those killed had a significant leadership or operational role in AQAP.[131]

The second problem is that drone strikes can produce backlashes from one's opposition. The day after Sa'id al-Shihri was killed in a drone strike, the Minister of Defence, Major General Muhammad Nasir Ahmad, survived an assassination attempt when a booby-trapped car exploded next to his motorcade, killing twelve.[132] The assassination of Ali Mahmud al-Qasaylah in 2007, the first al-Qa'ida attack since the prison break, was claimed in retaliation for the targeted killing of Abu Ali al-Harithi in 2002.[133] Equally, the attempted attacks of both Faisal Shahzad and Umar Farouk Abdulmutallab were claimed as retaliations to the deaths of Muslims at US hands in Yemen, the former saying 'I'm going to plead guilty a hundred times over until the hour the US … stops the drone strikes in Somalia and Yemen and in Pakistan.'[134]

The third and greatest problem with 'decapitation through targeted killing' is that it can create deep resentment and anger among local populations. When drone strikes form part of a longer campaign and bad targeting, civilian deaths and debates over the morality of the campaign are almost inevitable, local populations can begin to sympathise with, and often support, the opposition whose means one is trying to limit. US-Yemeni relations in late 2009 suggests that both governments were particularly concerned about this potential for what they termed 'blowback'. A leaked diplomatic cable of a meeting between President Saleh and General Petraeus just days before the attempted attack of Abdulmutallab in December 2009, suggests conclusively that the Yemeni regime would take the credit for US drone strikes in an attempt to lend the campaign legitimacy and to reduce anti-US sentiment:

> Saleh lamented the use of cruise missiles that are 'not very accurate' and welcomed the use of aircraft-deployed precision-guided bombs instead. 'We'll continue saying the bombs are ours, not yours,' Saleh said, prompting Deputy Prime Minister Alimi to joke that he had just 'lied' by telling Parliament that the bombs in Arhab, Abyan, and Shebwa were American-made but deployed by the ROYG.[135]

Further meetings between the Yemenis and the Ambassador focused on how to present US participation in and responsibility for air strikes if its role in leading the campaign came out into the open. One case was particularly problematic in that it involved the substantial loss of civilian life: Abdul Elah Hider Shayea, a Yemeni journalist, found evidence that the attack on al-

Ma'ajalah in May 2009 (which resulted in the tragic deaths of at least fourteen children and twenty-one women) had been an American operation.[136] In a meeting between the Yemenis and the US on 20 December 2009, the two parties discussed how to limit damage to both countries' reputations. The Yemenis felt that anti-US sentiment could be prevented by repeated assertions of the media line; the US recognised that the evidence was overwhelming and a more 'nuanced' position was required:

> [Deputy Prime Minister] Alimi told the Ambassador that Saleh was disturbed by press reports citing U.S. officials asserting American involvement in the [drone] operations, saying that the ROYG 'must maintain the status quo' with regard to the official denial of U.S. involvement in order to ensure additional 'positive operations' against AQAP ... The Ambassador cautioned Alimi that the ROYG may need to nuance its position regarding US involvement in the event more evidence surfaces, complicating its ability to adhere to the official line that ROYG forces conducted the operations independently. Alimi appeared confident that any evidence of greater US involvement—such as US munitions found at the sites—could be explained away as equipment purchased from the US.[137]

In the event, the US assessment was accurate. Yemeni journalists and opposition politicians had long claimed that the drone campaign was run by the US but definitive proof came with the release of diplomatic cables in the Wikileaks scandal. The role of the US in the drone campaigns led to significant loss of support for both the regime and the US in Yemen. In August and September 2012, there were anti-US protests, often joined by leading tribal sheikhs.[138] The mis-directed strike in May 2012 which killed Jaber al-Shabwani, the deputy governor of Ma'arib who was *en route* to a negotiation with local AQAP elements in an effort to persuade them to relinquish violence, provoked his tribe to sabotage Yemen's largest oil pipeline, costing the government more than a billion dollars in lost revenue.

Indeed, the difficulties in the drone campaign—as well as the nature of Yemeni society—suggest why the regime had to resort to different responses. Amongst these, the regime frequently sought to negotiate with violent Islamists, either by forming a working coalition with oppositions by bringing them in to the arena of legitimate political participation or to arrange a lasting truce or 'tacit non-aggression pact'.[139] In both cases, the dynamics and mechanisms of the patronage system were at play: inducements and rewards were offered to limit the behaviour of an opposition and the threat of retribution deterred transgressive actions.[140] Where 'red lines' were crossed, retribution was tailored to the magnitude of the infringement, most serious of which was violent opposition.[141] In this sense, negotiation is a strategy of control: it can either be preventative (which is to say it removes the means available to a potential opposition before it becomes a significant threat) or it can be preemptive (in that it entails 'emergency' action against a growing threat).[142]

The first negotiations with violent Islamists fall decidedly in to the 'preemptive' paradigm. In 1994, Saleh negotiated with the violent Islamist clusters that he had so keenly nurtured before and during the civil war, well aware that they represented a large if disorganised force. Negotiations with Tariq al-Fadhli were facilitated by his own background and political ambitions. His family had been ousted by the Marxists along with the British in 1967 and he had spent much of his life in virtual exile. In the aftermath of the civil war, al-Fadhli was offered a senior post in the General People's Congress, Saleh's own ruling party, and some of his lands were returned to him. This was not only a reward for his part in the civil war, but also an incentive to align with the regime and to play by the rules of the game; the coalition between al-Fadhli and Saleh was successful and long-lived and it was only in 2009 that al-Fadhli broke with the coalition and joined with the southern movement, *al-Hirak*. Negotiations with Abu Hassan of the AAIA were less successful in the long-term. After the civil war, the AAIA effectively entered into an unwritten truce with the regime. For four years, Yemen was relatively free of Islamist violence; the AAIA was unwilling to commit itself to mounting an attack on the regime, cognizant of the fact that they did not have the resources to present a serious challenge. By 1998, with global connections to prominent Islamists and increasing access to human and military resources, the AAIA broke the terms of the truce by planning an attack which was foiled in its early stages. The regime's response was uncompromising: they arrested all involved and, after the AAIA kidnapped a number of tourists, sent in troops to the AAIA's training camp in the al-Huttat mountains.

The regime's third attempt to negotiate with violent Islamist oppositions is perhaps the most interesting. According to a leaked diplomatic cable, in February 2009, President Saleh attempted to negotiate a truce with AQAP.

> The Republic of Yemen Government (ROYG) supposedly offered a truce to AQAP in early February … [offering] to cease attacks on AQAP if the organization halted attacks against ROYG elements, yet no further contact occurred—suggesting AQAP did not accept the truce.[143]

Unlike other strategies, negotiation is rarely an attempt to target the means of the opposition or to change their political ambitions. More frequently it is an attempt to bring about a change in the way that the opposition attempts to convert means to ends—it seeks to limit strategy. In this case, Saleh sought to consolidate his own power rather than to limit his opposition. As the same cable noted, 'it is highly likely Salih did indeed offer the truce, as recent information strongly suggests Salih's most pressing concern remains preserving his own power rather than eradicating Yemen's thriving extremist community'.[144] In the final analysis, however, violent Islamist organisations are deeply committed to their political goals; negotiations are likely to have a promising future only if the opposition judges a coalition or truce to be the best way of converting means to ends. In AQAP's analysis, the opposite was the case, as the cable noted:

> AQAP's rejection of the cease-fire highlights the already permissive security environment; AQAP leadership is aware even should ROYG security forces continue their counterterror campaign, such actions are unlikely to significantly affect operational planning and/or execution. President Salih's consideration of the political oppositionist movement as the priority threat to his regime strongly suggests the ROYG will continue attempts to appease or even co-opt extremist elements while attempting to quell secessionist sentiment in the south. Following this strategy, Yemeni counterterrorism operations against AQAP will likely wane, and the extremist organization will have even more freedom to plot attacks in both Yemen and in neighboring Saudi Arabia.[145]

In a country thick with oppositions, the regime long relied on coalitions and allegiances which it built through its extensive patronage network.[146] In the case of Islamist oppositions, co-optation into patronage networks was used as a method for maintaining control over parties whose objectives are often in conflict with those of the regime. Essentially, it is a method of crisis management under which, in the words of Sarah Phillips:

> solutions to problems are created through the dispersal of resources, benefits, and status, and the way to attract these is, therefore, to create a crisis and then negotiate a solution with the leadership... In a patronage system, ideological concerns take a backseat to the more material considerations of resources, benefits and status upon which the system is maintained.[147]

Rather than limiting political ends, therefore, bargains with violent Islamist groups limited the strategies used to achieve those ends (e.g. violence). By offering inducements and rewards for good behavior, the seductive promise of future rewards and benefits was intended to sweeten the bitter pill of co-operating with a rival and to ensure a certain level of loyalty to the regime. In return, the client:

> must also try to ensure the political quiescence of their constituency. In sum, they can take no action that either violently or non-violently threatens the

highly personalized nature of power around Salih. This includes everything from organizing a coup to building formal institutions with the capacity to limit executive authority.[148]

Equally, there are reprisals for bad behaviour when patronage clients transgress what April Longley Alley refers to as 'red lines'. 'Punishment', she notes, 'can be both individual and collective in nature. An individual may be punished directly or through the exclusion, harassment, or demotion of family members'.[149] Thus the logic of patronage and coalition forming was predicated on two parallel processes: on the one hand, there were political, reputational and economic inducements to initiate and maintain the coalition; on the other, the threat of exclusion and isolation from the patronage network was intended to coerce an opposition to remain within the alliance. In effect, coalitions survive or fail according to a strategic calculus: if the benefits (and costs) of political inclusion outweigh those of exclusion, as they did with non-violent Islamists in Yemen, then the coalition can function in the long-term. But it can also be a dangerous game: actors with different objectives can co-operate while it is expedient but the regime has little control over its rivals if their commitment to their own political agenda is very high. If the benefits of exclusion—the freedom to decide what one wants to do, when one wants to do it and how, without having to factor in the desires and aims of the benefactor—outweigh those of inclusion, then coalitions in Yemen were normally doomed to fail.

The calculation was particularly finely balanced in Yemen, where the dominant strategic logic of violence was to maximize existing means. For violent Islamists, it was precisely because they calculated their available means to be insufficient that they sought alternative strategies. For those with few resources like Yemen's violent Islamists, coalitions (even with those with very different outlooks) were a seductive option, offering the advantage and allure of participating in legitimate politics. But only up to a point: for violent Islamists who have already made the calculation that their means are too weak to warrant political inclusion and that violence is therefore the best course of action, the advantages of coalition with the regime (and the inducements offered) have to be extremely attractive to outweigh the perceived advantages of violence.

For this reason, coalitions tended to be fragile and transient, and the regime sought other strategies to cope with violent Islamism in Yemen. The most popular—and one of the most radical—were the de-radicalisation programmes established in Yemen. These broadly sought to 'turn' members of the opposition whilst they are in the community or, as was the case in Yemen, in prison.[150] The emergence of Yemen's de-radicalisation strategy, the first of its type in the world, took place in late August 2002. After announcing the establishment of *Lajnat Hiwar al-Fikri* (Committee for Intellectual Debate), Saleh proceeded to meet with the *ulema* in September to sketch out a broad framework in which the committee would work. The initiative ran into problems from the outset: based on an interview with Supreme Court Justice Judge Hamoud al-Hitar (who would run the Committee), Boucek *et al* suggest that fourteen of the fifteen clerics assembled by the president were so reluctant to be involved that they opted out of the initiative.[151] Their major issue was 'physical safety' and they drew parallels with the assassination of Muhammad al-Dhahabi by *Takfir wa'l-Hijra* in 1977, which they saw as an act of retribution against a cleric attempting to mediate with the group. In the end, al-Hitar ran the Committee with the aid of just three clerics. The dominant premise of the Committee was 'if you are right we will follow you, but if what we are saying is right, you have to admit it and follow us'.[152] The first meeting with prisoners, at the Political Security Organisation Centre in mid-September 2002, highlighted some of the problems with mounting this type of ideological challenge. The incarcerated Islamists accused their interlocutors of being little more than 'regime flunkies' and illegitimate by virtue of the simple fact that they disagreed with Islamist ideology and the politics of violence.

The initial dialogue sessions consisted largely of the prisoners presenting a grievance grounded in theology and a counter-challenge by al-Hitar. The first claim was that the regime was un-Islamic by virtue of its pro-Western stance (best encapsulated by their own imprisonment), to which the judge responded by providing a copy of the constitution and penal code for the prisoners with the challenge that if they could find anything in contravention of *shari'a* then the laws would be changed.[153] Another challenge was that President Saleh was an illegitimate leader because he did not govern as a *caliph*. Al-Hitar's counter-challenge was to ask the prisoners to show him where in the Qur'an such a requirement is presented; again they could not. As the programme progressed and seemed to be meeting with some success, the question arose of what to do with those who relinquished their views. At the beginning, there was talk of amnesty for those who signed declarations stating their rejection of violence but it was decided that those who had been primarily involved in lethal acts against others should be kept in prison for the duration of their sentences. Others, largely those who had been detained without charge, were released into society and sometimes provided with small amounts of money; release also required a commitment from family members and tribal figures to keep a watchful eye on former prisoners and to inform the authorities of any signs of recidivism.[154] In total, three hundred and sixty-four detainees entered into the dialogue process of which, it was estimated, forty per cent of interventions were successful and saw a release into society.

Although the work of the Committee was greeted with enthusiasm in Yemen and beyond while it was in its infancy, over time, doubts began to emerge over its effectiveness and after two former participants in the programme were identified as responsible for a suicide bombing on US forces in Baghdad, the programme was terminated after only three years in operation.[155] The academic and policy community is broadly split over whether the programme was effective. For some analysts, it was overtly a failure because AQAP re-emerged and re-engaged in terrorism from 2006 onwards.[156] Others have pointed to the initiative's flawed methodology, arguing that there were power imbalances between interlocutors and participants which simply did not permit a genuine dialogue, particularly where they thought that signing a declaration not to undertake violence could be interpreted as a confession of having not abided by these principles in the past.[157] Equally, the fact that the programme provided an all-too-easy route for release has meant that the initiative is widely interpreted as a piece of political theatre rather than a genuine attempt to restructure or realign the political views of violent Islamists.[158] Abu Jandal, bin Laden's former bodyguard, would later say that the Committee was little more than a political performance 'geared toward securing the detainees' acquiescence on several key points, including recognizing the legitimacy of the Yemeni government and obtaining assurance from progam participants that they would not engage in violence within Yemen'.[159] As Abu Jandal phrased it, 'we understood what the judge wanted and he understood what we wanted from him. The Yemeni Mujahideen in prison know Hitar is the way for them to get released, so they ingratiate themselves with him... There was no long or complex dialogue'.[160]

Others have pointed to the potential success of the Committee, arguing that its goal was never to bring about the de-radicalisation of all incarcerated Islamists but to 'facilitate the detainees' release and re-integration into society'.[161] Boucek et al, for example, suggest that the goals of the programme were to secure the recognition of the legitimacy of the Yemeni regime and the cessation of violence against Yemeni or western targets in Yemen and that by these lights, 'the dialogue committee has achieved relative successes'.[162] They respond to criticism that, for example, considerable numbers of Yemenis were present on other *jihadi* fronts, Iraq chief amongst them, by pointing out that detainees signed oaths stating that they would abstain from violence in Yemen, not beyond it.[163] Indeed, as al-Hitar himself said, 'Iraq wasn't part of the dialogue... I'm not responsible for Iraq. Nobody said to make a dialogue about that'.[164]

Whatever the potential success or failure of the strategy, it is clear that de-radicalisation was, essentially, a way of targeting a key weakness in violent Islamist oppositions: their means. The strategy sought to re-appropriate members from al-Qa'ida's ranks and in so doing de-legitimise the opposition's ideological underpinnings. When these initiatives are successful, this process of re-appropriation and de-legitimisation can de-mobilise an opposition by extending the gap between an opponent's resources and the political ambitions they are pursuing through violence. From a strategic point of view, then, de-radicalisation is decidedly a means-limiting script which seeks to prevent violence by making the tension between resources and goals unresolvable. In the case of Yemen, while the programme was in operation, it seems to have been at least partially responsible for the decline and eventual demise of al-Qa'ida. Although al-Qa'ida has re-emerged in Yemen, the de-radicalisation programme has not been restarted, although there were indications from the regime in 2010 that it intended to do so.[165] In the meantime, Yemen's violent Islamists have capitalised on the growing fragility of a financially weak, socially discontented and politically unstable country.

5

CONCLUSION: SCRIPTS OF TERROR

It is tough to make predictions. Especially about the future.

Yogi Berra

This book began by suggesting that terrorism is both a strategy and a choice. For those who perpetrate it, it is a choice made carefully with due consideration about how and whether violence will enable political goals to be reached. In part, the choice needs to be careful because the stakes are high: getting the strategy wrong will inevitably mean being on the receiving end of government retribution, losing popular support, being arrested, imprisoned, tortured and perhaps killed. It may also mean failure. But it is also a careful choice because terrorists not only want terrorism to work, but think it might work. They spend hours refining their strategies, and deliberating, not only because getting it wrong will have dire consequences, but because they think they can get it right, that they can achieve the political goals they so hanker after.

But the history of terrorism shows that it very rarely works: very few have ever achieved what they set out to get and most have been arrested or died in trying. Terrorism is so obviously risky and so rarely successful that one wonders that terrorists have not clocked that there are plenty of other, less violent and more legitimate ways through which they might achieve their political ambitions. Indeed, the choice of terror seems so starkly foolish and irrational that many look at terrorists and decide that they are little more than crazed fanatics with visions of grandeur and glory. Of course, the evidence shows that they are no more likely to have particular psychological traits than anyone else.

So why choose terrorism when it fails so often? I wanted to conclude this book by putting forward a different—and new—theory that goes some way to explaining why. This theory relies on some of the recent advances in behavioural sciences which suggests that rational decision-makers are beset by a host of biases, dissonances and heuristics which inevitably undermine the rationality and logic (and therefore outcomes) of our decisions. These biases are, sadly, myriad ranging from our predilection to trust tall, well-dressed, attractive people more than we do short, poorly-dressed, unattractive people (the halo effect) or to disbelieve anything that challenges our preconceived notions (confirmation bias).

One of the biases that seriously affects our judgement is the narrative delusion—the idea that stories are more convincing and compelling than simple facts.[1] Humans have a tendency to think through—and in terms of—stories. As Nassim Nicholas Taleb has argued, stories help humans to make sense of the world around them, to distil it into ready frameworks for interpretation and understanding. He says 'we like stories, we like to summarize, and we like to simplify'; we have a 'predilection for compact stories over raw truths' because 'explanations bind facts together... they help them make more sense'.[2] Charles Tilly similarly notes the human tendency to think in terms of narrative and to construct stories to explain sets of facts. Stories, he suggests:

> ... pop up everywhere. They lend themselves to vivid, compelling accounts of what has happened, what will happen or what should happen. They do essential work in social life, cementing people's commitments to common projects, helping people make sense of what is going on, channelling collective decisions and judgments, spurring people to action they would otherwise be reluctant to pursue.[3]

Even the ancient Greeks were aware of the power of stories. Odysseus—the great storyteller of the ancient world—had the power to make the 'falsehoods of a tale seem like the truth'.

What troubles all those who recognise the power of stories is their innate ability to mislead and beguile. This is because stories inevitably create causal links between things where there simply are none, or where they are weak. The classic 'rags to riches' tale might be an inspiration, but in reality it is a pretty rare occurrence. The very poor boy who finds fifty pence, buys a chocolate bar with a golden ticket, and goes to a spectacular chocolate factory that they then inherit makes for a fantastic tale, but probably should not be a model for anyone's life.

The same problems that apply to stories also apply to scripts. Scripts are basically stories: they describe situations, how different players interact in those situations, and sequences of events which can be expected to occur as a consequence. In the Aristotelian sense, they have 'a beginning, a middle and an end'.[4] They follow the same structure described by Charles Tilly who showed that stories consist of a limited number of characters with 'motives, capacities and resources', a set of objects with which to interact and a demarcated spatial and temporal environment; then 'set your characters in motion', 'make sure that all their actions follow your rules of plausibility' and 'trace the accumulated effects of their actions to some interesting outcome'.[5]

The problem with scripts is that, like stories, they have the power to seriously delude us. They can be hugely compelling, but also innately capricious, whimsical and unreliable. For the violent Islamists we have scrutinised in this book, there were only ever a handful of tried-and-tested scripts of terror (though, granted, there were far more peaceful ones available): survival (flight or fight), power play, provocation, de-legitimisation, mobilisation, attrition, co-operation, and de-mobilisation. Although more work would be needed to be certain, it is difficult to think of terrorist groups who have used wildly different scripts than the groups scrutinised in this book. In exploring these scripts, it is very clear that violent Islamists recognised that terrorism would be a risky choice and as such they gave it serious thought. Indeed, one pervasive characteristic of the violent Islamist organisations this book has explored is that they all spent a great deal of time debating (and, incidentally, disagreeing) over strategy. Indeed, by the time they were implementing their strategies, they often had surprisingly clear visions about how they intended them to unfold. A second key feature is that, despite the clarity of these scripts, most groups did not get what they wanted at all. Mostly, the scripts fell apart early on, or took an entirely different course than had been intended. Even where there were medium-term successes, such as the EIJ saw in Egypt, reality eventually kicked in and the situation deviated from the path that had been envisaged.

The most widely pursued, and in some senses, most important of these stories that we have seen was the survival script. Invariably a knee-jerk response, the survival script was the one that organisations turned to when they felt threatened. In these circumstances, they promptly dispensed with long-term goals in pursuit, by whatever means necessary, of the shorter-term goal of their own continued existence. This instinctive survival reaction mirrors the 'fight-or-flight' behaviour displayed by organisms under threat. As Walter Bradford Cannon, a leading physiologist in the first half of the twentieth century who coined the term, described it, 'The organism which... can best call forth sugar to supply the laboring muscles, can best lessen fatigue, and can best send blood to the parts essential in the run or the fight for life, is most likely to survive.'[6] Much the same could be said of violent Islamists whose instinctive reaction to a threat was to focus all energy, resources and effort on the short-term objective of survival.

Despite the knee-jerk reaction, those who fought, however ferociously, tended to perish swiftly. As they were increasingly threatened by the regime, both the Secret Apparatus and the 1965 Organisation, for example, sought to ward off the regime by resorting to violent self-defence. In practice, as they discovered, this succeeded only in causing significant casualties which could be weathered by the regime but not by their own embryonic movements.[7] Other groups, by contrast, sought not to fight to the death but to channel all their resources into fleeing from the opposition. Egyptian groups such as *Takfir wa'l-Hijra* and the Military Academy Group, for example, avoided regime repression by withdrawing into the mountains or hiding in plain sight respectively. By adopting this script, they were able to take advantage of the lull in hostilities to gather means and to recruit, although this inevitably resulted in difficult questions over when to dispense with survival and pursue more ends-oriented scripts.

Part of the problem with the survival script, however, was that violent Islamist resources were too weak to force the regime to back away and too meagre to withstand the inevitable storm of reprisals if they were caught. Violent Islamists, as we saw in the Egypt case study, understood this problem and recognised that they had to transition between the 'state of weakness' and the 'phase of power' before they could successfully confront the regime. One means-focused script which was used in an effort to transition was co-operation and, once again, it fell into two strands: alliances and coalitions. Violent Islamist alliances consisted of a union between organisations whose goals were analogous, but who differed on other matters—tactics, strategy, ideology and political vision, for instance. These alliances ranged from tenuous co-opera-tion (between bin Laden and Tariq al-Fadhli's cluster, for example, which was essentially a financial arrangement) to what amounted to formal unions between organisations (AQAP and Ansar al-Shari'a, for instance). Because violent Islamist goals were not only clearly defined but also held by all players, at least in a fundamental sense, alliances were relatively long-lasting and allowed players to increase pressure on their oppositions by pooling resources. Indeed, in the case studies, the only alliance which failed was the one between Farag and al-Zuhdi which formed Tanzim al-Jihad. Although the alliance was based on the logic of increasing meagre resources, the difficulty was that neither party could agree over the best way to deploy their increased means in the pursuit of political ends—that is, over strategy. The debate led to dissent between the Cairenes and Sa'idis, the disintegration of the alliance and, ultimately, to long-term animosity between the two groupings.

If, with the exception of the Tanzim al-Jihad, alliances were generally long-lasting and robust, then coalitions between violent Islamists and their regimes were transient, ephemeral and constantly on the precipice of dissolution. For violent Islamists, the strategic logic of coalitions was about garnering means: it was a way of putting the confrontation with the regime on hold while they devoted their energy to recruitment or turned their attention to a different, less contentious, opposition. For regimes, benefits came in the form of control: the coalition allowed them to limit Islamist violence or re-direct it towards another target. The problem with coalitions, in these case studies at any rate, was that violent Islamists calculated that they needed to pursue their own political ambitions if they were to keep the allegiance and interest of their members; at some stage, they inevitably broke the coalition as they pursued new, more violent, scripts against the regime. By breaking the coalition, violent Islamists transgressed established 'red lines' and, in so doing, inevitably stung their partners into punitive reprisals. In this sense, coalitions failed because violent Islamists failed to follow one of the four cardinal rules for successful co-operation identified by Robert Axelrod in his study of co-operation and the prisoner's dilemma. Here, he argued that 'the single best predictor' for the continued success of a co-operative relationship was whether or not a partner was the first to defect.[8] The difficulty for violent Islamists, particularly in Yemen, was that they always were the first to defect and the regime invariably reacted by dissolving the coalition on the one hand and with reprisals, normally fatal to violent Islamists, on the other.[9]

A third means-focused script which was implemented, albeit to a lesser extent than survival and co-operation, was power play. The script took two forms: in the first, violence was used in the face of organisational fracture to cement a leader's authority over dissenting factions and to reunite the organisation under that leader's control. For instance, al-Zawahiri ordered a suicide bombing in 1993 in an effort to rectify the damage to his reputation and to repair the organisational split in the EIJ over the appropriate targets of violence. Equally, Hasan al-Banna sought to repair the splits that emerged in the Brotherhood over the nature and need for violence by activating the Secret Apparatus. On the second and broader level, however, violence was used to improve an organisation's status in the eyes of supporters, both real and potential, when it had been outdone by a more active, ferocious or high-profile rival. This was surprisingly uncommon in the case studies: Shukri Mustafa ordered the kidnapping and subsequent execution of Muhammad al-Dhahabi in the face of a media smear campaign and the defection of several of his members to the Military Academy Group; equally, at least part of the logic of al-Zawahiri's campaign of violence in Egypt in 1993 was geared towards 'outbidding' the EIG.[10] Nevertheless, aside from these examples, there was a conspicuous lack of rivalry and one-upmanship between violent Islamists operating in the countries under study. There was, for example, no apparent use of the power play script by either al-Uyayri or al-Nashiri, despite the fact that the two were at loggerheads over their respective strategic vision; equally, there was no particular sense of animosity between AQAP and Ansar al-Shari'a, nor between the Saudi and Yemeni contingents which formed AQAP. It seems possible, bearing this in mind, to conclude tentatively that violent Islamists recognised that their means were meagre and rather than squandering these limited resources in an effort to eclipse rivals through displays of violent prowess, they preferred to 'co-operate' in order to accrue greater leverage.

Another script that was surprisingly underused, given its repeated implementation by other terrorist organisations from Narodnaya Volya to the FLN, was provocation.[11] Both bin Laden and al-Uyayri envisaged the provocation script although only the latter managed to implement it in one of the case study countries. Nevertheless, the basic premise of provocation—that extreme violence will elicit a response from an opposition which is so over- or underwhelming that the population loses faith in the regime and begins to favour the terrorists—remains clear. In this sense, provocation, which aims to produce specific behaviours in several audiences, several moves in advance, is an indirect strategy that attempts to pursue ends and gather means in equal measure. The sole deployment of the provocation script was by al-Uyayri who had been strong-armed into implementing the script prematurely by bin Laden. It is difficult to judge whether it would have had greater success had it been implemented when 'critical mass' has been reached as al-Uyayri envisaged; as it was, bin Laden laid considerable pressure on al-Uyayri to dispense with his survival script and 'get on with his job of hitting the opposition'.[12]

Nevertheless, al-Uyayri recognised that the problem with provocation was that the responses it was designed to elicit tended to be lethal and it was therefore a risky script which, without proper preparation, seriously threatened the organisation's existence. Indeed, this was precisely why he advocated the sur-

vival script in the first place: he sought to take advantage of the relative freedom to build up resources, recruit and train his personnel with a view to a
final provocative confrontation with the regime which violent Islamists would
be able to withstand. In practice, al-Uyayri's provocation script did elicit the
over-reaction he anticipated, but it failed to change the population's perception of the regime, not least because the regime had gone to great lengths to
ensure their legitimacy by implementing reforms which provided at least the
veneer of liberalisation; rather, the backlash was so repressive that it led not
only to the death of al-Uyayri but also to the dismantling of much of the
organisation which struggled to survive in the months that followed.

The fifth script used by the violent Islamist movements under study was
de-legitimisation.[13] By attacking an unpopular ally of the regime, so the
logic ran, violence would force a government to make impossible decisions
about whom to support. On the one hand, if the regime decided to support
its ally by cracking down on the perpetrators (catching moderates in the
crossfire) then it would be likely to lose legitimacy in the eyes of a population experiencing the negative effects of repression. On the other hand, the
regime could simply ignore the violence, but this would force a wedge
between the regime and valuable allies and impart legitimacy on the claims
made by terrorist violence. In the Saudi case study, de-legitimisation was
consistently configured as the second stage of the provocation script: the
provocation element sought to provoke the US into putting extreme pressure on the regime to deal with its violent Islamist 'problem' or risk losing a
valuable ally. This, in turn, was designed to force the regime to make impossible choices about whom to defend in which all options ended with the
regime's de-legitimisation. In this sense, the de-legitimisation script was a
way of harnessing the coercive force which the US was able to exert on the
regime in an effort to force it to make decisions which would inevitably lose
it popularity, power and legitimacy.

The problem with the script was not that the provocation element did not
work, but that it assumed that confronting violent Islamists would inevitably
deprive the regime of legitimacy. As the research argued, the Saudis mitigated
the potential loss of legitimacy by encasing their aggressive repression of violent Islamists in a legitimising frame of liberalisation and reform. On the one
hand, this had the effect of producing a 'schizophrenic' response to violent
Islamists who were confronted with repression and 'soft' de-radicalisation
initiatives in equal measure; on the other, it shored up the regime's political
base and deprived AQAP of the popular support they sought to acquire.

The sixth script identified in the case studies was mobilisation. In contrast to provocation which was under-used, this script was extremely prevalent. In its original format, the basic premise of mobilisation was that an act of violence which substantially changed the political landscape—through the assassination of a high-profile political figure, for example—had the capacity to persuade others of the weakness of the regime and to convince them to take up the cause. Farag envisaged the script in precisely these terms, arguing that the assassination of Sadat would liberate the Egyptian people and pave the way for an Islamic revolution. This vision was inherited by the EIJ after Farag's execution, although the organisation never had the opportunity to implement it because internal splits forced al-Zawahiri to deploy the power play script. Similarly, it formed a second stage in bin Laden's and al-Uyayri's strategic visions for Saudi Arabia. The problem with mobilisation was not so much in implementing violence and changing the landscape—although this understandably presented difficulties—but in inciting a population to take up the cause. The assassination of Sadat, for example, which Farag believed would create the conditions required for a popular, Islamic insurrection, in practice failed to have any substantial impact on the population.

AQAP in its Yemeni incarnation adapted the script to suit its own purposes. In contrast to the EIJ and al-Uyayri, AQAP sought to mobilise others not through the language of violence per se, but through their written materials. In the beginning, this material was essentially passive, amounting to little more than a call to arms in the form of statements concerning their ideology and politico-religious vision. By mid-2010, however, this material had become less about passive recruitment and more about active incitement. This material rejected the idea of would-be militants travelling to Yemen and urged them to construct their own jihadi enterprises at home. It delineated a strategic vision—'the strategy of a thousand cuts'—and urged its supporters to contribute to the cause by constructing their own grassroots jihad. This strategic vision was then enfolded in a motivational frame which intertwined local grievances with western interventionism in Yemen in order to provide a compelling rationale for participating in AQAP's de-centralised, grassroots *jihad*. In the short-term, this was successful: numerous individuals were motivated by this written material to take up the cause on AQAP's behalf. In the longer term, however, the grassroots campaign has been unsuccessful: western policy has not changed substantially, nor indeed has an Islamic state been established in Yemen.

The seventh script, attrition, was the pinnacle that most violent Islamists sought to attain. They hoped to garner sufficient resources through other scripts to be able to confront the regime with repeated acts of violence which would erode the regime's military, financial and political resources. In this sense, these attritional scripts reflected the standard 'guerrilla' paradigm: a long-term, grinding campaign which avoided open confrontation with the regime. For al-Zuhdi and the EIG, attrition was a way of inflicting costs on the regime by targeting their financial resources in the tourist trade, their legitimacy in the eyes of the Coptic community and their political support in the wider population. Both al-Nashiri and al-Muqrin pursued a similar script in which multiple acts of violence would force the US to withdraw from Saudi Arabia and, thus, weaken the regime. AQAP, similarly, constructed an insurgency against the Yemeni government in an effort to de-stabilise and overthrow the regime; simultaneously they incited a grassroots campaign which executed de-centralised terrorist attacks against the US in an attempt to force the US to leave the Arabian Peninsula.

The problem was that oppositions did not take multiple attacks on their forces and interests lightly. In the face of attrition, regimes responded ruthlessly: there were mass round-ups of Islamists, executions and assassinations of their figureheads and military operations against their strongholds. In this sense, the victor in the attrition script was the side which could best endure the inevitable casualties. As Edward Luttwak wrote 'there can be no victory in this style of war without overall material superiority, and there can be no cheap victories achieved by clever moves with few casualties and few resources expended'.[14] However, because attrition required significant resources this forced violent Islamists to make a tricky calculation: were sufficient means available to outlast the enemy? The point is made by John Mearsheimer:

> the attacker must believe that he has enough soldiers and equipment to compensate for his heavier losses, a point suggesting that success in a war of attrition largely depends on the size of the opposing forces. Allowing for the asymmetry in losses between offense and defense, the side with greater manpower and a larger material base will eventually prevail.[15]

Violent Islamists, however, did not have access to resources in abundance; not only were their means meagre in comparison to their political ambitions but also in relation to their opposition. As the attritional scripts were initiated, the disparity between their resources and those of the regimes they sought to coerce became patently clear. The Egyptian regime was able to deploy several thousand troops, arrest many thousands of Islamists and to maintain the aura of legitimacy in the eyes of its population without significantly stretching its military and security capabilities. The Saudi regime had to tread a finer line, largely because its own position was more precarious, but succeeded in snuffing out the Islamist threat whilst securing its own legitimacy in the form of a liberalisation programme. The Yemeni regime, by contrast, has not succeeded in treading this fine line, in part because its resources are limited and in part because its political authority is so contested; here, the attrition script continues to thrive.

The final script was de-mobilisation. This was an overt strategic choice made by violent Islamists when other scripts were deemed inappropriate or were perceived to have failed. As the Egypt case study demonstrated, the first stage of de-mobilisation involved re-evaluating the situation, recognising the flaws in previous strategic visions and identifying non-violent strategies as the most effective way to pursue political ends. The second stage was trickiest: here, the strategic evaluation had to be communicated to others, allies and enemies alike, in order to persuade them of the advantages of non-violence or, in the case of the latter, to convince them that the rejection of violence was genuine, rather than a ruse for some other purpose. The difficulty in persuading others of the need to de-mobilise was quite clear in the Luxor attack of 1997, in which elements of the EIG sent an authoritative, if brutal, message that violence was the only way to coerce the regime. Aside from this, however, both the EIG and EIJ were able to pursue the de-mobilisation script with some success, with the consequence that violence declined rapidly from 1997 onwards.

It is important to distinguish this script from disengagement, de-radicalisation and defeat. Clearly, some organisations rejected violence because they were defeated by the enemy's counter-terrorist operations which so deprived them of means that terrorism was no longer a viable option. Others rejected violence because they were convinced—by counter-propaganda, counter-extremism strategies or de-radicalisation initiatives—that their political ends were misguided or fallacious. But, between those who have not the resources for terrorism and those who have rejected the ambitious political goals for which terrorism was implemented, are those who pursue the same political ends through non-violent means. In this sense, defeat is a consequence of the debilitating loss of resources; disengagement and de-radicalisation are the product of shifting political priorities; de-mobilisation, by contrast, is a strategic shift for pursuing ambitions by other means. In practice, at least for the EIG and EIJ, that strategic shift required persuasion and this took the form of constructing a compelling narrative which identified the problem (the un-Islamic state and western interference in Egypt), provided a solution (non-violent political activism) and motivated supporters by laying emphasis on the need for this action.[16]

As all this suggests, the story of violent Islamism in the countries under study was, from their perspective at any rate, one of frustration and disappointment—of scripts which failed, means which were naggingly insufficient and ends which could only be left unreached. The only scripts which attained short-term strategic milestones—such as gaining resources or uniting the movement—were non-violent: 'flight', 'alliance formation', power play, and AQAP's adaptation of the 'mobilisation' script. Other, more violent, scripts stung the enemy into ruthless reprisals (fight and attrition) or failed to produce some desired reaction in the population (de-legitimisation and mobilisation) or simply collapsed of their own accord ('coalitions'). Even when different scriptual elements were glued together, they were unsuccessful: the hybridisation of mobilisation and attrition by Tanzim al-Jihad and al-Muqrin simultaneously failed to incite popular revolutions and to coerce their respective regimes. De-mobilisation was successful in terms of finding an alternative path that might lead to political ambitions, but it has not as yet attained those ambitions.

The Delusion of Terror

'The best-laid schemes o' mice an' men', wrote Robert Burns on uncovering a nest of mice with his plough share as an unforgiving Scottish winter loomed in 1785, promise much joy but often go awry, leaving little but grief and pain. His point was that one can plan furiously only for some unforeseen agent to plough up the whole carefully constructed scheme. Much the same could be said of scripts—at least if the experience of violent Islamists is anything to go by. Scripts promised much, but gave little; they offered tantalising images of hard battles won, oppressed populations liberated and coveted political goals reached, but in practice, they brought little but reprisals and repression.

The disparity between the way in which violent Islamists envisaged situations developing and the way in which events unfolded in reality—the strategic gap—was a central factor in the failure of the groups this book has looked at. In large part, this gap arises because scripts nearly always contain a fundamental cause-effect problem: as scripts, they describe a sequence of events (X, followed by Y, followed by Z) but, because they are used as stories about the future, they acquire a series of causal links (X causes Y which causes Z). The narrative element means the scripts acquire a cause-effect

135

structure which makes it all the more alluring to the decision-maker. Indeed, it is precisely because scripts are converted into narratives with causal structures that they encourage bad analogies, false assumptions, misinterpretations and fallacies. When it came to the groups at which this book looks, scripts offered tantalising promises of ambitions achieved through causally-linked sequences of events and lulled Islamists into pursuing them by fostering an 'illusion of inevitability'.[17]

If the theory provided the illusion of inevitability, then reality must have come as a shock. In practice, when violent Islamists put their scripts into play, the spurious cause-effect structures were invariably revealed as sequences of events failed to materialise, as other parties decided not to play their parts appropriately or pursued some script of their own and as political ambitions were left out of reach. An example usefully demonstrates the point. The 'mobilisation' script outlined in the previous section describes a chain of events which can be broken down into five component stages: violence | political change | weakened regime | popular revolution | further political change. The human tendency to recast sequences of events as stories means that we tend to explain these events by linking them in causal framework. This produces a little story: the assassination of a high-profile political figure substantially changes the political landscape by weakening the regime; this, in turn, appeals to a frustrated population who now recognise a regime's fragility with the consequence that the population rises up against the remnants of the regime, who are unable to suppress the insurrection and are thus driven out of power, allowing the people to institute a new, more favourable government. In this sense, the script has not only become a potentially compelling and convincing story but one which implies that each stage is a necessary and immutable product of the previous stage. For a violent Islamist strategist on the cusp of making a major decision about a future strategy, the script was compelling because it provided a set of rules for overthrowing the regime: all one needed to do was to attack a high-profile member of the enemy at the right moment when the population was restless and—to shorten the cause-effect structure yet further—the people will rise up and the regime fall.

The difficulty was that the cause-effect structures through which scripts explained sequences of events, were, for violent Islamists anyway, fundamentally flawed. They allowed little room for the accidental and unpredictable, they obscured the role of luck and overstated the role of human agency, and most importantly, they oversimplified complex causal structures, making them linear and one-dimensional. Not surprisingly, when implemented, the chain of events they forecast failed to emerge leaving a substantial gap between strategic vision and strategic action. Why did violent Islamists not recognise these flaws and produce more malleable scripts? At least part of the answer is because they suffered from narrative delusion: scripts were so compelling—because they explained sequences of events through stories—and violent Islamists were so eager to believe them, that they were blinded to the fallacies and assumptions in the cause-effect structures which characterised scripts.

The flaws in cause-effect structures come into particularly sharp focus when strategists draw analogies with similar situations and 'borrow' scripts. This process is a central part of script formation and decision-making. Just as the novelist cannot write a book which is not, in some sense, influenced by other stories, so the strategist cannot formulate scripts blindly, without (at least, subconscious) reference to other situations and scripts. As Taleb says 'it is literally impossible to ignore posterior information when solving a problem'. Strategists, like novelists, draw analogies with the scripts of other strategists, seeking to re-work their weaknesses and/or emulate their most successful elements in new situations.[18] This is not to say that strategists are closet plagiarists who thieve other people's scripts, but it is, however, to say that strategic scripts used by others act as a reference point for analogies and comparisons, whether positive or negative, in formulating scripts for the future.

Like most decision-makers, violent Islamist strategists drew numerous analogies with others, often seeking to replicate their successes by emulating them.[19] Abd al-Salam Farag, for example, formulated his mobilisation script on the paradigm of the Iranian Revolution, but his search for a new script was predicated on an explicit critique of the stories of his predecessors in which he argued that trying to avoid the regime by fleeing to the desert was a 'waste of time' and that attempting to put an end to imperialism through violence was 'not a useful act'. Bin Laden, similarly, borrowed from other strategists; he thought he could force the US to retreat from Saudi Arabia based on stories about their withdrawals from Aden, Lebanon and Somalia; al-Uyayri, in turn, formulated his script based on bin Laden's strategic vision; Abd al-Aziz al-Muqrin hybridised this script by combining the attrition and mobilisation elements of al-Uyayri's and al-Nashiri's strategic visions.

Violent Islamists who were lulled into emulating the compelling scripts of others suffered from narrative delusion: they remained blind to the crucial but fallacious assumption that the causal structures in the stories of others' successes could be 'transferred' to new environments. The case of Farag is particularly illuminating. He wanted to overthrow the regime in the same way as the

Iranian Revolution had overthrown the shah; therefore he needed to weaken the regime by assassinating Sadat and, in so doing, the Egyptian population, liberated from Sadat's authoritarianism, would recognise the regime's fragility and rise up against it, overthrowing the last remnants of the *jahili* government and establishing a truly Islamic state. Part of the problem was that the differences between Egypt and Iran outweighed the similarities. Sadat, although leading in a time of economic hardship and mild unpopularity, saw nothing on the scale of the long-term general strikes and animosity experienced by the shah in Tehran; Sadat had the full support of the US after Camp David whereas, after the election of Carter with his advocacy of human rights, the shah's relationship with the US was no longer unconditional; equally, Farag, although he had a following in Egyptian Islamist circles, was far from the charismatic rhetorician of Khomeini who was able to 'unify the various components, religious and secular, of a movement whose single point of departure was hatred of the shah'.[20]

Farag suffered from narrative delusion. His script carried a set of events broadly reflecting the Iranian model: violence | weakened regime | popular revolution | overthrow of the regime. The narrative aspect of the script, however, encased these components in a cause-effect framework which fostered the illusion that similar effects would stem from the same starting action in similar situations. So alluring was the cause-effect structure of the Iranian Revolution script, which he sought to re-deploy in Egypt, that Farag overlooked the flaws of emulation. The crucial difficulty was that the causal structure of the Iranian Revolution could not simply be transferred to the Egyptian theatre and, as we saw, the assassination of Sadat did not de-stabilise the Egyptian regime, nor did it incite a revolution, but it did produce an uncompromising backlash. In this sense, the strategic gap was the product of narrative delusion. Because violent Islamist strategists, like all humans, had a propensity to structure sequences of events as stories, they inevitably provided them with cause-effect structures. But the problem was that these causal models were not necessarily transferrable. An action that produces a particular effect in one environment may produce a completely different effect in another setting—and, as Farag found out, that effect may be detrimental, even lethal, to the strategist's own side.

Another consequence of narrative delusion was that strategists interpreted stories about the strategic successes (and failures) of others to suit their own purposes, distorting their causal structures, misconstruing crucial elements and even fabricating their outcomes. And yet, these 'recipes for success' were so compelling that strategists glossed over the flaws in their interpretations with the consequence that the scripts violent Islamists mimicked were fallacious. Bin Laden, for example, sought to coerce the US to withdraw from Saudi Arabia based on explicit references to Aden and Somalia. Bin Laden's analysis of Aden was clear:

> The United States wanted to set up a military base for US soldiers in Yemen so that it could send fresh troops to Somalia. The Arab *mujahideen* related to the Afghan *jihad* carried out two bomb explosions in Yemen to warn the United States, causing damage to some Americans staying in those hotels. The United States received our warning and gave up the idea of setting up its military bases in Yemen.[21]

For bin Laden, the US withdrawal from Aden provided evidence that provocation worked; by causing rapid loss of American life through violence, he calculated, it was possible to produce a recalibration of their cost-benefit analysis of occupying Muslim territory and to coerce them into withdrawal. The analogy with Somalia was equally important to bin Laden's advocacy of the 'provocation' script. In his 1996 '*fatwa*', he addressed US Secretary of Defense, William Perry, arguing that 'when tens of your soldiers were killed in minor battles and one American Pilot was dragged in the streets of Mogadishu you left the area carrying disappointment, humiliation, defeat and your dead with you. Clinton appeared in front of the whole world threatening and promising revenge, but these threats were merely a preparation for your withdrawal'.[22] Bin Laden interpreted the Battle of Mogadishu as evidence for American aversion to losses and, in his eyes, their cowardice. He calculated that the US could similarly be coerced into withdrawing from Saudi Arabia by inflicting heavy casualties of military personnel, thus altering the US government's perceptions of the advantages of their presence in Saudi Arabia.

The problem with bin Laden's analysis was not only that he assumed, like Farag, that the cause-effect structures in these analogous scripts could be re-used in the Saudi case, but that his interpretation of these cause-effect structures was flawed. In the case of Aden, he derived a script from a false story: the attacks did not actually kill any American soldiers and the subsequent 'withdrawal' of US forces was not a product of Islamist violence, but rather of operational requirements to enter the Somali theatre.[23] In the case of Somalia, the violence and loss of life in the Battle of Mogadishu did indeed bring about a departure of US troops; just four days after the gun battle in the streets of Mogadishu on 7 October 1993, Clinton announced that he would bring troops home in the next six months. The problem for bin Laden's analogy was that the events of Somalia had not been a 'provocation' script at all: as US forces attempted to capture two senior Somali National Alliance politicians, rumours spread throughout Mogadishu and Somali militants flocked to the scene. In contrast to the deliberative 'provocation' script in which violence forces an opposition to react and which bin Laden envisaged, the script actually implemented was a knee-jerk and instinctive reaction to US aggression broadly approximating the fight strand of the survival script. For violent Islamists, the impact of bin Laden's misinterpretation of these (and other) stories was considerable; bin Laden's 'provocation' script generated unreasonable expectations about the way in which a sequence of events should unfold and invariably elicited uncompromising responses from regimes when it was implemented. A further issue was that bin Laden's 'provocation' script acquired a lengthy 'ancestry'; it would later be used by al-Uyayri and, eventually, as part of al-Muqrin's hybridised script; on a broader level, it would be pursued by the wider al-Qa'ida movement in attacks like 9/11 and 7/7. And yet, because the script was based on flawed assumptions which led to a spurious cause-effect structure, it did not—and has not—succeeded in achieving strategic milestones or al-Qa'ida's long-term objectives.

When strategists formulate strategic visions based on the stories of others, an act of interpretation is required; the story to which analogy is drawn must be distilled into a sequence of events and the causal relationship between those events must then be identified accurately. But constructing new scripts based on interpretations of the past is far from easy. As Daniel Kahneman argued, 'we believe we understand the past which implies that the future also should be knowable, but in fact we understand the past less than we believe we do'.[24] The Aden and Mogadishu examples showed how easily interpretation of other stories can go awry. In the Aden case, bin Laden constructed a provocation script based on false perceptions about the outcome of a story; in the Mogadishu case, his perception of the outcomes were accurate, but his identification of the sequence of events and the causal relationship between those events—in other words, the script—which led to that outcome was false. The difficulty is that accurate interpretation of stories is far from easy; biases invariably creep in and when they do, the resulting script is likely to have a fundamentally flawed cause-effect structure which may promise much but, when put into practice, will make little headway in achieving one's ends.

Violent Islamist scripts, as stories, suffered from an underlying problem, whether they were the product of analogies and emulation or not: they invariably simplified the cause-effect structure which connected the various stages in their scripts, overstating human agency, underplaying the role of luck and excluding all but a handful of characters. The case of Abdulmutallab, for example, was extolled as a great success by AQAP in its first edition of *Inspire*, claiming that:

> He managed to penetrate all devices, modern advanced technology and security checkpoints in the international airports bravely without fear of death and defying the great myth of the American and international intelligence, and exposing how fragile they are, bringing their nose to the ground, and making them regret all that they spent on security technology.

In reality, Abdulmutallab was lucky; his father had been so concerned that he reported him to the US, who added him to the Terrorism Identities Datamart Environment database, but after a 'number of human errors', he was not added to the Terrorist Screening Database, nor was his visa revoked.[25] Another attack vigorously praised by AQAP was the attempted assassination of Prince Mohammed bin Nayef by Abdullah al-Asiri. Once again, luck played a significant role, not least in the fact that the prince agreed to the meeting, and, having agreed to it, in that al-Asiri was not searched by the prince's security guards. An issue of *Sada al-Malahim*, however, claimed that:

> [al-Asiri] was able to enter [Nayef's] palace and circulate amongst his bodyguards, thereupon igniting his explosive device ... after he passed through all the checkpoints in Najran and Jeddah airports, and was transferred aboard the plane that belongs to [the prince]."

This tendency to emphasise human agency in scripts and to omit the element of the unpredictable characterised most violent Islamist scripts. Bin Laden's provocation script, for example, was derived from stories about Aden and Mogadishu. In the case of Aden, there was very little human agency involved in coercing US forces to leave, not least because they left of their own accord. In the case of Mogadishu, the mass influx of Somali militiamen was essentially a random unpredictable event—a black swan, for academics like Taleb—rather than the product of human effort and yet, bin Laden re-told the story as one of violent Islamists forcing the US to withdraw. Equally, simplified causal structures permeated the stories violent Islamists told about the future: the *Tanzim al-Jihad*, for example, envisaged the assassination of Sadat by violent Islamists as a way of inciting a mass insurrection; al-Nashiri envisaged an attritional war in which violent Islamists inflicted heavy casualties which coerced the US into leaving the Arabian Peninsula; the Secret Apparatus imagined that Islamist violence would ward off regime oppression.

In relating these stories, violent Islamists constructed compelling narratives by lacing a causal thread through a sequence of events, pedestalling human agency and smothering the role of luck and the unpredictable. The difficulty with these stories was that cause could not be so easily linked to effect. In reality, successfully coercing enemies through meagre means required a whole range of factors to be present—economic hardship, a restless population, lack of international support for the regime, timing, luck, popularity for Islamist ideals and so on. Scripts, as stories, drastically simplified this causal nexus, linking Islamist violence to specific reactions of multiple players many moves in advance. They implied that ambitious ends could be achieved with even minimal resources through specific violent Islamist actions. The problem for violent Islamists, of course, was that they were deluded by the compelling narratives of scripts as stories. These stories were so alluring—and violent Islamists, committed to their political ambitions, so willing to be convinced— that their inherent flaws were glossed over, ignored or dismissed. This is a standard aspect of stories—as Kahneman has argued, compelling stories are 'simple; are concrete rather than abstract; assign a larger role to talent, stupidity and intentions than to luck; and focus on the few striking events that happened rather than on the countless events that failed to happen'.[26]

Perhaps violent Islamists would have had more success had they told better stories about the future, ones which allowed for the unpredictable and which understood a broader range of causes in producing effect.[27] In practice, however, violent Islamists did not just tell crudely constructed stories, they told extremely simple stories about the future which distilled situations to a handful of causes leading directly, immutably and inevitably to a single desired effect. This was a product of narrative delusion: because simple stories were compelling, violent Islamist strategists overlooked their inherent flaws. The simpler the story, the more compelling—and flawed—it was, and the more violent Islamists glossed over those flaws. The narrative delusion revolves around this simplicity; as Kahneman noted 'when there are fewer pieces to fit into the puzzle... [o]ur comforting conviction that the world makes sense rests on a secure foundation: our almost unlimited ability to ignore our ignorance'.[28] The simple stories of violent Islamists were compelling; they had the capacity to drive collective action; they described a series of simple, causally-linked events which led to desired goals; they made promises about the future; and, when it came to making decisions about the future, it is little wonder that particular scripts, offering tantalising images of political goals easily achieved, appealed to violent Islamists. And yet, violent Islamists rarely questioned the simplicity of these strategic visions nor the crucial factors that these stories omitted because compelling narratives deluded violent Islamists into 'ignoring their own ignorance'.

The underlying theory developed in this book—of scripts, strategies, stories and narrative delusion—could be fruitfully applied outside the world of violent Islamism. Indeed, it is precisely because all strategists tell stories about the future—and because all stories have cause-effect structures which offer tantalising images of goals achieved—that all strategists must, to some extent, suffer from narrative delusion. Nevertheless, there seems to be little choice for strategists other than to make stories out of sequences of events in order to make scripts which are useful and predictive. Without stories and their cause-effect structures, the outcomes of actions cannot be envisaged and decisions can only be made blindly in the vague hope that something advantageous might arise. Strategists are therefore engaged permanently in writing stories about the future based on their interpretation of stories about the past. From this perspective, good decisions and good strategy are a product of good story-telling about the future and good interpretation of past stories. By the same token, bad decisions and bad strategy, that is strategy unlikely to produce desired effects, are similarly the product of bad interpretation of past stories and bad story-telling about the future. If one is to convert means into ends, one must produce stories whose cause-effect structures are reasonable, whose assumptions are accurate and whose plots do not exclude crucial environmental factors such as the role of the unpredictable. The difficulty for strategists, and especially violent Islamist strategists for whom there is no room for mistakes, is that they must make extremely accurate predictions. As the eminently wise Yogi Berra noted, 'it is tough to make predictions. Especially about the future'. Strategists might well agree.

A NOTE ON DEFINITIONS

For the purposes of this study I primarily refer to the organisations examined as violent Islamist. The rationale for adopting this term is twofold. In the first place, it simultaneously encapsulates a set of political ambitions and the way in which the organisations under study seek to achieve those ambitions without conveying any sense of moral judgment. This neatly coincides with the definition of the strategy as a way of converting resources into political ambitions. In the second and more practical place, 'violent Islamist' is more clearly defined and demarcated than other terms, allowing for clarity and simplicity in its usage throughout the study. By contrast, the rival terms which are widely used in the secondary literature and over whose relative merits much ink has been spilled were either inherently pejorative or ambiguous. 'Fundamentalist', for example, carries with it an image of backwardness implying that these organisations have failed to appreciate the perceived advantages of modernity and democracy. 'Extremist' fares little better, encapsulating a variety of behaviours and beliefs perceived to be unacceptable and located beyond the boundaries of legitimacy.[1] Aside from the fact that the term has become intimately associated with Islamic terrorism, it also carries with it a sense of illegitimacy and immorality that lends it an uncomfortable political slant.[2]

The most commonly used term in the context of Islamist terrorism is *'jihadi'* (or *'jihadist'*). This term has been now widely been used when referring to those individuals and groups whose politico-religious beliefs fall under the broad mantle of Islamism, but whose method for bringing about the *Dar al-Islam* (the Islamic Society) is violence. But, despite these perceptions, *jihad* does not always entail violence.[3] The central meaning of *jihad* is 'to strive' or 'to struggle', and in a religious context, it incorporates 'any form of activity, either personal or communal, undertaken by Muslims in attempting to follow the path of God'.[4] It is precisely because the term conflates normal religious activity of many conservative Muslims with the political violence of the few that the term is avoided in this book.[5] *Salafi* has, like *jihadi*, come into usage to designate those individuals who base their religious behaviour on a literalist interpretation of the Qur'an and the *hadith*.[6] In contrast to *jihadi*, *Salafi* presents difficulties because it represents too broad a constituency.[7] Non-violent political parties, violent terrorist organisations, Saudi dissidents and supporters of the regime—all seem to fall under the banner of *Salafism*.[8] Indeed, it is because the term incorporates multiple and fluctuating identities, beliefs and ideologies that make it too unwieldy and slippery a term for this study.

In light of these problems and for the reasons suggested above, the research refers to the groups under study as violent Islamists. This is not, however, without its own problems because Islamism is a relatively broad term which encompasses a range of ideological perspectives.[9] Whilst the ideology of Islamism falls beyond the scope of this book, the critical fact is that, as a term, it encapsulates a relatively coherent set of political aims: the creation of a society which is Islamic in all aspects (politics, law, economics, civil society, education, foreign policy and so on), the establishment of an Islamic state and the implementation of *shari'a*.[10] Because this book examines terrorism as a strategy for converting resources into political ambitions, similarity in political ends provides a useful way of identifying groups under study—that is, they have adopted violence in order to achieve the specific goals of an Islamic state, free of external influence and the related desire to run that state according to *shari'a* and the precepts of the Qur'an. Less frequently, I refer to some of the organisations under study as terrorist. The briefest of glances at the secondary literature on the definition of terrorism will suggest that this is to play with fire.[11] However, the research only refers to groups as terrorist if they deploy violence as a strategy for achieving their goals.

NOTES

PREFACE: THE DILEMMA OF TERROR

1. Deborah A. Small, George Loewenstein, Paul Slovic, "Sympathy and callousness: The impact of deliberative thought on donations to identifiable and statistical victims," *Organizational Behavior and Human Decision Processes*, Volume 102, Issue 2, 2007: 143–53.

1. THE SEDUCTION OF TERROR

1. Lawrence Freedman, *Strategy: A History* (OUP, 2013), xii.
2. M. L. R. Smith and Peter Neumann, *The Strategy of Terrorism: How It Works, and Why It Fails* (Routledge, 2009) and "Strategic Terrorism: The Framework and Its Fallacies," *Journal of Strategic Studies* 28, no. 4 (2005). See also: Charles Tilly, "Terror as Strategy and Relational Process," *International Journal of Comparative Sociology* 46, no. 1–2 (2005); Andrew Kydd and Barbara Walter, "The Strategies of Terrorism," *International Security* 31, no. 1 (2006); Boaz Ganor, "Terrorism as a Strategy of Psychological Warfare," in *The Trauma of Terrorism: Sharing Knowledge and Shared Care, an International Handbook*, ed. Yael Danieli, Danny Brom, and Joe Sills (Binghampton, NY: Hawthorne Press, 2005); Freedman, "Terrorism as a Strategy"; "Strategic Terror and Amateur Psychology," *The Political Quarterly* 76, no. 2 (2005); Martha Crenshaw, "Terrorism, Strategies and Grand Strategies," in *Attacking Terrorism: Elements of a Grand Strategy*, ed. Audrey Kurth Cronin and James Ludes (Georgetown University Press, 2004); "The Logic of Terrorism: Terrorist Behavior as a Product of Strategic Choice," in *Origins of Terrorism: Psychologies, Ideologies, Theologies, States of Mind*, ed. Walter Reich (Woodrow Wilson Center Press: 1998); Max Abrahms, "Why Terrorism Does Not Work," *International Security* 31, no. 2 (2006).
3. Freedman, "Terrorism as a Strategy," 310; the coercive interpretation of terrorism is widely supported, see also: Max Abrahms, "What Terrorists Really Want: Terrorist Motives and Counterterrorism Strategy," *International Security* 32, no. 4; Peter

147

Neumann and M. L. R. Smith, "Strategic Terrorism: The Framework and Its Fallacies," *Journal of Strategic Studies* 28, no. 4; Kydd and Walter, "The Strategies of Terrorism"; Freedman, "Strategic Terror and Amateur Psychology."

4. Title 22 Chapter 38 U.S. Code § 2656f; Ariel Merari, "Terrorism as a Strategy of Insurgency", 217.

5. William Waugh, "The Values in Violence: Organizational and Political Objectives of Terrorist Groups," *Journal of Conflict Studies* 3, no. 4: e.g. 15; Kydd and Walter, "The Strategies of Terrorism," 52.

6. Max Abrahms, "The Political Effectiveness of Terrorism Revisited," *Comparative Political Studies* 45, no. 3: 360.

7. A point made in most studies of terrorist strategy: see, e.g. "Terrorism as a Strategy"; Smith and Neumann, *The Strategy of Terrorism*; Kydd and Walter, "The Strategies of Terrorism." Freedman has provided a specific definition that terrorism is a strategy which imposes 'a psychological effect—terror—with a view to creating a political effect that will be manifest in changes in the target's strategy'.

8. Kydd and Walter, "The Strategies of Terrorism," describe this as 'costly signalling'. Game theorists similarly see a variety of different signals at play in terrorism. For some, violence is an indication of the strength of an organisation in comparison to a government; see, e.g. Harvey Lapan and Todd Sandler, "Terrorism and Signalling," *European Journal of Political Economy* 9, no. 3; Per Baltzer Overgaard, "The Scale of Terrorist Attacks as a Signal of Resources," *Journal of Conflict Resolution* 38, no. 3. Violence is also viewed as a response to a government's willingness (or lack of it) to increase economic and/or political freedom; see e.g. Brock Blomberg, Gregory Hess, and Akila Weerapana, "Economic Conditions and Terrorism," *European Journal of Political Economy* 20, no. 2. It is also seen as a product of the refusal to make concessions, see Daniel Arce and Todd Sandler, "Terrorist Signalling and the Value of Intelligence," *British Journal of Political Science* 37, no. 4. Of course, it goes without saying that not all communications through violence are believed or even understood by their audiences, nevertheless that is a matter for the realities of terrorism rather than for the way it is intended to work. See Kydd and Walter, "The Strategies of Terrorism." Also Thomas Schelling, *Arms and Influence* (Yale University Press, 1967), 3f makes a similar point that coercion can only work if the coerced understands the ultimatum and demands presented by the coercer.

9. Cited by Bruce Hoffman, *Inside Terrorism* (Columbia University Press, 2006), 155.

10. Kydd and Walter, "The Strategies of Terrorism," 50f., also Arce and Sandler, "Terrorist Signalling and the Value of Intelligence."

11. Gilles Kepel et al., *Al Qaeda in Its Own Words* (Harvard University Press, 2010), 72.

12. Ibid., 204.

13. A point made by Freedman, "Terrorism as a Strategy," 321.

14. Thomas Thornton, "Terror as a Weapon of Political Agitation," in *Internal War: Problems and Approaches*, ed. Harry Eckstein (Greenwood Press, 1980); Crenshaw, "The Causes of Terrorism," 386.

15. Mikhail Bakunin, "Letters to a Frenchman on the Present Crisis," ed. Sam Dolgoff, *Bakunin on Anarchy. Selected works by the Activist-Founder of World Anarchism* (London: Allen and Unwin, 1973). On the propaganda of the deed model, see Marie Fleming, "Propaganda by the Deed: Terrorism and Anarchist Theory in Late Nineteenth-Century Europe," *Studies in Conflict & Terrorism* 4, no. 1.

16. Brian Michael Jenkins, "International Terrorism: A New Mode of Conflict," in *International Terrorism and World Security*, ed. David Carlton and Carlo Schaerf (London: Croom Helm), 15. This quotation was reworked by Simon and Benjamin (see n. 4 on p. 3) to highlight al-Qa'ida's unique lethality and indiscriminate targetting policy.

17. Alan Dershowitz, *Why Terrorism Works: Understanding the Threat, Responding to the Challenge*, new edition (Yale University Press, 2003), 86.

18. Ehud Sprinzak, "Rational Fanatics," *Foreign Policy* 120, September–October

19. Robert Pape, "The Strategic Logic of Suicide Terrorism," *American Political Science Review* 97, no. 3: 351f; *Dying to Win: The Strategic Logic of Suicide Terrorism* (Random House, 2005).

20. Thomas Schelling, "What Purposes Can 'International Terrorism' Serve?," in *Violence, Terrorism, and Justice*, ed. Raymond Frey and Christopher Morris (Cambridge University Press, 1991). See also Smith and Neumann, *The Strategy of Terrorism*.

21. David Lake, "Rational Extremism: Understanding Terrorism in the Twenty-First Century," *Dialog-IO* 1, no. 1.

22. Eric Gould and Esteban Klor, "Does Terrorism Work?," *The Quarterly Journal of Economics* 125, no. 4: 1507.

23. Andrew Kydd and Barbara Walter, "Sabotaging the Peace: The Politics of Extremist Violence," *International Organization* 56, no. 02.

24. Abrahms, "Why Terrorism Does Not Work."

25. Paul Wilkinson, *Terrorism Versus Democracy: The Liberal State Response* (Frank Cass Publishers, 2000), 21.

26. Freedman, "Terrorism as a Strategy," 335. The reasons for the strategic failure of terrorism are less examined. For Neumann and Smith, terrorism fails not only because it tends to fall into an 'escalation trap', but also because it seeks to attain political ambitions through 'the exploitation of the psychological rather than the destructive effects of armed action'; this, they argue, is ineffective against states who view the outcomes of conflict in terms of the resulting balance of military power. Abrahms, by contrast, argues that terrorism is a largely unsuccessful strategy because it fails to communicate terrorist objectives. Target governments, he

argues, interpret terrorist acts in terms of their immediate effects (the death of its civilians) which are then viewed as a threat to the social order rather than in terms of stated terrorist objectives. See Neumann and Smith, "Strategic Terrorism"; Abrahms, "The Political Effectiveness of Terrorism Revisited."

27. Daniel Kahneman, *Thinking, Fast and Slow* (Penguin, 2012); he adopts the terms System 1 and System 2 from Keith Stanovich and Richard West, "Individual Differences in Reasoning: Implications for the Rationality Debate?," *Behavioral and Brain Sciences* 23, no. 5. The latter now prefer Type 1 and Type 2.

28. Jonathan St B. T. Evans, "Dual-Processing Accounts of Reasoning, Judgment, and Social Cognition," *Annual Review of Psychology* 59, no. 1: 256.

29. Kahneman, *Thinking, Fast and Slow*, 36.

30. Ibid., 24.

31. Roger Schank and Robert Abelson, *Scripts, Plans, Goals, and Understanding: An Inquiry into Human Knowledge Structures* (Psychology Press, 1977), 41. See also Robert Abelson, "Script Processing in Attitude Formation and Decision-Making," in *Cognition and Social Behavior*, ed. John S. Carroll and John W. Payne (Oxford: Lawrence Erlbaum); "Psychological Status of the Script Concept," *American Psychologist* 36, no. 7; Roger Schank and Robert Abelson, "Scripts, Plans, and Knowledge," in *Proceedings of the 4th International Joint Conference on Artificial intelligence* (Tblisi: Morgan Kaufmann, 1975).

32. Deborah Welch Larson, "The Role of Belief Systems and Schemas in Foreign Policy Decision-Making," *Political Psychology* 15, no. 1: 24. Geva and Mintz similarly differentiate between schemata and scripts which refer to 'sequences of events in the environment'. Nehemia Geva and Alex Mintz, *Decision-Making on War and Peace: The Cognitive-Rational Debate* (New York: Lynne Rienner, 1997), 73; see also Susan Fiske and Shelley Taylor, *Social Cognition* (McGraw-Hill, 1991).

33. Ibid., 621.

34. This is a major feature described in Freedman, *Strategy: A History*.

35. Kydd and Walter, "The Strategies of Terrorism." They refer to this as 'intimidation'.

36. Ibid., 51. The fullest treatment of outbidding is in Mia Bloom, *Dying to Kill: The Allure of Suicide Terror* (Columbia University Press, 2005). See also Andrew Kydd and Barbara Walter, "Outbidding and the Overproduction of Terrorism," (n.p., 2009); Mia Bloom, "Palestinian Suicide Bombing: Public Support, Market Share, and Outbidding," *Political Science Quarterly* 119, no. 1 (2004). A critique is provided by Robert Brym and Bader Araj, "Palestinian Suicide Bombing Revisited: A Critique of the Outbidding Thesis," ibid. 123, no. 3.

37. Martha Crenshaw, "Terrorism and Global Security," in *Leashing the Dogs of War: Conflict Management in a Divided World*, ed. Chester A. Crocker, Fen Osler Hampson, and Pamela R. Aall (US Institute of Peace Press, 2007), 73; Kydd and Walter, "The Strategies of Terrorism"; Audrey Kurth Cronin, *How Terrorism Ends:*

Understanding the Decline and Demise of Terrorist Campaigns (Princeton University Press, 2009), 118f.

38. A point made similarly by Cronin, *How Terrorism Ends*, 119.

39. Smith and Neumann, *The Strategy of Terrorism*, 581 refers to this as 'power deflation'.

40. A number of academics argue that de-legitimisation is a product of a broader strategy of polarisation which 'tries to divide and de-legitimise the state... [by] driving regimes sharply to the right and ultimately forcing populations to choose between the terrorist cause and brutal state repression... the goal is to force divided populations further apart, fragmenting societies to the extent that it is impossible to maintain a stable, moderate middle within a functioning state': Cronin, *How Terrorism Ends*, 119. See also Frantz Fanon, *The Wretched of the Earth* (Les Damnés de la Terre), trans. Constance Farrington (New York: Grove Press); Jean-Paul Sartre, "Preface," in ibid.

41. The same point is also made by Kydd and Walter, "The Strategies of Terrorism," 69–70; Smith and Neumann, *The Strategy of Terrorism*, 580f.

42. Abu Mus'ab al-Suri, for example, imagined that by attacking the US in Saudi Arabia, the regime would be forced 'to defend the US and ... lose their legitimacy in the eyes of Muslims leading the religious establishment to defend [the Americans] which in turn will make them lose their legitimacy'. Peter Bergen, *The Osama Bin Laden I Know: An Oral History of Al Qaeda's Leader* (Free Press, 2006), 115–16. See also Carlos Marighella, *Minimanual of the Urban Guerrilla* (Red and Black Publishers, 2008), who noted in his chapter on popular support: 'The role of the urban guerrilla, in order to win the support of the population, is to continue fighting, keeping in mind the interests of the people and heightening the disastrous situation within which the government must act. These are the conditions, harmful to the dictatorship, which permit the guerrillas to open rural warfare in the middle of an uncontrollable urban rebellion'.

43. Social movement theorists make a similar point, e.g. Doug McAdam, Sidney Tarrow, and Charles Tilly, *Dynamics of Contention* (Cambridge University Press, 2001); Charles Tilly and Sidney G. Tarrow, *Contentious Politics* (Paradigm Publishers, 2007).

44. Joel Beinin and Frédéric Vairel, *Social Movements, Mobilization, and Contestation in the Middle East and North Africa* (Stanford University Press, 2011); Jeroen Gunning, "Social Movement Theory and the Study of Terrorism," in *Critical Terrorism Studies: A New Research Agenda*, ed. Richard Jackson, Marie Breen Smyth, and Jeroen Gunning (Routledge, 2009); Ziad Munson, "Islamic Mobilization: Social Movement Theory and the Egyptian Muslim Brotherhood," *The Sociological Quarterly* 42, no. 4 (2001); Peter Neumann and Brooke Rogers, "Recruitment and Mobilisation for the Islamist Militant Movement in Europe," (ICSR, 2007); Mohammed M. Hafez and Quintan Wiktorowicz, "Violence as

Contention in the Egyptian Islamic Movement," in *Islamic Activism: A Social Movement Theory Approach*, ed. Quintan Wiktorowicz (Indiana University Press, 2004); Wiktorowicz, "Anatomy of the Salafi Movement"; *Islamic Activism*.

45. Bader Araj, "Harsh State Repression as a Cause of Suicide Bombing: The Case of the Palestinian–Israeli Conflict," *Studies in Conflict & Terrorism* 31, no. 4; Smith and Neumann, *The Strategy of Terrorism*; Kydd and Walter, "The Strategies of Terrorism," 59–66.

46. This is much as it was described by Delbrück in his *History of the Art of War* in which 'the battle is merely one of several equally effective means of attaining the political ends of the war and is essentially no more important than the occupation of territory, the destruction of crops or commerce and the blockade'. Gordon A. Craig, "Delbrück: The Military Historian," in *Makers of Modern Strategy from Machiavelli to the Nuclear Age*, ed. Peter Paret, Gordon A. Craig, and Felix Gilbert (OUP, 1986), 341–2. See also John Mearsheimer, *Conventional Deterrence* (Ithaca: Cornell University Press, 1983); John Fearon, "Bargaining, Enforcement, and International Cooperation," *International Organization* 52, no. 2 (1998).

47. Kydd and Walter, "The Strategies of Terrorism," 60–63 describes three conditions favourable to success: the degree to which the state has interests in the disputed issue, constraints over the nature and magnitude of response and the capacity for tolerating the effects of a campaign of violence.

48. The definition of alliances is broadly derived from that of Stephen M. Walt, *The Origins of Alliances* (Cornell University Press, 1990). His definition of an alliance (p. 12) is 'a formal or informal arrangement for security cooperation between two or more sovereign states'. For the purposes of non-state actors, the nature of the political objective—security—can be dispensed with, but not the fact that objectives and ambitions are aligned. See also "Alliance Formation and the Balance of World Power," *International Security* 9, no. 4 (1985); Hans J. Morgenthau, Kenneth W. Thompson, and David Clinton, *Politics among Nations* (McGraw-Hill Higher Education, 2005); George Liska, *Nations in Alliance: The Limits of Interdependence* (The Johns Hopkins University Press, 1962). The definition of coalitions echoes that of William A. Gamson, "A Theory of Coalition Formation," *American Sociological Review*: 374; see also "An Experimental Test of a Theory of Coalition Formation," *American Sociological Review*; William H. Riker, *Theory of Political Coalitions* (Greenwood Press, 1984).

49. E.g. April Longley Alley, "The Rules of the Game: Unpacking Patronage Politics in Yemen," *The Middle East Journal* 64, no. 3.

50. Conceivably, there is a ninth script, 'rejection or alteration of political goals'. This is not studied in this book, as no examples were found. This, one suspects, is because rejecting political goals is what social scientists might refer to as a 'non-choice', that is an option that is explicitly kept off the table (James Jasper, "A Strategic Approach to Collective Action: Looking for Agency in Social Movement Choices,"

Mobilization: An International Quarterly 9, no. 1: 10–11). It is not discussed further because the terrorist organisations under study are so committed to their ambitions that the option of changing or discarding one's political goals is rarely addressed.

51. For the purposes of this book, disengagement therefore refers to a 'behavioural change, such as leaving a group or changing one's role within it ... [i]t does not necessitate a change in values or ideals, but requires relinquishing the objective of achieving change through violence. De-radicalisation, however, implies a cognitive shift—i.e., a fundamental change in understanding': Naureen Fink and Ellie Hearne, "Beyond Terrorism: Deradicalization and Disengagement from Violent Extremism," *International Peace Institute Report*: 1.

52. Gilles Kepel, *Roots of Radical Islam* (Saqi Books Publishers, 2005). See also *Muslim Extremism in Egypt: The Prophet and Pharaoh, with a New Preface for 2003* (University of California Press, 2003).

2. EGYPT: TERROR AND REPRESSION

1. On socio-economic crisis and the violent Islamist movement in Egypt, see R. Hrair Dekmejian, *Islam in Revolution: Fundamentalism in the Arab World* (Syracuse University Press, 1994); James Toth, "Islamism in Southern Egypt: A Case Study of a Radical Religious Movement," *International Journal of Middle East Studies* 35, no. 4 (2003); Mahmud A. Faksh, *The Future of Islam in the Middle East: Fundamentalism in Egypt, Algeria and Saudi Arabia* (Greenwood Press, 1997); Ali Dessouki, *Islamic Resurgence in the Arab World* (Praeger, 1982); Lucien Vandenbroucke, "Why Allah's Zealots? A Study of the Causes of Islamic Fundamentalism in Egypt and Saudi Arabia," *Middle East Review* 16, no. 1 (1983); 'Cassandra', "The Impending Crisis in Egypt," *The Middle East Journal* 49, no. 1. On the clash of cultures, see Ernest Gellner, *Islamic Dilemmas: Reformers, Nationalists, Industrialization: The Southern Shore of the Mediterranean* (Walter de Gruyter, 1985); François Burgat, *L'islamisme Au Maghreb: La Voix Du Sud* (Payot, 2008); Jacques Waardenburg, "Islam as a Vehicle of Protest," in *Islamic Dilemmas: Reformers, Nationalists, Industrialization: The Southern Shore of the Mediterranean*, ed. Ernest Gellner (Mouton, 1985); Roy, *The Failure of Political Islam*; *Globalised Islam: The Search for a New Ummah*; Kepel, *Roots of Radical Islam*; *The Prophet and Pharaoh*; *Jihad: The Trail of Political Islam*.

2. See for example Hafez and Wiktorowicz, "Violence as Contention."; Wiktorowicz, *Islamic Activism*; Munson, "Islamic Mobilization: Social Movement Theory and the Egyptian Muslim Brotherhood."; Beinin and Vairel, *Social Movements, Mobilization, and Contestation in the Middle East and North Africa*; Christine Sixta Rinehart, "Volatile Breeding Grounds: The Radicalization of the Egyptian Muslim Brotherhood," *Studies in Conflict & Terrorism* 32, no. 11 (2009).

3. A point made by Hafez and Wiktorowicz, "Violence as Contention." See, for example, the work of Roel Meijer, "Commanding Right and Forbidding Wrong as a Principle of Social Action: The Case of the Egyptian Al-Jama'a Al-Islamiyya," in *Global Salafism: Islam's New Religious Movement*, ed. Roel Meijer (Columbia University Press); Paul Berman, *Terror and Liberalism* (W.W. Norton, 2004); Faisal Devji, *Landscapes of the Jihad* (Hurst and Co., 2005); Roxanne Euben and Muhammad Zaman, *Princeton Readings in Islamist Thought: Texts and Contexts from Al-Banna to Bin Laden* (Princeton University Press, 2009); Bernard Lewis, *What Went Wrong?: The Clash between Islam and Modernity in the Middle East* (Harper Perennial, 2003).

4. See e.g. Gabriel Almond, Scott Appleby, and Emmanuel Sivan, *Strong Religion: The Rise of Fundamentalisms around the World* (University of Chicago Press, 2003); Emmanuel Sivan, *Radical Islam: Medieval Theology and Modern Politics* (Yale University Press, 1990).

5. Brynjar Lia, *The Society of the Muslim Brothers in Egypt: The Rise of an Islamic Mass Movement, 1928–1942* (Ithaca Press, 2006), 256.

6. Indeed, the extent of their concern had been demonstrated only a few months earlier when the palace had been forced to release a number of Brotherhood detainees from prison, in contravention of British demands, fearing 'a "religious revolution" if we keep these people interned'. This caused great consternation to the British ambassador, who became convinced that the regime was trying to 'whitewash the Ikhwan in the eyes of the British'. Ibid., 266. See also Munson, "Islamic Mobilization: Social Movement Theory and the Egyptian Muslim Brotherhood," 488; Richard P. Mitchell, *The Society of the Muslim Brothers* (Oxford University Press, 1993), 27.

7. *Muslim Brothers*, 28–42; James Heyworth-Dunne, *Religious and Political Trends in Modern Egypt*, 50.

8. Mark Huband, *Warriors of the Prophet: The Struggle for Islam* (Basic Books, 1999), 84f.

9. Lia, *The Society of the Muslim Brothers*, 268.

10. The letter was titled *Risala bayn al-Ams wal-Yawm* (Letter between Today and Yesterday) and can be found in Mitchell, *Muslim Brothers*, 30.

11. Indeed, this section of the letter was titled 'Obstacles in our path'. Ibid., 29.

12. Huband, *Warriors of the Prophet: The Struggle for Islam*, 85; Alison Pargeter, *The Muslim Brotherhood: The Burden of Tradition* (Saqi Books, 2010), 29; Abd al-Fattah M. El-Awaisi, *The Muslim Brothers and the Palestine Question 1928–1947* (I. B. Tauris, 1998). Mitchell notes somewhat dryly 'Arms gathering "for the Arabs" and "training", thus apparently vindicated, went on apace' (Mitchell, *Muslim Brothers*, 61).

13. Ana Belen Soage and Jorge Fuentelsaz Franganillo, "The Muslim Brothers in Egypt," in *The Muslim Brotherhood: The Organization and Policies of a Global*

Islamist Movement, ed. B. Rubin (Palgrave Macmillan, 2010), 40–41; Mitchell, *Muslim Brothers*, 62.

14. *Muslim Brothers*, 61f; Soage and Franganillo, "The Muslim Brothers in Egypt," 41. On al-Banna's fluctuating relationship with the Palace, see Huband, *Warriors of the Prophet: The Struggle for Islam*, 84f.

15. The assassination is widely believed to have been ordered by King Farouk. See Kepel, *Roots of Radical Islam*, 29; also Barry Rubin, *Islamic Fundamentalism in Egyptian Politics* (Palgrave Macmillan, 2002) and *The Muslim Brotherhood: The Organization and Policies of a Global Islamist Movement* (Palgrave Macmillan, 2010); Lia, *The Society of the Muslim Brothers*.

16. For a full discussion of political violence in Egypt in the 1940s, see Donald Reid, "Political Assassination in Egypt, 1910–1954," *International Journal of African Historical Studies* 15, no. 4.

17. Ibid., 633.

18. In the final years of the war, Anwar al-Sadat was arrested for providing German spies living on a houseboat in Cairo with weapons to attack the British: Mohamed Heikal, *Autumn of Fury: The Assassination of Sadat* (Corgi, 1984), 17–26. Sadat also had close contact with the Muslim Brotherhood and may have provided them with materiel as a way of challenging the pro-British monarchy. Rubin, *Islamic Fundamentalism in Egyptian Politics*, 11; Heikal, *Autumn of Fury: The Assassination of Sadat*, 16. Similarly, Sadat's associate Husayn Tewfiq regularly attacked British soldiers in Ma'adi, before he was caught red-handed in an attempt on the prime minister in 1946. Reid, "Political Assassination in Egypt, 1910–1954," 633. Also Heikal, *Autumn of Fury: The Assassination of Sadat*, 24f. On the communist groups, see Peter Mansfield, *A History of the Middle East* (Penguin, 2004), 135. On nationalists, see Reid, "Political Assassination in Egypt, 1910–1954," 633f. In February 1945, one of their members (and a suspected Secret Apparatus operative) shot the prime minister, Ahmad Mahir Pasha.

19. Both points are made by Lapan and Sandler, "Terrorism and Signalling," 385.

20. For a first-hand account, see Heikal, *Autumn of Fury: The Assassination of Sadat*.

21. Only Sheikh Hassan al-Baquri accepted. He was dismissed by the Guidance Council for taking a part in *jahili* politics. See Maye Kassem, *Egyptian Politics: The Dynamics of Authoritarian Rule* (Lynne Rienner Publishers Inc, 2004), 138.

22. Mitchell, *Muslim Brothers*, 296. Despite his mismanagement of the Secret Apparatus, al-Banna had a remarkable ability to inspire loyalty. One anecdote describes a follower saying, 'if Banna were to sneeze in Cairo, the Brothers in Aswan would say "Bless You".' On the charisma of al-Banna, see Rinehart, "Volatile Breeding Grounds: The Radicalization of the Egyptian Muslim Brotherhood." For an analysis of the 'myth' of al-Banna, see Pargeter, *The Muslim Brotherhood: The Burden of Tradition*. On Hudaybi, see Barbara Zollner, *The Muslim Brotherhood: Hasan Al-Hudaybi and Ideology* (Taylor & Francis, 2009).

23. Al-Hudaybi was also given the death sentence, but it was commuted to life imprisonment on the grounds that 'perhaps he had fallen under the influence of those around him, a view supported by his bad health and age'. Mitchell, *Muslim Brothers*, 160.

24. John Calvert, *Sayyid Qutb and the Origins of Radical Islamism* (Columbia University Press, 2010), 242. See also Omar Ashour, *The De-Radicalization of Jihadists: Transforming Armed Islamist Movements* (Routledge, 2009), 76 and n. 69, p. 164 in particular; Calvert, *Sayyid Qutb and the Origins of Radical Islamism*, 29f; Nazih Ayubi, "The Political Revival of Islam: The Case of Egypt," *International Journal of Middle East Studies* 12, no. 4: 137–43.

25. This work is also called 'Milestones' and 'Signs along the Way'. "The Political Revival of Islam: The Case of Egypt." The quotation is from Calvert, *Sayyid Qutb and the Origins of Radical Islamism*, 259, and Kepel, *Roots of Radical Islam*, 29.

26. Calvert, *Sayyid Qutb and the Origins of Radical Islamism*, 29; Zollner, *The Muslim Brotherhood: Hasan Al-Hudaybi and Ideology*, 416f., points out that Qutb had succeeded in disseminating early drafts of *Milestones* in the form of letters. Ashour, *The Deradicalization of Jihadists*, 76., points out that the work had been formally authorized by al-Hudaybi.

27. *The Deradicalization of Jihadists*, 76.; cf. Zollner, *The Muslim Brotherhood: Hasan Al-Hudaybi and Ideology*. She refers to it as Organisation 1965 and suggests that al-Hudaybi knew about, if not encouraged, its existence.

28. Interview with former Egyptian violent Islamist 2, Cairo, 14 June 2011. This is supported by Calvert, *Sayyid Qutb and the Origins of Radical Islamism*, 242.

29. Ibid., 243.

30. Ibid., 239.

31. Ibid., 248. Nasser claimed that a huge plot had been found; in reality, it is likely that he was attempting to galvanise public support in the wake of a stream of foreign and domestic policy disasters, see Kepel, *Roots of Radical Islam*, 31.

32. *Roots of Radical Islam*, 32f; John Waterbury, *The Egypt of Nasser and Sadat: The Political Economy of Two Regimes* (Princeton University Press, 1992), 340.

33. Sivan, *Radical Islam*, 27; Zollner, *The Muslim Brotherhood: Hasan Al-Hudaybi and Ideology*, 419. Four of the younger members—Sabri Arfa, Ahmad Abd al-Majid, Majdi Abd al-Aziz and Ali Ashmawi—had their sentences commuted to life imprisonment.

34. Sayyid Qutb, *Milestones* (Islamic Book Service), 21.

35. On the broader concept of *jahiliyya* in Qutb, see William Shepard, "Sayyid Qutb's Doctrine of Jahiliyya," *International Journal of Middle East Studies* 35, no. 04. On *juhl* in the work of al-Hudaybi see Zollner, *The Muslim Brotherhood: Hasan Al-Hudaybi and Ideology*, 422.

36. Ibrahim, *Egypt, Islam and Democracy: Critical Essays*, 19, suggests there was a substantial membership. 'Between three and five thousand active members', notes

"Egypt's Islamic Militants," *MERIP Reports*, no. 103: 5; Jeffrey B. Cozzens, "Al-Takfir Wa'l Hijra: Unpacking an Enigma," *Studies in Conflict & Terrorism* 32, no. 6: 494 suggests that there were 4000 members. On the structure of the organisation, in particular, the messianic image of Shukri Mustafa, see Ayubi, "The Political Revival of Islam: The Case of Egypt," 79.

37. On the organisation's ideology, see Kepel, *Roots of Radical Islam*, 78; Ibrahim, *Egypt, Islam and Democracy: Critical Essays*, 22; "Egypt's Islamic Militants," 6f.; David Zeidan, "Radical Islam in Egypt: A Comparison of Two Groups," *Middle East* 3, no. 3: 3f.; Cozzens, "Al-Takfir Wa'l Hijra: Unpacking an Enigma," 493f.

38. This was one among many examples of power play which I do not examine, largely because details of the defections and reprisals are scant.

39. A number of spurious claims were made, amongst them Shukri's *droit de seigneur*. Kepel, *Roots of Radical Islam*, 89.

40. Al-Dhahabi had recently written an article on the Society that was less than favourable. On the demands (which were extensive), see ibid., 92. Cozzens, "Al-Takfir Wa'l Hijra: Unpacking an Enigma," 493.

41. Kepel, *Roots of Radical Islam*, 99, notes that some Islamists claim he was murdered by the police, though no evidence has emerged to confirm this.

42. Ibid., 83.

43. Ibid., 92. In his trial, he went still further: 'The Society of Muslims is the first Islamic Movement to be founded in centuries. As for the Muslim Brethren, God did not grant them power and that is irrefutable proof that they were not a true and legitimate Islamic movement'.

44. Ibrahim, "Egypt's Islamic Militants."

45. *Egypt, Islam and Democracy: Critical Essays*, 20f.

46. Kepel, *Roots of Radical Islam*, 94–5.

47. See ibid., 94–6.

48. Particularly bearing in mind the fact that *Tanzim al-Jihad*, as we shall see in the next section, employed the same script. Although it was successful operationally, it was a strategic failure.

49. The *jama'at* are not to be confused with the singular *Gama'a*. The former were effectively student unions, who began as non-violent groups advocating discursive *hisba* (best translated as commanding right and forbidding wrong) before progressing to a form of physical *hisba*, manifested as vigilantism. See Meijer, "Commanding Right and Forbidding Wrong as a Principle of Social Action: The Case of the Egyptian Al-Jama'a Al-Islamiyya," 195f; Ayubi, "The Political Revival of Islam: The Case of Egypt," 75. See Kepel, *Roots of Radical Islam*, 134f., for an entertaining description of campus life. The *Gama'a*, by contrast, were a terrorist organisation on which much more can be found in the next section.

50. *Roots of Radical Islam*, 154. It is worth noting that this is another example of the 'flight' strand of the survival script.

51. Heikal, *Autumn of Fury: The Assassination of Sadat*, 134–5.

52. It is worth noting in passing that these two loosely formulated groups implicitly selected the 'alliance' script with the aim of increasing their resources and ability to coerce the regime. Available evidence suggests that the alliance of the Sa'idis and the Cairenes was not officially named *Tanzim al-Jihad* until 1982; nevertheless, I use it to refer to the alliance from 1980 for the sake of simplicity. Figures on the number of cells vary from between four and six: Sageman, *Understanding Terror Networks*, 30. 'Five or six', Lawrence Wright, *The Looming Tower: Al Qaeda's Road to 9/11* (Penguin), 42. Both Kepel and Ibrahim suggest four: Kepel, *Roots of Radical Islam*; Ibrahim, *Egypt, Islam and Democracy: Critical Essays*; "Egypt's Islamic Militants." On the geographic differences between the groups, see Mamoun Fandy, "Egypt's Islamic Group: Regional Revenge?," *Middle East Journal* 48, no. 4; and Toth, "Islamism in Southern Egypt: A Case Study of a Radical Religious Movement." It is worthwhile noting that neither of the constituent groups had a name. Almost all analyses of the organisation suggest that the Cairo branch was called 'al-Jihad' and the Assyut branch *al-Gama'a*. See Sageman, *Understanding Terror Networks*; Hamied N. Ansari, "The Islamic Militants in Egyptian Politics," *International Journal of Middle East Studies* 16, no. 1; Hoffman, *Inside Terrorism*; Kepel, *Jihad: The Trail of Political Islam*; *Roots of Radical Islam*; Sivan, *Radical Islam*; Wright, *Looming Tower*. I found no evidence for this in my research or my interviews, indeed, it seems likely that this is the consequence of applying the names of the two groups which they would become in the mid-1980s to their pre-merger identities.

53. Ansari, "The Islamic Militants in Egyptian Politics."

54. For a copy of the text, see Johannes Jansen, *The Neglected Duty: The Creed of Sadat's Assassins and Islamic Resurgence in the Middle East* (Macmillan, 1986). Tracts are reproduced in Euben and Zaman, *Princeton Readings in Islamist Thought: Texts and Contexts from Al-Banna to Bin Laden*.

55. Ansari, "The Islamic Militants in Egyptian Politics."

56. Kepel, *Roots of Radical Islam*, 171. See also, Heikal, *Autumn of Fury: The Assassination of Sadat*, 222.

57. Interview with former British diplomat, Cambridge, 7 May 2012.

58. Kepel, *The Prophet and Pharaoh*.

59. Heikal, *Autumn of Fury: The Assassination of Sadat*, 182.

60. Kepel, *Roots of Radical Islam*, 198.

61. To use Kepel's phrase, see e.g. Ibid., passim.

62. As Stein phrases it, 'environmental influences, particularly the Iranian Revolution, certainly created a general atmosphere of possibility for Islamists as a whole'. Ewan Stein, "An Uncivil Partnership: Egypt's Jama'a Islamiyya and the State after the Jihad," *Third World Quarterly* 32, no. 5 (2011): 866; see also Shahrough Akhavi, "The Impact of the Iranian Revolution on Egypt," in *The Iranian Revolution: Its*

Global Impact, ed. John Esposito (Miami: Florida International University Press, 1990); Kepel, *Jihad: The Trail of Political Islam*, 118f.

63. Some of these interrogation reports are in the possession of the author, although there is no way to verify their authenticity. This point, however, is supported by Kepel, *Jihad: The Trail of Political Islam*, 87.

64. *The Prophet and Pharaoh*, 212–13.

65. Euben and Zaman, *Princeton Readings in Islamist Thought: Texts and Contexts from Al-Banna to Bin Laden*, 332–37 §57, §62 and §70.

66. Kepel, *Roots of Radical Islam*, 209.

67. Coptic communities were engaged in an exerted effort to recruit through proselytism and police raids discovered caches of arms and weaponry. See ibid., 164f.

68. François Burgat, *Face to Face with Political Islam* (London: I. B. Tauris), 82. There was also a conspiracy theory that these weapons were brought in under the personal supervision of Rosalynn Carter (p. 83).

69. Kepel, *Roots of Radical Islam*, 215.

70. Interview with Official, London, 14 April 2012.

71. The Emergency Law had been reactivated in 1967 and ran continuously until early 1980; an 18-month hiatus came to an end with the assassination of Sadat and the Emergency Law was continuously in place until June 2012, when the Military Council partially lifted the laws, stating that they would still remain for acts of thuggery (*beltagiyya*). Amnesty International, "Egypt: Arbitrary Detention and Torture under Emergency Powers," (1989); International Federation for Human Rights (FIDH), "Egypt: Counter-Terrorism against the Background of an Endless State of Emergency," (FIDH, 2010).

72. Sageman, *Understanding Terror Networks*, 32–3.

73. Al-Zawahiri was reportedly tortured to get information on the whereabouts of his close friend Essam al-Qamari Montasser al-Zayyat, *The Road to Al-Qaeda: The Story of Bin Laden's Right-Hand Man* (London: Pluto Press), 31. Al-Qamari was an army officer and close friend of al-Zawahiri, who had recruited him some years earlier. Other cases of torture are too numerous to recount here: suffice to say that there is widespread acknowledgement that torture was (and is) 'standard practice' in Egyptian security facilities. See e.g. Heba Saleh, "Egyptian Report Denounces Torture," BBC, http://news.bbc.co.uk/1/hi/world/middle_east/4433303.stm. Specific examples had an impact on violent Islamist groups; most infamously, the treatment of Sayyid Qutb shaped the nature and attitudes of *Ma'alim f'il-Tariq* towards the *jahili* regime. For fuller discussions of torture in Egypt see, "Egypt: Grave Human Rights Abuses Amid Political Violence"; "Egypt: Arbitrary Detention and Torture under Emergency Powers"; "Human Rights Watch World Report 1993"; "Human Rights Watch World Report 1994"; "Behind Closed Doors: Torture and Detention in Egypt"; Egyptian Organisation for Human Rights, "When Will the Crime of Torture Stop?"; International Federation

for Human Rights (FIDH), "Egypt: Counter-Terrorism against the Background of an Endless State of Emergency".

74. Kepel et al., *Al Qaeda in Its Own Words*, 154 (with minor additions for clarity). After his treatment al-Zawahiri would long remain passionate on the subject of torture. In 1992, he devoted an entire book, entitled *The Black Book* to cataloguing the torture of Islamists and non-Islamists, arguing that the former received the most brutal treatment.

75. This particular aspect of the debate would continue well into the 1990s; see Hisham Mubarak, "What Does the *Gama'a Islamiyya* Want? Tal'at Fu'ad Qasim, Interview with Hisham Mubarak," in *Political Islam: Essays from Middle East Report*, ed. Joel Beinin and Joe Stork (University of California Press, 1997).

76. Kepel, *Jihad: The Trail of Political Islam*, 221; Wright, *Looming Tower*, 56–7.

77. Gerges, *The Far Enemy*, 99–101. Abdel Bari Atwan, *The Secret History of Al Qaeda: Updated Edition* (Abacus, 2008), 69.

78. The part played by the EIG in Afghanistan falls outside the remit of this research. There are a number of excellent studies, e.g. Ahmed Rashid, *Descent into Chaos: The World's Most Unstable Region and the Threat to Global Security* (Penguin, 2009); Burke, *Al-Qaeda: The True Story of Radical Islam*; Hoffman, *Inside Terrorism*; Sageman, *Understanding Terror Networks*; Gerges, *The Far Enemy*; Alex Strick van Linschoten and Felix Kuehn, *An Enemy We Created: The Myth of the Taliban/Al-Qaeda Merger in Afghanistan, 1970–2010* (C. Hurst & Co., 2012); Wright, *Looming Tower*.

79. Al-Rahman made a number of trips into Afghanistan before he was re-arrested in Egypt in 1986; one interviewee said that the last trip was in 1988 and that he took his two oldest sons, Mohammed and Asim. Interview with Abdallah, Cairo, January 2012. Burke, *Al-Qaeda: The True Story of Radical Islam*, 76–7; Kepel, *Jihad: The Trail of Political Islam*, 282–3.

80. Hafez and Wiktorowicz, "Violence as Contention," 71. Further figures can be found in Ibrahim, *Egypt, Islam and Democracy: Critical Essays*, 88; Meijer, "Commanding Right and Forbidding Wrong as a Principle of Social Action: The Case of the Egyptian Al-Jama'a Al-Islamiyya," 199.

81. Kepel, *Jihad: The Trail of Political Islam*, 282.

82. Hafez and Wiktorowicz, "Violence as Contention," 77 cites Abdel Azim Ramadan as saying that the EIG 'established roving bands that often engaged in "forbidding vice"—segregating the sexes, preventing girls from engaging in sporting activities at schools and breaking up concerts'.

83. Interview with 'John', 13 Apr. 2012; Interview with Charles, London, 12 Apr. 2011.

84. Kepel, *Jihad: The Trail of Political Islam*, 283; Hafez and Wiktorowicz, "Violence as Contention," 72f.

85. Alan Cowell, "Mideast Tensions: Egypt's Parliament Speaker Is Assassinated by Gunmen," *New York Times*, 13 Oct. 1990.

86. Wright, *Looming Tower*, 184.

87. Kepel, *Jihad: The Trail of Political Islam*, 288.

88. Ibid., 289.

89. Hafez and Wiktorowicz, "Violence as Contention," 76.

90. Interview with John. Cambridge, UK, 28 May 2012

91. This is based on informal conversations with residents of Imbaba. It is corroborated by Kepel, *Jihad: The Trail of Political Islam*, 290, who argues that the EIG 'were organizing everything: sporting activities, schools, militias that maintained Islamic order in the quarter and opposed any attempt by the Police to assert control'. The slogan became representative of the unity of the Islamist movement—a fact which caused great concern in the government. Tents with *Islam howa al-Hal* marked on the side were confiscated by the government when the Brotherhood was distributing them after the 1992 earthquake.

92. Toth, "Islamism in Southern Egypt: A Case Study of a Radical Religious Movement," 563.

93. Mubarak, "What Does the *Gama'a Islamiyya* Want? Tal'at Fu'ad Qasim, Interview with Hisham Mubarak," 322.

94. Robert Taber, *The War of the Flea* (Paladin, 1977), 29. There were, of course, differences in the way that terrorist attrition and insurgent attrition were implemented, but the point is that the way in which the script aimed to coerce the opposition remained the same.

95. This point is widely made, normally with the rider that these assassinations were in response to the assassination of Ala Muhieddin by the regime in September 1990. Meijer, "Commanding Right and Forbidding Wrong as a Principle of Social Action: The Case of the Egyptian Al-Jama'a Al-Islamiyya," 207; Mohammed M. Hafez, *Why Muslims Rebel: Repression and Resistance in the Islamic World* (Lynne Rienner Publishers, 2004), 83; Burgat, *Face to Face with Political Islam*, 98.

96. Hafez and Wiktorowicz, "Violence as Contention," 78. The 1992 figure is from Burgat, *Face to Face with Political Islam*, 98–9. The 2000 figure is from the U.S. Department of State, "2000 Country Report on Human Rights in Egypt," (Bureau of Public Affairs).

97. Kassem, *Egyptian Politics: The Dynamics of Authoritarian Rule*, 155.

98. International Federation for Human Rights (FIDH), "Egypt: Counter-Terrorism against the Background of an Endless State of Emergency," 12.

99. Kassem, *Egyptian Politics: The Dynamics of Authoritarian Rule*, 155; Hafez and Wiktorowicz, "Violence as Contention," 78.

100. Kepel, *Jihad: The Trail of Political Islam*, 291.

101. Burgat describes the rationale: 'in order to arrest the members of the Gama'a

Islamiyya, their wives, sisters and even their mothers were punished by embargoes, sometimes by the destruction of their homes and, in at least one case, the destruction of an entire hamlet'. Burgat, *Face to Face with Political Islam*, 99.

102. Neumann and Smith, "Strategic Terrorism," 588–9.

103. Neumann and Smith (ibid.) argue that lack of resources and public support are key difficulties for organisations attempting to escalate.

104. This became a key text for Afghan Arabs. For a biography of Dr Fadl, see Lawrence Wright, "The Heretic," *The Guardian*, 13 July 2008.

105. Linschoten and Kuehn, *An Enemy We Created*, 93.

106. Sageman, *Understanding Terror Networks*, 36; Linschoten and Kuehn, *An Enemy We Created*, 92–4.

107. Numerous studies suggest that this was the work of the EIG. I have found no evidence for this; indeed, based on the analysis of both organisations' strategy it is unrealistic for four reasons. First, there was considerable animosity between the EIG and the EIJ, and it seems unlikely that the former would have used the latter's support network, particularly when negotiations over an alliance had just fallen through. Second, the EIG were completely preoccupied with their attritional campaign in Egypt and, in their written material, demonstrate little interest in attacking outside Egyptian territory. Third, the operation was run by Mustafa Hamza, an Egyptian who had, after the Afghan *jihad*, followed bin Laden to Sudan and worked in one of his businesses in Khartoum (Burke, *Al-Qaeda: The True Story of Radical Islam*, 312, n31). Fourth, the attack was also helped by Sudanese intelligence, with whom bin Laden was close; that Sudanese intelligence would have been sufficiently close to the EIG to help with logistics seems unlikely. See Wright, *Looming Tower*, 214f; National Commission on Terrorist Attacks, *The 9/11 Commission Report: Final Report of the National Commission on Terrorist Attacks Upon the United States* (W. W. Norton & Company), 62. I follow Burke, *Al-Qaeda: The True Story of Radical Islam*, 115 (it is worth noting, however, that he contradicts this position on p. 154).

108. Al-Zayyat, *The Road to Al-Qaeda*, 68. He says 'I announced at the time that the Vanguards of Conquest was not a separate group, and that Islamic Jihad [EIJ] and the Vanguards of Conquest were two names for the same group led by Zawahiri. This was clear from the fact that the four accused in the Vanguards of Conquest cases that were tried by a military court were shouting their allegiance to Zawahiri from behind bars'. Sageman, *Understanding Terror Networks*, 41.

109. Nimrod Raphaeli, "Ayman Muhammad Rabi' Al-Zawahiri: The Making of an Arch-Terrorist," *Terrorism and Political Violence* 14, no. 4: 12.

110. Al-Zayyat, *The Road to Al-Qaeda*, 84. The quotation is extended by Raphaeli, "Al-Zawahiri: The Making of an Arch-Terrorist," 12.

111. Michael Scheuer, *Through Our Enemies' Eyes: Osama Bin Laden, Radical Islam, and the Future of America, Revised Edition* (Potomac Books Inc., 2006), 184.

112. Internally, the EIJ had fractured along the lines of those loyal to al-Zawahiri and Dr Fadl and those younger members who were clamouring for action—particularly when they saw the repeated attacks of their rivals in the EIG. As Camille Tawil puts it: 'there is no question that many EIJ members were unhappy with the way in which al-Gama'a al-Islamiyya was hogging the [media] spotlight at the time': Camille Tawil, *Brothers in Arms: Al Qa'ida and the Arab Jihadists* (Saqi Books, 2010), 103.

113. Burke, *Al-Qaeda: The True Story of Radical Islam*, 154.

114. See for example, Mubarak, "What Does the *Gama'a Islamiyya* Want? Tal'at Fu'ad Qasim, Interview with Hisham Mubarak." in which Qasim repeatedly distances the EIG from the EIJ (although he does note that 'there are efforts' towards forming a union).

115. Excerpts can be found in Kepel et al., *Al Qaeda in Its Own Words*, 47–50.

116. The majority of the remaining membership of EIJ rebelled against the decision, furious that al-Zawahiri had not informed or consulted with them. Gerges, *The Far Enemy*, ch. 3.

117. Sheikh Mir Hamza for the Pakistani *Jamiat-ul-Ulema* and Fazlul Rahman, leader of the *Jihad* Movement in Bangladesh also signed; Wright, *Looming Tower*, 260. Bearing in mind their recent rejection of violence, the EIG historic leadership were livid when they found out that Taha had acted unilaterally and responded by dismissing him from the organisation. See Ashour, *The Deradicalization of Jihadists*, 94.

118. Sageman, *Understanding Terror Networks*, 47f, Gerges, *The Far Enemy*, 158f.

119. Wright, *Looming Tower*, 260.

120. Ibid., 257–60.

121. Sageman, *Understanding Terror Networks*, 42. Al-Fadhli is discussed in detail in chapter 4.

122. To return to a previously cited quotation from Richard K. Betts, "Is Strategy an Illusion?," *International Security* 25, no. 2: 5.

123. Smith and Neumann, *The Strategy of Terrorism*, 93.

124. John Stone, "Al Qaeda, Deterrence, and Weapons of Mass Destruction," *Studies in Conflict & Terrorism* 32, no. 9: 765.

125. Smith and Neumann, *The Strategy of Terrorism*, 93.

126. These figures are taken from Hafez, *Why Muslims Rebel*, 85–6.

127. Conceivably, either organisation could have re-evaluated their political goals in an effort to render them more attainable. Not surprisingly, bearing in mind the fact that both were deeply committed to their political ambitions, this did not appeal to either.

128. See, in particular, Hamed El-Said and Jane Harrigan, *Deradicalising Violent Extremists: Counter-Radicalisation and Deradicalisation Programmes and Their*

Impact in Muslim Majority States (Routledge, 2012); Ashour, *The Deradicalization of Jihadists.*

129. Goerzig, *Talking to Terrorists: Concessions and the Renunciation of Violence*; Rohan Gunaratna and Mohamed Bin Ali, "De-Radicalization Initiatives in Egypt: A Preliminary Insight," *Studies in Conflict & Terrorism* 32, no. 4 (2009).

130. Stein, "An Uncivil Partnership: Egypt's Jama'a Islamiyya and the State after the Jihad."; Nicole Stracke, "Arab Prisons: A Place for Dialogue and Reform," *Perspectives on Terrorism* 1, no. 4. Blaydes and Rubin, "Ideological Reorientation and Counterterrorism: Confronting Militant Islam in Egypt."

131. Hamed el-Said, "De-Radicalising Islamists: Programmes and Their Impact in Muslim Majority States," (The International Centre for the Study of Radicalization and Political Violence (ICSR), 2012); El-Said and Harrigan, *Deradicalising Violent Extremists*; Dia'a Rashwan, "The Renunciation of Violence by Egyptian Jihadi Organizations," in *Leaving Terrorism Behind: Individual and Collective Disengagement*, ed. Tore Bjørgo and John Horgan (Routledge, 2009); "The Obstacle Course of Revisions: Gamaah Versus Jihad," in *al-Ahram Commentary* (Cairo: al-Ahram Centre for Political and Security Studies, 2007); Ashour, *The Deradicalization of Jihadists*; "De-Radicalization of Jihad? The Impact of Egyptian Islamist Revisionists on Al-Qaeda," *Perspectives on Terrorism* 2, no. 5 (2010); Blaydes, L. and L. Rubin, "Ideological Reorientation and Counterterrorism: Confronting Militant Islam in Egypt." *Terrorism and Political Violence* 20, 4 (2008): 461–79.

132. See e.g. *The Deradicalization of Jihadists*, 98–101; Gunaratna and Ali, "De-Radicalization Initiatives in Egypt," 288; Rashwan, "The Renunciation of Violence," 121f.

133. "The Renunciation of Violence," 124.

134. Ashour, *The Deradicalization of Jihadists*, 100.

135. Cited in Hafez, *Why Muslims Rebel*, 87; see also Hafez and Wiktorowicz, "Violence as Contention."; and, in a different context Araj, "Harsh State Repression as a Cause of Suicide Bombing: The Case of the Palestinian–Israeli Conflict."

136. To borrow a phrase from Ashour, *The Deradicalization of Jihadists*, 91–6. Little, the close reader of this study will note, is said about what constitutes the charismatic leader and, surprisingly, no reference is made to Weber, arguably the standard theorist on charisma, in Max Weber, *The Theory of Social and Economic Organization*, trans. Talcott Parsons and A. M. Henderson (Martino Fine Books, 2012 [1947]). Indeed, Ashour goes no further than citing the work of Lia, *The Society of the Muslim Brothers*; and Caron Gentry, "The Relationship between New Social Movement Theory and Terrorism Studies: The Role of Leadership, Membership, Ideology and Gender," *Terrorism and Political Violence* 16, no. 2 (2004).

137. Lisa Blaydes and Lawrence Rubin, "Ideological Reorientation and Counterterrorism: Confronting Militant Islam in Egypt," ibid.20, no. 4: 470; see also Lisa Blaydes, "Makram Mohammed Ahmed Interviews the Historic Leadership of Al-Gama'a Al-Islamiyya inside the 'Scorpion' Prison," (n.p.).

138. Ashour, *The Deradicalization of Jihadists*, 138.

139. Stracke, "Arab Prisons: A Place for Dialogue and Reform."

140. El-Said, "De-Radicalising Islamists: Programmes and Their Impact in Muslim Majority States," 18.

141. Personal Interview cited in Goerzig, *Talking to Terrorists: Concessions and the Renunciation of Violence*, 34.

142. Ashour, *The Deradicalization of Jihadists*, 96.

143. Meijer, "Commanding Right and Forbidding Wrong as a Principle of Social Action: The Case of the Egyptian Al-Jama'a Al-Islamiyya," 208–9; Ashour, *The Deradicalization of Jihadists*, 92.

144. El-Said and Harrigan, *Deradicalising Violent Extremists*; Ashour, *The Deradicalization of Jihadists*; Meijer, "Commanding Right and Forbidding Wrong as a Principle of Social Action: The Case of the Egyptian Al-Jama'a Al-Islamiyya"; Rashwan, "The Renunciation of Violence."

145. Numbers vary: six is suggested by Blaydes and Rubin, "Ideological Reorientation and Counterterrorism: Confronting Militant Islam in Egypt." Four is proposed by Ashour, *The Deradicalization of Jihadists*, 51. Twenty-seven is proposed by Rashwan who argues that only four were approved by the leadership, Rashwan, "The Renunciation of Violence," 126. Sherman Jackson, "Beyond Jihad: The New Thought of the Gamā'a Islāmiyya," *Journal of Islamic Law and Culture* 11, no. 1: 57 argues along the same lines. During fieldwork, the author found six books: Usamah Hafiz, Muhammad Asim Abd al-Majid, and Karam al-Zuhdi, *Mubadarat Waqf Al-Unf: Ru'yah Waqi'iyah Wa Nazrah Shar'iyah* (An Initiative for Stopping Violence: A Practical Vision and Legal Framework) (Cairo: Maktabat al-Turath al-Islami, 2002); Karam al-Zuhdi, *Istiratijiyat Wa Tafjirat Al-Qa'idah: Al-Akhta' Wal-Akhtar* (The Strategy and Bombings of al-Qa'ida: Dangers and Mistakes) (Cairo: Maktabat al-Turath al-Islami, 2004); Hamdi al-Rahman et al., *Taslit Al-Adwa Ala Ma Waqa'a Fil-Jihad Min Akhta* (Shining a Light on the Mistakes of the Jihad) (Cairo: Maktabat al-Turath al-Islami, 2002); Ibrahim Najih, *Hurmat Al-Ghulu Fi Al-Din Wa Takfir Al-Muslimin* (The Illegality of Excess in Declaring Muslims Apostate), ed. Ali Sharif and Karam al-Zuhdi (Cairo: Maktabat al-Turath al-Islami, 2002); Ibrahim Najih and Ali Sharif, *Tafjirat Al-Riyad: Al-Ahkam Wal-Athar* (The Bombings in Riyadh: Rulings and Effects) (Cairo: Maktabat al-Turath al-Islami, 2003); Ali Sharif, *Nahr Al-Dhirkrayat: Al-Muraja'at Al-Fiqhiyah Lil-Jama'a Al-Islamiya* (The River of Memories: Interpretative Revision in the Gama'a Islamiyya) (Cairo: Maktabat al-Turath al-Islami, 2003). For interviews, see Lisa Blaydes' translation of the interview of the EIG with the

editor of *al-Musawwar*, Makram Mohammed Ahmed. Blaydes, "Makram Mohammed Ahmed Interviews the Historic Leadership of Al-Gama'a Al-Islamiyya inside the 'Scorpion' Prison."

146. Jackson, "Beyond Jihad: The New Thought of the Gamā'a Islāmiyya," 56. Ashour, *The Deradicalization of Jihadists*, 51. The idea that EIG elements had not heard about the ceasefire seems unlikely to have been the case, not least because it was plastered over the newspapers and, more importantly, because five months had passed between the declaration of non-violence and the massacre—ample time for instructions to be passed on to even the most remote of militants. The point about this attack standing out in the history of Egyptian violence was made by the EIG leadership in their written material Hafiz, al-Majid, and al-Zuhdi, *Mubadarat Waqf Al-Unf: Ru'yah Waqi'iyah Wa Nazrah Shar'iyah*, 7f.

147. Ashour, *The Deradicalization of Jihadists*, 98.

148. Goerzig, *Talking to Terrorists: Concessions and the Renunciation of Violence*, 34.

149. Jackson, "Beyond Jihad: The New Thought of the Gamā'a Islāmiyya," 61.

150. Hafiz, al-Majid, and al-Zuhdi, *Mubadarat Waqf Al-Unf*; this is also quoted in El-Said and Harrigan, *Deradicalising Violent Extremists*, 83. For an interesting Islamist perspective on *haram* see Yusuf al-Qaradawi, *The Lawful and the Prohibited in Islam* (Islamic Books, 1997).

151. Hafiz, al-Majid, and al-Zuhdi, *Mubadarat Waqf Al-Unf*, 35; this translation is from Goerzig, *Talking to Terrorists: Concessions and the Renunciation of Violence*, 35.

152. Najih, *Hurmat Al-Ghulu Fi Al-Din Wa Takfir Al-Muslimin*, 4.

153. Blaydes, "Makram Mohammed Ahmed Interviews the Historic Leadership of Al-Gama'a Al-Islamiyya inside the 'Scorpion' Prison," 12–13.

154. Goerzig, *Talking to Terrorists: Concessions and the Renunciation of Violence*, 35.

155. Al-Zayyat, *The Road to Al-Qaeda*, 63; Goerzig, *Talking to Terrorists: Concessions and the Renunciation of Violence*, 35f.

156. Al-Zayyat, *The Road to Al-Qaeda*, 76.

157. Goerzig, *Talking to Terrorists: Concessions and the Renunciation of Violence*, 35.

158. On frames, see Robert Benford and David Snow, "Framing Processes and Social Movements: An Overview and Assessment," *Annual Review of Sociology*.

159. Meijer, "Commanding Right and Forbidding Wrong as a Principle of Social Action: The Case of the Egyptian Al-Jama'a Al-Islamiyya."

160. A charge that he denies at considerable length. al-Zayyat, *The Road to Al-Qaeda*, 79f.

161. Ibid., 77.

162. Sayyid Imam al-Sharif, *Wathiqat Tarshid Al-Jihad Fi Misr Wal-'Alam* (Document for Guiding Jihad in Egypt and the World) (Al-Jarida, 2007); see also Goerzig, *Talking to Terrorists: Concessions and the Renunciation of Violence*, 37; El-Said and Harrigan, *Deradicalising Violent Extremists*, 89.

163. Amr Hamzawy and Sarah Grebowski, "From Violence to Moderation: Al-Jama'a Al-Islamiya and Al-Jihad," in *Carnegie Papers* (Washington DC: Carnegie Endowment for International Peace), 7.

164. Blaydes, "Makram Mohammed Ahmed Interviews the Historic Leadership of Al-Gama'a Al-Islamiyya inside the 'Scorpion' Prison," 20.

165. Al-Zayyat, *The Road to Al-Qaeda*, 78.

166. El-Said and Harrigan, *Deradicalising Violent Extremists*, 89.

167. Ashour, *The Deradicalization of Jihadists*, 103f.

168. A violent Islamist movement, called Ansar al-Sharia, is, as of early 2019, beginning to emerge in the Sinai. It was mentioned in two off the record interviews as being primarily the work of the young and disaffected rather than the older EIJ membership.

169. Benford and Snow, "Framing Processes and Social Movements," 617f; Kahneman, *Thinking, Fast and Slow*, 363–70.

170. Thomas Schelling, "What Purposes Can 'International Terrorism' Serve?," in *Violence, Terrorism and Justice*, ed. Raymond Gillespie Frey and Christopher W. Morris (Cambridge University Press, 1991), 21.

171. Charles Tilly, "The Trouble with Stories," in *Stories, Identity and Political Change*, ed. Charles Tilly (Rowman & Littlefield, 2002).

3. SAUDI ARABIA: TERROR AND LEGITIMACY

1. Translated by Norman Cigar, *Al-Qaida's Doctrine for Insurgency: Abd Al-Aziz Al-Muqrin's "a Practical Course for Guerrilla War"* (Potomac Books Inc., 2009), 127.

2. Al-Qa'ida in the Arabian Peninsula is a moniker that has also been adopted by an organisation in Yemen. As we shall see in the next chapter, this was a deliberate manoeuvre designed to suggest continuity between the organisation in Saudi Arabia and its latest incarnation in Yemen. I do not differentiate between the groups by providing multiple acronyms which can become confusing. Where clarity is needed, I refer to 'AQAP in Saudi Arabia' and 'AQAP in Yemen'; in all other cases, the AQAP mentioned is the one which operated in the case study country.

3. A point made by Bruce Riedel and Bilal Saab, "Al Qaeda's Third Front: Saudi Arabia," *Washington Quarterly* 31, no. 2: 34. Bin Laden engaged in a number of discussions with senior figures in the Saudi regime, offering to help with the South Yemen problem in 1989/1990 as well as the invasion of Kuwait in 1990. For a fuller discussion, see e.g. Peter Bergen and Paul Cruickshank, "Revisiting the Early Al Qaeda: An Updated Account of Its Formative Years," *Studies in Conflict & Terrorism* 35, no. 1. Wright, *Looming Tower*, 155f., provides a useful general overview.

4. Steve Coll, *The Bin Ladens: Oil, Money, Terrorism and the Secret Saudi World* (Penguin, 2008), 373.

5. Bergen, *The Osama Bin Laden I Know*, 112.

6. Thomas Hegghammer, *Jihad in Saudi Arabia: Violence and Pan-Islamism since 1979* (Cambridge University Press, 2010), 104f., argues that the 1994 Saudi clamp down on the Islamist movement *al-Sahwa* was the trigger for this strategic change.

7. Bergen, *The Osama Bin Laden I Know*, 115. A point made by Pascal Ménoret, *The Saudi Enigma: A History*, trans. Patrick Camiller (Zed Books Ltd, 2005), 5–9, notes that (p. 7) 'What bin Laden is really saying is that Saudi Arabia is in the situation of a colony; that the Americans have robbed the Saudi people of their wealth and their potential for economic development'.

8. This was the assessment of Prince Turki, former head of Saudi Intelligence. Wright, *Looming Tower*, 158.

9. This is not intended to be a full examination of the non-violent Islamist movement in Saudi Arabia which falls beyond the scope of this study. For more on the Islamist movement in Saudi Arabia, see Stéphane Lacroix, *Awakening Islam: The Politics of Religious Dissent in Contemporary Saudi Arabia*, ed. George Holoch (Harvard University Press, 2011); al-Rasheed, *Contesting the Saudi State: Islamic Voices from a New Generation*; Fandy, *Saudi Arabia and the Politics of Dissent*.

10. Gwenn Okruhlik, "Making Conversation Possible: Islamism and Reform in Saudi Arabia," in *Islamic Activism: A Social Movement Theory Approach*, ed. Quintan Wiktorowicz (Indiana University Press, 2004), 254.

11. A translated copy of the letter is provided by Lacroix, *Awakening Islam: The Politics of Religious Dissent in Contemporary Saudi Arabia*, 180f.

12. Okruhlik, "Making Conversation Possible: Islamism and Reform in Saudi Arabia," 261–2. See also Andrzej Kapiszewski, "Saudi Arabia Steps toward Democratization or Reconfiguration of Authoritarianism?," *Journal of Asian and African Studies* 41, no. 5–6.

13. Roel Meijer, "The Cycle of Contention and the Limits of Terrorism in Saudi Arabia," in *Saudi Arabia in the Balance: Political Economy, Society, Foreign Affairs*, ed. Paul Aarts and Gerd Nonneman (C. Hurst & Co., 2005), 275.

14. Indeed, for social movement theorists like Gwenn Okruhlik and Roel Meijer, it was precisely this repressive atmosphere which brought about the narrowing of participatory political space that led to the emergence of violent forms of contention. Okruhlik, "Making Conversation Possible: Islamism and Reform in Saudi Arabia"; Meijer, "The Limits of Terrorism in Saudi Arabia"; Anouar Boukhars, "At the Crossroads: Saudi Arabia's Dilemmas," *Journal of Conflict Studies* 26, no. 1.

15. Joshua Teitelbaum, *Holier Than Thou: Saudi Arabia's Islamic Opposition* (Brookings Institution, 2000), 40.

16. These two were known as the 'sheikhs of Awakening' (*shuyukh al-sahwa*). There is a full discussion in Lacroix, *Awakening Islam*, 202f.; Ménoret, *The Saudi Enigma*, 123f.

17. Lacroix, *Awakening Islam*, 195; Wright, *Looming Tower*, 195.

18. Madawi al-Rasheed, *A History of Saudi Arabia*, 175; Meijer, "The Limits of Terrorism in Saudi Arabia," 276.

19. Lacroix, *Awakening Islam*, 193f.

20. Interview with 'Matthew', London, 3 Mar. 2011.

21. Teitelbaum, *Holier Than Thou*, 73. For a discussion of the timing of the attack and the reaction of the *Sahwa*, see Lacroix, *Awakening Islam*, 198f.

22. The identity of the perpetrators remains controversial because three different and previously unknown organisations claimed responsibility for the attacks: *Numur al-Khalij* (The Tigers of the Gulf), *Harakat al-Taghyir al-Islamiyya, al-Janah al-Jihadi f 'il-Jazeera al-Arabiyya* (Islamic Change Movement, the *Jihad* Wing in the Arabian Peninsula) and the *Munazzamat Ansar Allah al-Muqatila* (Fighting Organisation of the Supporters of God): Teitelbaum, *Holier Than Thou*, 73–6. As others have pointed out, there is no evidence to suggest that this attack had any direct link with bin Laden, although one of the attackers, Riyadh al-Hajri did say that he had a fax machine and 'received the publications of Mas'ari [another cleric with Islamist leanings] and bin Laden'. See Thomas Hegghammer, "Jihad, Yes, but Not Revolution: Explaining the Extraversion of Islamist Violence in Saudi Arabia," *British Journal of Middle Eastern Studies* 36, no. 3; Fandy, *Saudi Arabia and the Politics of Dissent*, 1–2 (on Mas'ari, see 115–45).

23. On al-Utaybi, see Thomas Hegghammer and Stéphane Lacroix, "Rejectionist Islamism in Saudi Arabia: The Story of Juhayman Al-Utaybi Revisited," *International Journal of Middle East Studies* 39, no. 1; Dekmejian, *Islam in Revolution: Fundamentalism in the Arab World*, 133–7; Nazih Ayubi, *Political Islam: Religion and Politics in the Arab World* (Routledge, 1993), 99–104.

24. Robert Lacey, *Inside the Kingdom* (Arrow), 178.

25. The 9/11 Report noted that 'the operation was carried out principally, perhaps exclusively, by Saudi Hezbollah, an organization that had received support from the government of Iran. While the evidence of Iranian involvement is strong, there are also signs that al-Qaida played some role, as yet unknown': (*The 9/11 Commission Report: Final Report of the National Commission on Terrorist Attacks Upon the United States*, 60. I agree with the analysis of most scholars that in the absence of better evidence, the attack was at the very least supported by the Iranians. See, e.g. Teitelbaum, *Holier Than Thou*, 83–97; Thomas Hegghammer, "Deconstructing the Myth About Al-Qa'ida and Khobar," Combating Terrorism Centre at Westpoint, http://www.ctc.usma.edu/posts/deconstructing-the-myth-about-al-qaida-and-khobar. An interesting case for al-Qa'ida's responsibility is that of Gareth Porter, "Khobar Towers Investigated: How a Saudi Deception Protected Osama Bin Laden." On bin Laden's support for the attacks, see: "Bin Laden's Fatwa Aug. 23, 1996," http://www.pbs.org/newshour/updates/military/july-dec96/fatwa_1996.html. Anthony Cordesman and Nawaf Obaid, *National Security in*

Saudi Arabia: Threats, Responses, and Challenges (Praeger Security International, 2005), 122 tentatively ascribes the attack to bin Laden's organisation.

26. F. Gregory Gause III, *The International Relations of the Persian Gulf* (Cambridge University Press, 2009), 140. On the stripping of bin Laden's citizenship, see Tim Niblock, *Saudi Arabia: Power, Legitimacy and Survival* (Routledge, 2006), 154.

27. A point made by one interviewee. Interview with Peter, London, 27 Mar. 2012.

28. Sageman, *Understanding Terror Networks*; Linschoten and Kuehn, *An Enemy We Created*.

29. To employ the language of Gerges, *The Far Enemy*. It is worth noting that Gerges sees the change in simpler terms: 'unlike his religious nationalist counterparts, bin Laden viewed local regimes, including the house of Saud, as insignificant tools and agents in the hands of the Americans. He considered Saudi Arabia an occupied country and its regime incapable of forcing the Americans out. Therefore, he declared war on the United States, not on Saudi Arabia'. (p. 149)

30. Bergen and Cruickshank, "Revisiting the Early Al Qaeda: An Updated Account of Its Formative Years," 26–7.

31. Ibid.

32. Cordesman and Obaid, *National Security in Saudi Arabia: Threats, Responses, and Challenges*, 114.

33. Brynjar Lia and Thomas Hegghammer, "Jihadi Strategic Studies: The Alleged Al Qaida Policy Study Preceding the Madrid Bombings," *Studies in Conflict & Terrorism* 27, no. 5: 373, n. 28.

34. It is certain that he met al-Awda whilst raising funds for the Bosnian *jihad* in Dammam; his future father-in-law, Sheikh Sulayman al-Ulwan, was a high profile member of the *al-Sahwa* movement. For further details and biography of al-Uyayri, see Roel Meijer, "Yusuf Al-Uyairi and the Transnationalisation of Saudi Jihadism," in *Kingdom without Borders: Saudi Arabia's Political, Religious and Media Frontiers*, ed. Madawi al-Rasheed (Hurst, 2008), 226f.

35. For al-Uyayri's criticism of the *Sahwa* and Safar al-Hawali in particular, see "Yusuf Al-'Uyairi and the Making of a Revolutionary Salafi Praxis," *Die Welt des Islams* 47, no. 3–4: 439f. See also Lacroix, *Awakening Islam: The Politics of Religious Dissent in Contemporary Saudi Arabia*, 251f.

36. Roel Meijer, "Re-Reading Al-Qaeda Writings of Yusuf Al-Ayiri," *ISIM Review* 18; "Yusuf Al-Uyairi and the Transnationalisation of Saudi Jihadism." Others have put the date as late as 1999 or 2000, see Hegghammer, *Jihad in Saudi Arabia*, 119–20.

37. Al-Uyayri established his al-Qa'ida website, *al-Nida'* just before 9/11 and well before the internet had been widely explored by *jihadi* propagandists. Prior to that he had also contributed regularly to *Sawt al-Qawqaz*, the home page of the Chechen *mujahideen*, as well as the burgeoning Saudi online presence on websites such as *al-Salafyoon* and *al-Ansar*. See *Jihad in Saudi Arabia*, 122f.; Meijer,

"Yusuf Al-Uyairi and the Transnationalisation of Saudi Jihadism," 228f. On al-Uyayri's influence on the propagandists more generally, see Lia and Hegghammer, "Jihadi Strategic Studies: The Alleged Al Qaida Policy Study Preceding the Madrid Bombings," 358f.

38. See Hegghammer, *Jihad in Saudi Arabia*, 120, who suggests that these meetings with high-level Taliban figures is good evidence for bin Laden's role in recommending and organising the trip.

39. A point made by ibid., 120.

40. Michael Scott Doran, "The Saudi Paradox," *Foreign Affairs* 83, no. 1: 43.

41. Meijer, "Yusuf Al-Uyairi and the Transnationalisation of Saudi Jihadism," 229.

42. Interview with Peter, London, 27 Mar. 2012. See also Hegghammer, *Jihad in Saudi Arabia*, 162.

43. Indeed, so important was Saudi Arabia that there is anecdotal evidence that it was Sayf al-Adl, now military commander for al-Qa'ida, that was despatched to the Kingdom: ibid., 165.

44. Ibid., 165, estimates that between three hundred and a thousand mujahideen returned to Saudi from Afghanistan.

45. For further details on al-Qa'ida's organisational structure, see Cordesman and Obaid, *National Security in Saudi Arabia: Threats, Responses, and Challenges*, 113; Anthony Cordesman and Nawaf Obaid, "Al-Qaeda in Saudi Arabia: Asymmetric Threats and Islamist Extremists," (Washington: Centre for Strategic and International Studies). They describe five discrete cells: the first headed by Turki al-Dandani, the second by Ali Abd al-Rahman al-Faqasi al-Ghamdi, the third by Khaled al-Hajj, the fourth by the future leader, Abd al-Aziz al-Muqrin, and fifth which was never fully established. It is worth noting that these were discrete, semi-autonomous entities without knowledge of the others' existence; indeed, al-Uyayri was so keen on operational secrecy that he was known as *al-Battar*, 'the Sabre', and was not, according to some, identified by US intelligence until April 2003. See Ron Suskind, *The One Percent Doctrine: Deep inside America's Pursuit of Its Enemies since 9/11* (Simon and Schuster, 2006), 217–18.

46. Interview with Matt, Cairo, 8 Feb. 2011. *The One Percent Doctrine*, 235 describes an interesting exchange between al-Uyayri and one of al-Nashiri's commanders. 'Tucked inside the sigint chatter in April of possible upcoming attacks inside the kingdom was evidence of a tense dialogue between al-Ayeri [an alternative spelling of al-Uyayri] and another, less senior operative in the Gulf, Ali Abd al-Rahman al-Faqasi al-Ghamdi, over whether the Saudi al Qaeda operation had enough men, weapons, and organization to truly challenge and overthrow the Saudi regime. Al-Ayeri said no, it was too soon, the organization had not yet matured, while al-Ghamdi strongly recommended pushing forward'.

47. This organisation would eventually become AQAP: Hegghammer, *Jihad in Saudi Arabia*, 177f; "Islamist Violence and Regime Stability in Saudi Arabia,"

International Affairs 84, no. 4: 711f. *Jihad in Saudi Arabia*, 179 also cites evidence from the Interior Ministry that between May 2003 and January 2004, they seized '24 tons of explosive material, 300 rocket-propelled, 430 hand grenades, 300 explosive belts and 674 detonators'. As with all figures from the Saudi Interior Ministry, extreme caution is required when approaching them.

48. A view also propounded by *Jihad in Saudi Arabia*, 170–3.

49. Khalid al-Hammadi, "The inside Story of Al-Qaʻida," *al-Quds al-Arabi*, 22 Mar. 2005.

50. Wikileaks: The Guantánamo Files, "Abd Al Rahim Hussein Mohammed Al Nashiri."

51. Bruce Riedel, *The Search for Al Qaeda: Its Leadership, Ideology, and Future*, 2nd ed. (Brookings Institution), 107.

52. Interview with John, Cambridge May 2012. Wikileaks: The Guantánamo Files, "Abd Al Rahim Hussein Mohammed Al Nashiri."

53. Hegghammer, *Jihad in Saudi Arabia*, 167—68.

54. A number of media reports released on 22 November suggest that he was arrested earlier that month (Philip Shenon, "Threats and Responses: Terror Network; a Major Suspect in Qaeda Attacks Is in U.S. Custody," *The New York Times* 22 Nov. 2002; Oliver Burkeman, "US Captures Key Al-Qaida Suspect," *The Guardian*, 22 Nov. 2002; "Al-Qaeda Gulf Chief' Held by US," http://news.bbc.co.uk/1/hi/world/middle_east/2501121.stm.). However, it is likely that the waterboarding and interrogation of al-Nashiri led to the identification of and drone strike against Abu Ali al-Harithi on 3 Nov. 2002 (on which see chapter 4). On al-Nashiri's waterboarding see, e.g. Human Rights Watch, "Abd Al-Rahim Al-Nashiri," http://www.hrw.org/news/2012/10/26/abd-al-rahim-al-nashiri.

55. Cordesman and Obaid, "Al-Qaeda in Saudi Arabia: Asymmetric Threats and Islamist Extremists," 4f.

56. Cordesman and Obaid, *National Security in Saudi Arabia: Threats, Responses, and Challenges*, 113f.

57. Riedel and Saab, "Al Qaeda's Third Front: Saudi Arabia"; Cordesman and Obaid, *National Security in Saudi Arabia: Threats, Responses, and Challenges*, 113f.

58. Cigar, *Al-Qaida's Doctrine for Insurgency*, 10 refers to an Arabic source which estimates that half of AQAP's effort was devoted to media operations. It is also worth noting that there were—and are—conflicting views on who ran AQAP after the death of al-Uyayri. For some, including Hegghammer, it was Khalid al-Hajj; for others such as Norman Cigar, it was Abd al-Aziz al-Muqrin. The latter seems more likely, bearing in mind the former's absence from AQAP literature. See Hegghammer, *Jihad in Saudi Arabia*, 203f; Cigar, *Al-Qaida's Doctrine for Insurgency*, 11f.

59. Hegghammer, "Terrorist Recruitment and Radicalization in Saudi Arabia," 41.

60. *Jihad in Saudi Arabia*, 204–5.

61. Cigar, *Al-Qaida's Doctrine for Insurgency*, 49.

62. Neil MacFarquhar, "Among the Saudis, Attack Has Soured Qaeda Supporters," *New York Times*, 11 Nov. 2003.

63. Hegghammer, *Jihad in Saudi Arabia*, 206.

64. Cordesman and Obaid, *National Security in Saudi Arabia: Threats, Responses, and Challenges*, 115.

65. Respectively, see Brian Whitaker, "Saudis Brandish 'Iron Fist' against Militants Who Threaten Foreigners," *The Guardian*; Abdul Hameed Bakier, "Lessons from Al-Qaeda's Attack on the Khobar Compound," *Terrorism Monitor* 4, no. 16 (2006).

66. See, in order mentioned above, "Two BBC Men Shot in Saudi Capital," http://news.bbc.co.uk/1/hi/world/middle_east/3781803.stm; Associated Press, "Americans Targeted Again in Riyadh," http://www.cbsnews.com/8301–224_162–622798.html; PBS Newshour, "American Hostage in Saudi Arabia Beheaded by Captors," (18 June 2004).

67. Two further issues were released in April 2005 and January 2007, however these were the work of individuals, both of whom were promptly arrested.

68. Cigar, *Al-Qaida's Doctrine for Insurgency*, 95.

69. Ibid., 99.

70. Ibid., 101.

71. Prince Bandar bin Sultan bin Abdulaziz al-Saud, "A Diplomat's Call for War," *Washington Post*. Also quoted in Boukhars, "At the Crossroads: Saudi Arabia's Dilemmas."

72. The 2005 figure can be found in Cordesman and Obaid, "Al-Qaeda in Saudi Arabia: Asymmetric Threats and Islamist Extremists," 122; the other figures are taken from Riedel and Saab, "Al Qaeda's Third Front: Saudi Arabia," 38.

73. Human Rights Watch, "Precarious Justice: Arbitrary Detention and Unfair Trials in the Deficient Criminal Justice System of Saudi Arabia," (Human Rights Watch, 2008).

74. There were at least two large-scale amnesties: the first in November 2007 in which around 1,500 detainees were released and the second in June 2008, when approximately a hundred and eighty individuals were released ibid., 6; "Human Rights and Saudi Arabia's Counterterrorism Response: Religious Counseling, Indefinite Detention, and Flawed Trials," 4. It is also worth noting that it is impossible to be precise in stating what proportion of those held in detention were violent Islamists because the Saudi regime regularly used counter-terrorism legislation to apprehend non-violent political opposition as well as violent Islamists. See "Precarious Justice: Arbitrary Detention and Unfair Trials in the Deficient Criminal Justice System of Saudi Arabia," e.g. p. 5.

75. Hegghammer, *Jihad in Saudi Arabia*, 203.

76. Meijer, "The Limits of Terrorism in Saudi Arabia," 282.

77. It is worth noting that it was the attacks on the Muhayya Housing Compound

which brought condemnation from the EIG, in the form of al-Zuhdi, *Istiratijiyat Wa Tafjirat Al-Qa'idah: Al-Akhta' Wal-Akhtar*

78. Hegghammer, *Jihad in Saudi Arabia*, 219f.

79. See el-Said, "De-Radicalising Islamists: Programmes and Their Impact in Muslim Majority States," 37f. Also Fink and Hearne, "Beyond Terrorism," 7.

80. Kapiszewski, "Saudi Arabia Steps toward Democratization or Reconfiguration of Authoritarianism?," 466.

81. A full list is provided by ibid., 467.

82. Toby C. Jones, "Social Contract for Saudi Arabia," *Middle East Report* (2003), 228.

83. Mai Yamani, "The Two Faces of Saudi Arabia," *Survival* 50, no. 1: 147.

84. Cordesman and Obaid, *National Security in Saudi Arabia: Threats, Responses, and Challenges*, 125.

85. U.S. Treasury, "Treasury Designates Al Haramain Islamic Foundation."

86. The programme's full title is The Advisory Committee Counselling Program. The precise date is uncertain, but most analysts suggest that it was launched after the November 2003 attacks. E.g. John Horgan and Kurt Braddock, "Rehabilitating the Terrorists?: Challenges in Assessing the Effectiveness of De-Radicalization Programs," *Terrorism and Political Violence* 22, no. 2: 276; Chris Boucek, "Extremist Re-Education and Rehabilitation in Saudi Arabia," in *Leaving Terrorism Behind: Individual and Collective Disengagement*, ed. Tore Bjørgo and John Horgan (Routledge, 2009), 212; Marisa Porges, "The Saudi Deradicalization Experiment," *Council on Foreign Relations, Expert Brief* (2010).

87. As Marisa Porges and Jessica Stern, "The Saudi Deradicalization Experiment", have pointed out, the programme has been refined since its inception, particularly in light of very public acts of recidivism, most notably those Saudis who completed the programme after their return from Guantánamo and then promptly absconded to Yemen to join an emergent AQAP as leaders. One development was to create the 'Mohammed bin Nayef Center for Counseling and Advice', which acts as a halfway house, simultaneously helping offenders re-integrate into Saudi society whilst providing the Security subcommittee with the opportunity for further monitoring and assessment. This improvement was so popular that further Care and Rehabilitation Centres were established. For a full discussion, see Chris Boucek, "Saudi Arabia's 'Soft' Counterterrorism Strategy: Prevention, Rehabilitation, and Aftercare," in *Carnegie Papers 97* (Carnegie Endowment for International Peace, 2008), 17–19.

88. Boucek, "Saudi Arabia's 'Soft' Counterterrorism Strategy," 11.

89. Horgan and Braddock, "Rehabilitating the Terrorists?: Challenges in Assessing the Effectiveness of De-Radicalization Programs," 278.

90. Boucek, "Extremist Re-Education," 213.

91. See the discussion in chapter 4.

92. Porges, "The Saudi Deradicalization Experiment"; Jessica Stern and Marisa L. Porges, "Getting Deradicalization Right," *Foreign Affairs*; Boucek, "Extremist Re-Education".

93. An argument put forward by, for example, Hegghammer, "Islamist Violence"; *Jihad in Saudi Arabia*; Riedel, *The Search for Al Qaeda*; Riedel and Saab, "Al Qaeda's Third Front: Saudi Arabia."

94. Hegghammer, "Islamist Violence," 713.

4. YEMEN: COALITIONS OF TERROR

1. E.g. Tawil, *Brothers in Arms: Al Qa'ida and the Arab Jihadists*; Atwan, *The Secret History of Al Qaeda*, 160; Wright, *Looming Tower*, 319–30 provides a full account of the attack on the USS Cole, but rarely returns to Yemen thereafter. Some academic literature, focusing only tangentially on security issues, was in existence: William Harold Ingrams, *The Yemen: Imams, Rulers & Revolutions* (J. Murray, 1963); J. E. Peterson, *Yemen: The Search for a Modern State* (The Johns Hopkins University Press, 1982); G. R. Smith, *The Yemens: The Yemen Arab Republic and the People's Democratic Republic of Yemen*, World Bibliographical Series (Clio, 1984); Robert D. Burrowes, *The Yemen Arab Republic: The Politics of Development 1962–1986*, Westview Special Studies on the Middle East (Boulder, 1987); Paul Dresch, *A History of Modern Yemen* (Cambridge University Press, 2001); Fred Halliday, *Revolution and Foreign Policy: The Case of South Yemen, 1967–1987* (Cambridge University Press, 2002); Sheila Carapico, *Civil Society in Yemen: The Political Economy of Activism in Modern Arabia* (Cambridge University Press, 2007).

2. Paul Dresch and Bernard Haykel, "Stereotypes and Political Styles: Islamists and Tribesfolk in Yemen," *International Journal of Middle East Studies* 27, no. 4 (1995): 420.

3. Dresch, *A History of Modern Yemen*, 87.

4. Ibid., 99.

5. Ibid., 115.

6. See Noel Brehony, *Yemen Divided: The Story of a Failed State in South Arabia* (I. B. Tauris, 2011), 60f.

7. For a fuller discussion see Bryce Loidolt, "Managing the Global and Local: The Dual Agendas of Al Qaeda in the Arabian Peninsula," *Studies in Conflict & Terrorism* 34, no. 2; Peter Bergen and Paul Cruickshank, "Revisiting the Early Al Qaeda: An Updated Account of Its Formative Years," ibid. 35, no. 1.

8. "Revisiting the Early Al Qaeda: An Updated Account of Its Formative Years," 13.

9. Bergen, *The Osama Bin Laden I Know*, 109.

10. For a biography of Wadi'i, the founder of Salafism in Yemen, see Laurent Bonnefoy, "Muqbil Al-Wadi'i," in *Global Salafism: Islam's New Religious Movement*, ed. Roel

Meijer. For an in-depth study, see "Varieties of Islamism in Yemen: The Logic of Integration under Pressure". Also, "How Transnational Is Salafism in Yemen"; *Salafism in Yemen: Transnationalism and Religious Identity* (Hurst, 2012). On the *Islah* party more generally see Nathan J. Brown and Amr Hamzawy, *Between Religion and Politics* (Carnegie Endowment, 2010), 136–59; Janine Clark, "Islamist Women in Yemen: Informal Nodes of Activism," in *Islamic Activism: A Social Movement Theory Approach*, ed. Quintan Wiktorowicz (Indiana University Press, 2004); Dresch and Haykel, "Stereotypes and Political Styles"; April Longley, "The High Water Mark of Islamist Politics? The Case of Yemen," *The Middle East Journal* 61, no. 2 (2007); Jillian Schwedler, "The Islah Party in Yemen: Political Opportunities and Coalition Building in a Transitional Polity," in *Islamic Activism: A Social Movement Theory Approach*, ed. Quintan Wiktorowicz (2004); *Faith in Moderation: Islamist Parties in Jordan and Yemen*.

11. Cited in Bergen and Cruickshank, "Revisiting the Early Al Qaeda: An Updated Account of Its Formative Years," 13–14.

12. Muqbil al-Wadi'i would later address bin Laden in uncompromising terms: 'O toi le *muflis* (le "faille"), je veux dire, Oussama Ben Laden, tu n'es entouré de rien d'autre que de mâcheurs de qât, de fumeurs et de malodorants.' (You're bankrupt, yes you, Osama bin Laden; you're surrounded by no-one but those who chew *qat*, smoke and stink), cited in François Burgat and Mu'hammad Sbitli, "Les Salafis Au Yémen Ou... La Modernisation Malgré Tout," *Chroniques Yéménites*, no. 10.

13. Boucek, "Yemen: Avoiding a Downward Spiral," 12. In 2001, Hussayn al-Arab, the former Minister of the Interior, estimated that by 1993, as many as 29,000 Afghan Arabs had returned to Yemen. Schwedler, *Faith in Moderation: Islamist Parties in Jordan and Yemen*, 208. The figure seems large, but it is supported elsewhere, see, e.g. Victoria Clark, *Yemen: Dancing on the Heads of Snakes* (Yale University Press, 2010), 161.

14. On business models and al-Qa'ida, see Peter Bergen, *Holy War, Inc.: Inside the Secret World of Osama Bin Laden* (Free Press, 2002).

15. Clark, *Yemen*, 160 suggests that Tariq al-Fadhli spent three months in bin Laden's camp in Jaji, but he has repeatedly denied this, saying that he met bin Laden briefly only in 1989 at the battle of Jalalabad. See Rafid Ali, "The Jihadis and the Cause of South Yemen: A Profile of Tariq Al-Fadhli," *Terrorism Monitor* 7, no. 35 (2009).

16. In a 2005 interview, Tariq al-Fadhli acknowledged that 'Osama bin Laden provided me with funding', but denied that he was part of al-Qa'ida, however, saying, 'I have only heard about al-Qaeda recently because there was no such thing when I was in Afghanistan'. Cited from Gregory Johnsen, "The Resiliency of Yemen's Aden-Abyan Islamic Army," in *Global Terrorism Analysis* (The Jamestown Foundation). I use the name of the groups provided by Dresch, *A History of Modern Yemen*, 187. According to Schwedler, *Faith in Moderation: Islamist Parties in Jordan*

and Yemen, 209 the group was known as *Harakat al-jihad al-Islami* (Islamic Jihad Movement), but I have found no references to this name.

17. Much of this biography was provided in my interviews with Bob and Abu Hadhram. Clark, *Yemen*, 162. See also Wright, *Looming Tower*, 217. Scheuer, *Through Our Enemies' Eyes: Osama Bin Laden, Radical Islam, and the Future of America, Revised Edition*, 139 suggests that bin Laden also provided militants from Sudan.

18. So vituperative was it that Dresch and Haykel, "Stereotypes and Political Styles," 409, assert that 'there is little doubt that Zindani ... anathematised the YSP [Yemeni Socialist Party]'. Clark, *Yemen*, 162.

19. Abu Hassan was a *kunya* (a teknonym often used as a *nom de guerre*); his real name was Zayn al-Abdin al-Mihdhar. Brian Whitaker, "Abu Al-Hassan and the Islamic Army of Aden-Abyan", http://www.al-bab.com/yemen/hamza/hassan.htm. I refer to Abu Hassan's organisation as AAIA, despite the fact that it did not formally use this name until 1998. This has led most commentators to assume that it was formed in the years after the Civil War in 1996, or 1997 and to over-emphasise the links to al-Qa'ida. In all probability, this was an autonomous group in the beginning whose ideology was similar enough to that of bin Laden to allow co-operation in the future, but it should not be understood as part of bin Laden's global *jihad* per se.

20. Fred Halliday, "The Third Inter-Yemeni War and Its Consequences," *Asian Affairs* 26, no. 2 (1995): 132; Dresch and Haykel, "Stereotypes and Political Styles," 409.

21. Despite his denials of involvement in the incident (which continue to this day: see Clark, *Yemen*, 156f.), Tariq al-Fadhli was widely seen as the leader of the violent Islamist movement and was promptly arrested on the mere suspicion of involvement (although he was released in time for the 1994 Civil War). While it is far from clear whether al-Fadhli played a role in the affair, it is reasonably certain that the attack was at the very least funded by bin Laden. In the months that followed, US intelligence reports concluded along the same lines that '[bin Laden's] group almost certainly played a role' in the attack, although little further information is provided about the actual perpetrators. The quotation is from an Intelligence Community paper of April 1993, cited in U. S. House of Representatives, *Report of the Joint Inquiry into the Terrorist Attacks of September 11, 2001—by the House Permanent Select Committee on Intelligence and the Senate Select Committee on Intelligence, Volume I*, 194. With regards to the anonymity of the attacks, the exception is Jamal al-Nahdi, a Sana'ani businessman about whom little else seems to be known. See John Burns, "Yemen Links to Bin Laden Gnaw at F.B.I. In Cole Inquiry," *New York Times*, 26 Nov. 2000.

22. Halliday, "The Third Inter-Yemeni War and Its Consequences," 132; Brehony, *Yemen Divided: The Story of a Failed State in South Arabia*, 194.

23. Brehony, *Yemen Divided: The Story of a Failed State in South Arabia*, 196; Mark

Katz, "U.S.-Yemen Relations and the War on Terror: A Portrait of Yemeni President Ali Abdullah Salih," *Terrorism Monitor* 7, no. 2 (2005).

24. Brehony, *Yemen Divided: The Story of a Failed State in South Arabia*, 195.

25. Scheuer, *Through Our Enemies' Eyes*, 151; Burns, "Yemen Links to Bin Laden Gnaw at F.B.I. In Cole Inquiry."

26. Halliday, "The Third Inter-Yemeni War and Its Consequences," 138–9. See also Schwedler, "The Islah Party in Yemen: Political Opportunities and Coalition Building in a Transitional Polity."

27. Christina Hellmich, "Fighting Al Qaeda in Yemen? Rethinking the Nature of the Islamist Threat and the Effectiveness of U.S. Counterterrorism Strategy," *Studies in Conflict & Terrorism* 35, no. 9 (2012): n.42, 632.

28. Chris Boucek and Marina Ottaway, eds., *Yemen on the Brink* (Carnegie Endowment for International Peace, 2010), 12.

29. Brian Whitaker, "Extracts from Supporters of Shari'a Newsletters," Yemen Gateway, http://www.al-bab.com/yemen/hamza/sos3.htm. See also, Jonathan Schanzer, "Yemen's War on Terror," *Orbis* 48, no. 3 (2005).

30. Some accounts differ over the date, stating that the kidnapping took place on 27 December; equally, there were reports that suggested that it was his stepson who was caught; however, in interviews, Abu Hamza always referred to him as his godson, see Rory Carroll, "Terrorists or Tourists?," Guardian Article Reprinted at http://www.al-bab.com/yemen/artic/gdn42.htm.

31. Schanzer, "Yemen's War on Terror," 525.

32. It is worth reiterating the point made in chapter 1 that alliances are co-operative relationships between those whose political objectives are broadly similar while coalitions are formed with political actors whose objectives are different. Walt, *The Origins of Alliances*; Gamson, "A Theory of Coalition Formation."

33. Bergen, *The Osama Bin Laden I Know*, 108–9.

34. Boucek and Ottaway, *Yemen on the Brink*, 12. Several EIJ members settled in Yemen, see chapter 2.

35. Schwedler, *Faith in Moderation: Islamist Parties in Jordan and Yemen*; "The Islah Party in Yemen: Political Opportunities and Coalition Building in a Transitional Polity." See also Alley, "The Rules of the Game: Unpacking Patronage Politics in Yemen"; "Shifting Light in the Qamariyya: The Reinvention of Patronage Networks in Contemporary Yemen," (unpublished doctoral dissertation, Georgetown University, 2008); Vincent Durac, "The Joint Meeting Parties and the Politics of Opposition in Yemen," *British Journal of Middle Eastern Studies* 38, no. 3 (2011).

36. Alley, "The Rules of the Game: Unpacking Patronage Politics in Yemen."

37. Schanzer, "Yemen's War on Terror."

38. Brian Whitaker, "Abu Hamza and the Islamic Army," http://www.al-bab.com/yemen/hamza/day.htm.

39. This was a fairly typical characteristic of al-Qa'ida at the time; in the 1998

U.S. Embassy bombings in East Africa, two of the perpetrators had refused to swear allegiance in case bin Laden refused to allow them to become *shaheed* (martyrs—that is, suicide bombers) and given them logistics roles. See Marc Sageman, *Leaderless Jihad: Terror Networks in the Twenty-First Century* (University of Pennsylvania Press, 2008), 30.

40. Hegghammer, *Jihad in Saudi Arabia*, 117f.; Bergen and Cruickshank, "Revisiting the Early Al Qaeda: An Updated Account of Its Formative Years," 25–8.

41. Paul Dixon, "'Hearts and Minds'? British Counter-Insurgency Strategy in Northern Ireland," *Journal of Strategic Studies* 32, no. 3 (2009); Harry Eckstein, *Internal War: Problems and Approaches* (Greenwood Press, 1980). Brehony, *Yemen Divided: The Story of a Failed State in South Arabia*, 185, identifies the influx of around 800,000 Yemeni migrant workers from Saudi Arabia as 'all but destroying the economic dividend of unity and of the promised riches of oil exports'. Nora Ann Colton, "Yemen: A Collapsed Economy," *The Middle East Journal* 64, no. 3: 414–16, also notes the impact on unemployment.

42. The role of local grievances rather than global ideology in 'Islamist' violence in Yemen is noted by Dresch and Haykel, "Stereotypes and Political Styles."

43. In an interview with Ahmad Zaidan, al-Jazeera's Bureau Chief in Pakistan, bin Laden admitted that the attack had been centrally planned. Further evidence that the attack was al-Qa'ida rather than the AAIA is in a poem which he read at his son's wedding in Kandahar in early 2001: 'A destroyer: even the brave fear its might / it inspires horror in harbor and in the open sea / she sails into the waves / flanked by arrogance, haughtiness and false power. / To her doom she moves slowly / a dinghy awaits her, riding the waves (Bergen, *The Osama Bin Laden I Know*, 256).

44. See Wright, *Looming Tower*, 328f., who provides evidence that Fahd al-Quso shipped $36,000 to Malaysia to 'Khallad' and provided on-the-ground logistics.

45. See Sheila Carapico, "No Quick Fix: Foreign Aid and State Performance in Yemen," in *Rebuilding Devastated Economies in the Middle East*, ed. Leonard Binder (Palgrave MacMillan, 2007), who notes that 'aid per capita slipped from US$22 to US$15 between 1997 and 2000' (p. 197).

46. "Sanaa Security Environment Profile Questionnaire—Spring 2009," (Embassy Sanaa (Yemen): Wikileaks, 2009); "Royg Operation against Terrorists in Abyan," (Embassy Sanaa (Yemen): Wikileaks, 2003); "August 29, 2003, Security Environment Profile Questionnaire Response," (Embassy Sanaa (Yemen): Wikileaks, 2003); "Yemen: 2003 Annual Terrorism Report," (Embassy Sanaa (Yemen): Wikileaks, 2003).

47. Interview with Bob, April 2012.

48. For the corruption figures, see World Bank, "Republic of Yemen—Poverty Reduction Strategy Paper Annual Progress Report and Joint Ida-IMF Staff Advisory Note," (The World Bank, 2006).

49. Curt Tarnoff, "Millennium Challenge Corporation," in *CRS Report for Congress*

(Congressional Research Service), 14. See also, Phillips, *Yemen and the Politics of Permanent Crisis*, 42–4.

50. Gregory Johnsen cited in Sarah Phillips, "Yemen: Developmental Dysfunction and Division in a Crisis State," in *Developmental Leadership Program Research Paper*, 14, n. 31 (2011).

51. An interpretation echoed in US diplomatic cables, see "Al-Qa'ida Escape: Update," (Embassy Sanaa (Yemen): Wikileaks).

52. "Embassy Follow-up to MCC Signing Ceremony Postponement," (Embassy Sanaa (Yemen): Wikileaks). In November, the ambassador attempted bargaining rather than intimidation, reiterating to al-Dhabbi the US government's desire to have al-Badawi handed over into their custody. He went on to 'point to material gains for Yemen as a result of al-Badawi's surrender to US custody', suggesting 'that these measures might include, in the first instance, a rescheduling of the MCC Threshold Program signing'. He even went so far as to suggest that 'the USG would be prepared to work towards the return of Yemeni nationals currently held at Guantanamo'. "Ambassador Presses Foreign Ministry on Badawi Case," (Embassy Sanaa (Yemen): Wikileaks).

53. I call this organisation al-Qa'ida in Yemen for ease.

54. Barfi, "Yemen on the Brink? The Resurgence of Al Qaeda in the Arabian Peninsula."

55. Gabriel Koehler-Derrick, *A False Foundation? Aqap, Tribes and Ungoverned Spaces in Yemen* (Combatting Terrorism Centre, 2011).

56. He was one of three brothers all of whom had been heavily involved in violent Islamism. His younger brother, Faris, fought in Afghanistan before returning to Yemen; and his elder brother, Ali, who trained at the al-Farouq camp in Afghanistan in 2001, was detained in Guantánamo Bay. See Wikileaks: The Guantánamo Files, "Ali Yahya Al-Raimi," http://wikileaks.org/gitmo/prisoner/167.html. Also Barfi, "Yemen on the Brink? The Resurgence of Al Qaeda in the Arabian Peninsula"; Gregory Johnsen, "Tracking Yemen's 23 Escaped Jihadi Operatives Parts I," *Terrorism Monitor* 5, no. 18; "Tracking Yemen's 23 Escaped Jihadi Operatives Parts II," *Terrorism Monitor* 5, no. 19. His current status is unknown: he has reportedly been killed in twice, in 2007 and 2010, but videos of him have been released since.

57. Some quickly turned themselves in to the authorities; others were killed in confrontations with security forces and by July, ten were left unaccounted for. "Al-Qa'ida Escape: Update." See also Johnsen, "Tracking Yemen's 23 Escaped Jihadi Operatives Parts I"; "Tracking Yemen's 23 Escaped Jihadi Operatives Parts II".

58. But despite this, the nascent organisation was also markedly international: of those who escaped, eleven were Yemenis born outside their homeland (mainly in Saudi Arabia) and thirteen of them had been involved in *jihadi* exploits in at least one other country (mainly Afghanistan). These figures are based on biographies compiled by Johnsen, "Tracking Yemen's 23 Escaped Jihadi Operatives Parts I"; "Tracking Yemen's 23 Escaped Jihadi Operatives Parts II".

59. Batch 10 was adopted as a slogan by Peter Taylor. See "Yemen Al-Qaeda Link to Guantanamo," BBC, http://news.bbc.co.uk/1/hi/programmes/newsnight/8454804.stm.

60. His real name, according to his Guantánamo file, was Mohamed Atiq Awayd al-Harbi. Wikileaks: The Guantánamo Files, "Mohamed Atiq Awayd Al-Harbi," http://wikileaks.org/gitmo/ prisoner/333.html.

61. He was subsequently interviewed by the BBC, see Peter Taylor, "Generation Jihad," (BBC 2). Evan Kohlmann, "'The Eleven': Saudi Guantanamo Veterans Returning to the Fight," (NEFA Foundation).

62. The biography is compiled from the Guantánamo files; see Wikileaks: The Guantánamo Files, "Sa'id Ali Jabir Al Khathim Al Shihri," http://wikileaks.org/gitmo/prisoner/372.html.

63. Al-Qa'ida in the Arabian Peninsula, "Communiqué #4: Expel the Infidels from the Arabian Peninsula," (al-Malahim Media, 2008).

64. "Yemen Bomb Kills Spanish Tourists," http://news.bbc.co.uk/1/hi/6262302.stm; Ellen Knickmeyer, "Attack against U.S. Embassy in Yemen Blamed on Al-Qaeda," http://www.washingtonpost.com/wp-dyn/content/article/2008/09/17/AR2008091700317.html; Matthew Weaver, "Britain's Deputy Ambassador to Yemen Survives Rocket Attack," *The Guardian*, 6 Oct. 2010.

65. Harris, "Exploiting Grievances: Al-Qaeda in the Arabian Peninsula," 3–4. The second incident is reported on the "National Consortium for the Study of Terrorism and Responses to Terrorism (Start)," (Global Terrorism Database).

66. Data derived from "National Consortium for the Study of Terrorism and Responses to Terrorism (Start)."

67. See also "Exploiting Grievances: Al-Qaeda in the Arabian Peninsula"; Page, Challita, and Harris, "Al Qaeda in the Arabian Peninsula: Framing Narratives and Prescriptions." They describe a reverse process through which grievances are identified and solutions are provided in the form of a 'diagnostic' and a 'prognostic' stage. They argue that this material attempts to remove the psychological barriers to participating in such a high-value, high-risk form of political opposition. In the first eight issues, *Sada al-Malahim* contained a regular feature called *Madrassat Yusuf* (the School of Yusuf) which aimed to provide particular elements of tradecraft to would-be *mujahideen*; these sections outlined how the captured militant could survive their time in prison, how they could deal with questioning and interrogation and how they could cope with the psychological impact. Harris *et al* have noted that the School of Yusuf was 'likely aimed at … [building] increased confidence among recruits in their ability to confront the potentially deadly consequences of their involvement in jihadi activities'. Ibid., 162.

68. Al-Qa'ida in the Arabian Peninsula, "An Interview with One of the Most Wanted Men: Abu Hummam Al-Qahtani (Translated by the Nefa Foundation)," (al-Malahim Media, 2008).

69. Benford and Snow, "Framing Processes and Social Movements."

70. With minor editing, from al-Qa'ida in the Arabian Peninsula, "The Fragility of the Administration and the Loss of Control," (al-Malahim Media, 2008).

71. Phillips, "Al-Qaeda and the Struggle for Yemen," 105.

72. Al-Qa'ida in the Arabian Peninsula, "From Here We Start and in Al-Aqsa We Shall Meet," (al-Malahim Media, 2009).

73. Ibid.

74. Ibid. There is a certain irony in this, bearing in mind that, only a few weeks after the release of the video, al-Awfi would recant his views and admit himself into the Saudi Counselling Programme.

75. Thomas Hegghammer, "The Failure of Jihad in Saudi Arabia," (DTIC Document).

76. "Saudi and Yemeni Branches of Al-Qaida Unite," *Jihadica*. See also Gregory Johnsen, "Al-Qaida in the Arabian Peninsula in Yemen," in *Talk of the Nation* (NPR).

77. Jonathan Masters, "Al-Qaeda in the Arabian Peninsula (Aqap)," http://www.cfr.org/yemen/al-qaeda-arabian-peninsula-aqap/p9369; "Al Qaeda in Arabian Peninsula (Aqap)," http://www.huffingtonpost.com/jonathan-masters/yemen-al-qaeda_b_1028389.html; BBC, "Profile: Al-Qaeda in the Arabian Peninsula," http://www.bbc.co.uk/news/world-middle-east-11483095; al-Jazeera, "Profile: Al Qaeda in the Arabian Peninsula," http://www.aljazeera.com/news/middleeast/2012/05/2012597359456359.html.

78. The phrase is from "Inspire 3," (al-Malahim Media, 2010).

79. At the beginning of 2009, it was estimated that AQAP consisted of approximately two or three hundred members ("Frontline: Al-Qaeda in Yemen," Waq al-Waq, http://bigthink.com/waq-al-waq/frontline-al-qaeda-in-yemen?page=all.). By 2012, John Brennan, assistant to the president for Homeland Security and Counterterrorism, estimated there were more than 1000 members ("Killing of Al Qaeda Leader in Yemen Evidence of New U.S.-Yemeni Offensive," CNN Security Clearance [Blog], http://security.blogs.cnn.com/2012/05/07/killing-of-al-qaeda-leader-in-yemen-evidence-of-new-u-s-yemeni-offensive.)

80. Koehler-Derrick, *A False Foundation? Aqap, Tribes and Ungoverned Spaces in Yemen*, 47f; "Tourists Die in Yemen Explosion," http://news.bbc.co.uk/1/hi/7945013.stm. Shibam is a small town in the Hadhramout replete with mud-brick tower blocks which rise out of the cliffs and which date back to the sixteenth century; it is, according to UNESCO, one of the 'oldest and best examples of urban planning based on the principle of vertical construction'. "Old Walled City of Shibam," http://whc.unesco.org/en/list/192.

81. "Bomber Targets S Koreans in Yemen," http://www.aljazeera.com/news/middleeast/2009/03/200931871130679609.html. For a full discussion, see James Spencer, "Al-Qa'ida in the Arabian Peninsula: Mos & Deductions," *Small Wars Journal*, 2011.

82. Informal conversation with British Intelligence Officer, 2 Aug. 2012

83. Informal conversation with British Intelligence Official, 18 Aug. 2012

84. The conversation was recorded by al-Asiri's opposite number and released as part of an audio recording in al-Qa'ida in the Arabian Peninsula, "The Descendents of Muhammad Bin Maslamah," ed. Sada al-Malahim (Translated by NEFA Foundation). Full details of the attack were obtained in informal conversation with a UK intelligence official, 18 Aug. 2012 who was absolutely clear about the positioning of the explosives on which there are multiple stories concerning the attack on Mohammed bin Nayef; some are unclear as to where the explosives were e.g. Koehler-Derrick, *A False Foundation? Aqap, Tribes and Ungoverned Spaces in Yemen*, 48–9. Others suggest that the explosives were inserted into the rectum: Chris McGreal and Vikram Dodd, "Cargo Bombs Plot: Us Hunts Saudi Extremist," *The Guardian*, 31 Oct. 2010; "Ibrahim Hassan Al-Asiri: The Prime Bombmaking Suspect," 31 Oct. 2010; "Cargo Plane Bomb Plot: Saudi Double Agent 'Gave Crucial Alert'," *The Guardian*, 1 Nov. 2010.

85. The author has seen photographs of the scene and analysis of the blast which was directed to the sides of al-Asiri rather than forward.

86. Gregory Johnsen, "Aqap in Yemen and the Christmas Day Terrorist Attack," in *CTC Sentinel* (Combatting Terrorism Centre at West Point). A previous and similar shoot out, without the disguises took place in late September 2009, see Thomas Joscelyn, "Former Gitmo Detainee Killed in Shootout," The Long War Journal, http://www.longwarjournal.org/archives/2009/09/former_gitmo_detaine.php.

87. For a fuller biography of Yusuf al-Shihri, see "Another Former Gitmo Detainee Killed in Shootout," The Long War Journal http://www.longwarjournal.org/archives/2009/10/another_former_gitmo.php. Also, Kohlmann, "'The Eleven': Saudi Guantanamo Veterans Returning to the Fight," 7–10.

88. Al-Qa'ida in the Arabian Peninsula, "Masha'l Al-Shadukhi: Limadha Nuqatil Fi Jazirat Al-'Arab?," *Sada al-Malahim* 10. Cited in Loidolt, "Managing the Global and Local: The Dual Agendas of Al Qaeda in the Arabian Peninsula," 108.

89. Koehler-Derrick, *A False Foundation? AQAP, Tribes and Ungoverned Spaces in Yemen*, 49.

90. Gregory Johnsen, *The Last Refuge: Yemen, Al-Qaeda, and America's War in Arabia* (W. W. Norton & Company, 2012), 257. See also Koehler-Derrick, *A False Foundation? AQAP, Tribes and Ungoverned Spaces in Yemen*, 52.

91. His travel route is derived from that provided by "Profile: Umar Farouk Abdulmutallab," http://www.bbc.co.uk/news/world-us-canada-11545509.

92. Shiraz Maher, "Instant Analysis: New Issue of Inspire Magazine," FreeRad!cals Blog, International Centre for the Study of Radicalisation, http://icsr.info/2010/11/instant-analysis-new-issue-of-inspire-magazine-2. The fact that one of the packages contained a copy of Great Expectations has caused much ink to be spilled over the role of al-Awlaqi in this last attack. For some it is evidence for

his central role, citing an interview with *Inspire* magazine in which he said that it had been his favourite book when he was in prison. This does not, however, sit easily with al-Awlaqi's role in AQAP as it has been described above. More likely is that the book appealed to core members of AQAP like al-Wuhayshi precisely because it brought al-Awlaqi, now viewed by the US as an arch enemy, to mind. It also goes without saying that the book's title had a symbolism which appealed to AQAP: this was an attack which broke the mould by focusing on cargo rather than passenger planes and by cutting out the suicide bomber and the networks of communication and security that presented ample opportunity for interception. By contrast, this involved little financial input, little in the way of personnel and materiel and yet could provide substantial coercive force.

93. Although there is evidence he went to Afghanistan, it was in 1993, see Bobby Ghosh, "How Dangerous Is the Cleric Anwar Al-Awlaki?," *Time*, 13 Jan. 2009. On the hijackers, see *The 9/11 Commission Report: Final Report of the National Commission on Terrorist Attacks Upon the United States*, 215f. It will be noticed that Khaled al-Mihdhar shares the same name as Abu Hassan (also known as Zayn al-Abdin al-Mihdhar); both were involved in the AAIA, the latter as a leader. There is no evidence to suggest that they were related, or indeed, that they were not related.

94. J. M. Berger, "Exclusive: U.S. Gave Millions to Charity Linked to Al Qaeda, Anwar Awlaki," http://news.intelwire.com/2010/04/us-gave-millions-to-charity-linked-to.html.

95. Berger, "Anwar Al-Awlaki's Links to the September 11 Hijackers," *The Atlantic*, 9 Sep. 2011.

96. Thomas Hegghammer, "The Case for Chasing Al-Awlaki," in *Foreign Policy*; Frank Ciluffo and Clinton Watts, "Yemen & Al Qaeda in the Arabian Peninsula: Exploiting a Window of Counterterrorism Opportunity," in *HSPI Issue Brief Series* (Homeland Security and Policy Institute), are the main exponents; "Countering the Threat Posed by Aqap: Embrace, Don't Chase Yemen's Chaos," Selected Wisdom Blog, http://selectedwisdom.com/?p=352. See also Chris Boucek, "The New Face of Al-Qaeda?," *Foreign Policy*, 18 May 2011; "The Killing of Al-Awlaqi: A Crippling Blow"; Clausewitz: The Economist's Defence, Security and Diplomacy Blog, http://www.economist.com/blogs/clausewitz/2011/10/killing-anwar-al-awlaki; Hakim Almasmari, Margaret Coker, and Siobhan Gorman, "Drone Kills Top Al Qaeda Figure," *Wall Street Journal*, 1 Oct. 2011; Adrian Blomfield, "Analysis: Awlaki's Death Is a Boost for the West," http://www.telegraph.co.uk/news/worldnews/al-qaeda/8799991/Analysis-Awlakis-death-is-a-boost-for-the-West.html.

97. Gregory Johnsen, "The Al-Awlaki Debate Continues," Waq al-Waq, http://bigthink.com/waq-al-waq/the-al-awlaki-debate-continues; "A False Target in Yemen," http://www.nytimes.com/2010/11/20/opinion/20johnsen.html; Jerrold M. Post,

"The Generation of Vipers: The Generational Provenance of Terrorists," *SAIS Review* 31, no. 2: 115–16; Denis MacEoin, "Anwar Al-Awlaki: 'I Pray That Allah Destroys America,'" *Middle East Quarterly* XVIII, no. 2; Michael Clarke and Valentina Soria, "Terrorism: The New Wave," *RUSI Journal* 155, no. 4; Dean Alexander, "Al Qaeda and Al Qaeda in the Arabian Peninsula: Inspired, Homegrown Terrorism in the United States," *Journal of Applied Security Research* 6, no. 4.

98. Hegghammer, "The Case for Chasing Al-Awlaki." The blog he mentions is now defunct.

99. He signed off on articles in the first three editions of *Inspire*. The second question is also posed by Johnsen, "The Al-Awlaki Debate Continues".

100. Osama bin Laden, "Letter to 'Sheikh Mahmood' (Socom-2012–0000003)," (Combatting Terrorism Centre at West Point).See also Nelly Lahood et al., "Letters from Abbottabad: Bin Ladin Sidelined," in *Harmony Program* (Combatting Terrorism Center at West Point, 2012).

101. A phrase of Evan Kohlmann's, cited in Josh Meyer, "Fort Hood Shooting Suspect's Ties to Mosque Investigated," *Los Angeles Times*, 9 Nov. 2009.

102. Scott Shane, "U.S. Approves Targeted Killing of American Cleric," *The New York Times*, 7 Apr. 2010; Philip Johnston, "Anwar Al Awlaki: The New Osama Bin Laden?," *The Telegraph*, 17 Sep. 2010; Catherine Herridge, "Awlaki Tops Bin Laden as Top Terror Threat to U.S., Counterterrorism Official Says," Fox News, http://www.foxnews.com/us/2011/02/09/awlaki-tops-bin-laden-terror-threat-counterterrorism-official-says/; Voice of America, "Al-Awlaki's Death Leaves Gap in Al-Qaida," 29 Sep. 2011.

103. The legal literature on the killing of al-Awlaqi is considerable and beyond the scope of this research. Useful articles include: Mark Hosenball, "Secret Panel Can Put Americans on Kill List," Reuters, http://www.reuters.com/article/2011/10/05/us-cia-killlist-idUSTRE79475C20111005; Robert Chesney, "Who May Be Killed? Anwar Al-Awlaki as a Case Study in the International Legal Regulation of Lethal Force," *SSRN eLibrary* (2011), http://papers.ssrn.com/sol3/papers.cfm?abstract_id=1754223; "Al-Awlaki as an Operational Leader Located in a Place Where Capture Was Not Possible," http://www.lawfareblog.com/2011/09/al-awlaki-as-an-operational-leader-located-in-a-place-where-capture-was-not-possible/; Daniel Bethlehem, "Mopping up the Last War or Stumbling into the Next?," *Harvard Law School National Security Journal* (2011); Bruce Ackerman, "Obama's Death Panel," *Foreign Policy*, 7 Oct. 2011.

104. Evan Perez, "U.S. Terror Suspect Arrested," *Wall Street Journal*, 3 June 2010. Anwar al-Awlaqi, "44 Ways to Support Jihad," (n.p.).

105. The quotation is left precisely as was written by Hassan. For the publicly available emails, see William H. Webster Commission, "The Federal Bureau of

Investigation, Counterterrorism Intelligence, and the Events at Fort Hood, Texas on November 5, 2009."

106. Joseph Lieberman, *Ticking Time Bomb: Counter-Terrorism Lessons from the US Government's Failure to Prevent the Fort Hood Attack* (DIANE Publishing, 2011). The report actually makes very little comment about al-Awlaqi, other than acknowledging his role in other cases of 'lone wolf' terrorism.

107. Thomas Joscelyn, "Awlaki's E-Mails to Terror Plotter Show Operational Role," Long War Journal, http://www.longwarjournal.org/archives/2011/03/anwar_al_awlakis_ema.php#ixzz1HXMb3Cp (2 Mar. 2012).

108. J. M. Berger, "Two E-Mails from Anwar Awlaki," http://news.intelwire.com/2012/06/two-e-mails-from-anwar-awlaki.html.

109. Bruce Golding, "Times Sq. Bomber's Vile Rant as He Gets Life in Jail," *New York Post*, 6 Oct. 2010.

110. "Al Qaeda in Yemen," (PBS); "Frontline: Al-Qaeda in Yemen", ibid.; "In Case You Missed It: The 'Al Qaeda in Yemen' Live Chat," http://www.guardian.co.uk/commentisfree/cifamerica/2012/may/29/frontline-al-qaida-yemen-live-chat.

111. Benedict Wilkinson, "What Is the Link between Ansar Al-Sharia and Al-Qa'ida in the Arabian Peninsula?," RUSI Analysis, 25 May 2012, https://www.rusi.org/commentary/what-link-between-ansar-al-sharia-and-al-qaida-arabian-peninsula.

112. Al-Qa'ida in the Arabian Peninsula, "Yahya Ibrahim: $4200," in *Inspire 3* (al-Malahim Media, 2010), 15.

113. Ibid., "Abu Mus'ab Al-Suri: *Jihadi* Experiences," in *Inspire 2* (al-Malahim Media, 2010), 21.

114. Ibid., *Inspire 3*.

115. Ibid. Taber, *The War of the Flea*, 29.

116. *Inspire 2*, (al-Malahim Media, 2010), 55.

117. *Inspire 3*.

118. Human Rights Watch, "Human Rights Watch World Report 2002—Yemen."

119. Amnesty International, "Amnesty International Report 2002—Yemen," 3. My own informal interviews suggested that 'several hundred' were picked up.

120. "Yemen: The Rule of Law Sidelined in the Name of Security," 6.

121. "Amnesty International Report 2002—Yemen," 2.

122. "Amnesty International Report 2003—Yemen," 2.

123. "Yemen: The Rule of Law Sidelined in the Name of Security," 8.

124. Human Rights Watch, "No Direction Home: Returns from Guantanamo to Yemen," 43.

125. Hafez and Wiktorowicz, "Violence as Contention," 78.

126. Byman, "Do Targeted Killings Work," 103–4.

127. These figures are taken from Bill Roggio and Bob Barry, "The Covert US Air Campaign in Yemen," Long War Journal http://www.longwarjournal.org/multimedia/Yemen/code/Yemen-strike.php.

128. Ibid.

129. Howard LaFranchi, "US Covert Attacks in Yemen: A Better Template for the War on Terror?," *Christian Science Monitor*, 15 June 2011; Patrik Jonsson, "Will Yemen Air Strike Change View of Fort Hood Shooting?," ibid., 24 Dec. 2009; Bobby Ghosh, "Has the Alleged Fort Hood Gunman's Imam Been Silenced?," *Time*, 24 Nov. 2009; CNN, "Most Wanted: Anwar Al-Awlaki," CNN Security Clearance [Blog], http://security.blogs.cnn.com/2011/06/17/most-wanted-anwar-al-awlaki/; Agence France Presse, "Drone Attack Kills 10 Qaeda Suspects in South Yemen," http://www.google.com/hostednews/afp/article/ALeqM5ig SCJQYllvvvaI-70o66azhP9JwA?docId=CNG.0d3bf3dd466de4d0317f3f205 dba2ee1.2f1.

130. Al-Qaʻida in the Arabian Peninsula, "Letter from the Editor, Yahya Ibrahim," in *Inspire 9* (al-Malahim Media, 2012), 4.

131. In 2012, there were two attempts against Qasim al-Raymi, the first on 7 April (Agence France Presse, "Yemen Air Force, U.S. Drone Kill 24 Qaeda Suspects," http://english.alarabiya.net/articles/2012/04/08/206235.html.); the second was on 10 May ("Yemen 'Al-Qaeda Fighters' Killed in Air Raids," http://www.aljazeera.com/news/middleeast/2012/05/2012511145648893973.html.). There was one attempt against Nasir al-Wuhayshi (7 April). On 30 April, Abu Hummam al-Zarqawi, nephew of Abu Musʻab al-Zarqawi, was targeted and killed. Salah al-Jawhari, a bomb-maker attached to Ansar al-Shariʻa was killed; on 22 April, Ghareeb al-Taizi was eliminated. Further deaths, already noted, were those of Fahd al-Quso and Saʻid al-Shihri.

132. CNN, "Yemeni Defense Minister Survives Apparent Assassination Attempt," 11 Sep. 2012; "13 Die in Blast Targeting Yemen's Defense Minister," *USA Today*, 11 Sep. 2012.

133. Gregory Johnsen, "Is Al-Qaeda in Yemen Regrouping," *Terrorism Focus* 4, no. 15 (2007).

134. Benjamin Weiser and Colin Moynihan, "A Guilty Plea in Plot to Bomb Times Square," *The New York Times*, 22 June 2010.

135. Wikileaks: available at https://wikileaks.org/plusd/cables/10SANAA4_a.html.

136. The Yemeni regime responded, typically, with repression. In the first instance he was repeatedly threatened and then arrested on charges of supporting al-Qaʻida and acting as a media advisor to Anwar al-Awlaqi. The story goes on: although he was to receive a presidential pardon in 2011, a telephone call between Ali Abdullah Saleh and President Obama (in which the latter expressed concerns over the release) ensured his continued detention. Jeremy Scahill, "Why Is President Obama Keeping a Journalist in Prison in Yemen?," *The Nation*, 13 Mar. 2012. Molly Ochs, "Yemen: New Government, Same Challenges to Press Freedom," (International Press Institute, 2012). The truth behind Shayea's story is verified by Wikileaks cables: see, "US Embassy Cables: Yemen Trumpets Strikes

on Al-Qaida That Were Americans' Work," http://www.guardian.co.uk/world/us-embassy-cables-documents/240955.

137. "Us Embassy Cables: Yemen Trumpets Strikes on Al-Qaida That Were Americans' Work".

138. "Suspected U.S. Drone Strike Kills Civilians in Yemen, Officials Say," http://www.cnn.com/2012/09/03/world/meast/yemen-drone-strike/index.html; "Protesters Storm Us Embassy in Yemen over Anti-Islam Film," *The Guardian*, 13 Sep. 2012; Xinhua, "Yemenis Protest Botched U.S. Drone Strikes," 4 Sep. 2012.

139. To use a phrase employed by Boucek, "Yemen: Avoiding a Downward Spiral," 13.

140. Sarah Phillips, *Yemen's Democracy Experiment in Regional Perspective: Patronage and Pluralized Authoritarianism* (Palgrave Macmillan, 2008); Alley, "The Rules of the Game: Unpacking Patronage Politics in Yemen."

141. "The Rules of the Game: Unpacking Patronage Politics in Yemen."

142. Freedman, "Prevention, Not Preemption."

143. "Diplomatic Security Daily," (Department of State: Wikileaks). The cable suggests that the information was passed on by the *Mabahith* (Saudi Intelligence) but came originally from Mohammed al-Awfi, who turned himself into Saudi authorities shortly after his appearance in the merger video of January 2009.

144. Ibid.

145. Ibid.

146. The literature on Yemen's patronage system is extensive, but key articles include, see April Longley Alley, "Yemen's Multiple Crises," *Journal of Democracy* 21, no. 4 (2010); Carapico, *Civil Society in Yemen: The Political Economy of Activism in Modern Arabia*; Durac, "The Joint Meeting Parties and the Politics of Opposition in Yemen"; Schwedler, *Faith in Moderation: Islamist Parties in Jordan and Yemen*; "The Islah Party in Yemen: Political Opportunities and Coalition Building in a Transitional Polity"; Stacey Yadav, "Antecedents of the Revolution: Intersectoral Networks and Post-Partisanship in Yemen," *Studies in Ethnicity and Nationalism* 11, no. 3 (2011); Alley, "Shifting Light in the Qamariyya: The Reinvention of Patronage Networks in Contemporary Yemen"; "The Rules of the Game: Unpacking Patronage Politics in Yemen."

147. Phillips, *Yemen's Democracy Experiment in Regional Perspective: Patronage and Pluralized Authoritarianism*, 5.

148. Alley, "The Rules of the Game: Unpacking Patronage Politics in Yemen," 399–400.

149. Ibid., 403.

150. See Schwedler, *Faith in Moderation: Islamist Parties in Jordan and Yemen*; "The Islah Party in Yemen: Political Opportunities and Coalition Building in a Transitional Polity."

151. Chris Boucek, Shazadi Beg, and John Horgan, "Opening up the *Jihadi* Debate: Yemen's Committee for Dialogue," in *Leaving Terrorism Behind: Individual and*

Collective Disengagement, ed. Tore Bjørgo and John Horgan (Routledge, 2009), 185.

152. "Growing Repression in Yemen May Feed Al Qaeda," in *All Things Considered* (National Public Radio). I am grateful to the late Chris Boucek for this reference.

153. "Opening up the *Jihadi* Debate: Yemen's Committee for Dialogue," 187.

154. Ibid., 189. See also Kevin Peraino, "The Reeducation of Abu Jandal," Newsweek Magazine, http://www.thedailybeast.com/newsweek/2009/05/28/the-reeducation-of-abu-jandal.html.

155. Gregory Johnsen, "Yemen's Passive Role in the War on Terrorism," *Terrorism Monitor* 4, no. 4 (2006).

156. Angel Rabasa et al., "Deradicalizing Islamist Extremists," in *RAND Corporation Monograph Series* (RAND, 2010).

157. Ane Skov Birk, "Incredible Dialogues: Religious Dialogue as a Means of Counter-Terrorism in Yemen," in *Developments in Radicalisation and Political Violence* (ICSR, 2009), 14.

158. Fink and Hearne, "Beyond Terrorism."

159. Blomberg, Hess, and Weerapana, "Economic Conditions and Terrorism," 53.

160. Tim Whewell, "Yemeni Anti-Terror Scheme in Doubt," in *Crossing Continents* (BBC, 2005).

161. Birk, "Incredible Dialogues," 4.

162. Boucek, Beg, and Horgan, "Opening up the *Jihadi* Debate: Yemen's Committee for Dialogue," 189.

163. The presence (or lack of it) of Yemenis in Iraq has been a topic of debate in studies of de-radicalisation. For differing perspectives, see Rabasa et al., "Deradicalizing Islamist Extremists"; Boucek, Beg, and Horgan, "Opening up the *Jihadi* Debate."

164. Rabasa et al., "Deradicalizing Islamist Extremists," 53; Whewell, "Yemeni Anti-Terror Scheme in Doubt." Indeed, Hamoud al-Hitar has been on record as saying that 'resistance in Iraq is legitimate, but we cannot differentiate between terrorism and resistance in Iraq's case because things are not clear'.

165. Rabasa et al., "Deradicalizing Islamist Extremists," 85.

5. CONCLUSION: SCRIPTS OF TERROR

1. Others have referred to this as the narrative fallacy: Taleb, *The Black Swan*; Kahneman, *Thinking, Fast and Slow*; Freedman, *Strategy: A History*; Lawrence Freedman and Jeffrey Michaels, eds., *Scripting Middle East Leaders: The Impact of Leadership Perceptions on US And UK Foreign Policy* (Bloomsbury Academic, 2013). I refer to it as narrative delusion in order to lend the phenomenon a more active role on strategists.

2. Nassim Nicholas Taleb, *The Black Swan: The Impact of the Highly Improbable* (Penguin, 2008), 64.

3. Tilly, "The Trouble with Stories," 258.

4. Rudolf Kassel, *Aristotelis De Arte Poetica Liber*, repr. of 1966 ed. (Clarendon Press, 1968), 1450b21–50b34; a translation can be found in Aristotle, "Poetics," in *Complete Works of Aristotle, Volume 2*, ed. Jonathan Barnes (Princeton University Press, 1984). The text I have translated above is from 1450b26: ὅλον δέ ἐστιν τὸ ἔχον ἀρχὴν καὶ μέσον καὶ τελευτήν.

5. Tilly, "The Trouble with Stories," 257.

6. Walter Bradford Cannon, "The Emergency Function of the Adrenal Medulla in Pain and the Major Emotions," *American Journal of Physiology* 33, no. 2 (1914): 372. See also: *Bodily Changes in Pain, Hunger, Fear and Rage: An Account of Recent Researches into the Function of Emotional Excitement* (New York: Appleton, 1915).

7. Fanon, *The Wretched of the Earth*, 89.

8. Robert Axelrod, *The Evolution of Co-Operation* (Penguin, 1990), passim; esp 109–23; Robert Axelrod and William D. Hamilton, "The Evolution of Cooperation," *Science* 211, no. 4489.

9. The Yemeni regime, it is worth noting, followed all four of Axelrod's rules: 'Don't be envious, don't be the first to defect, reciprocate both cooperation and defection and don't be too clever'. Axelrod, *The Evolution of Co-Operation*, 110.

10. This is the term used by Kydd and Walter, "Outbidding and the Overproduction of Terrorism"; Brym and Araj, "Palestinian Suicide Bombing Revisited: A Critique of the Outbidding Thesis"; Kydd and Walter, "The Strategies of Terrorism."

11. Cronin, *How Terrorism Ends*, 118f.

12. Interview with Jane, 2 May 2013

13. For some, this is merely a desirable by-product of terrorist violence (e.g. Kydd and Walter, "The Strategies of Terrorism"). Others have referred to this as polarisation: Cronin, for example, argues that 'this strategy directs itself at the effects of terrorist attacks on the domestic politics of a state, driving regimes sharply to the right and ultimately forcing populations to choose between the terrorist cause and brutal state repression. The goal is to force divided populations further apart...'. (Cronin, *How Terrorism Ends*, 119.)

14. Edward Luttwak, *Strategy: The Logic of War and Peace*, 2nd ed. (Harvard University Press, 2002), 114.

15. Mearsheimer, *Conventional Deterrence*, 34.

16. Benford and Snow, "Framing Processes and Social Movements."

17. Kahneman, *Thinking, Fast and Slow*, 200.

18. Similar points are made by Larson, "The Role of Belief Systems"; Yuen Foong Khong, *Analogies at War: Korea, Munich, Dien Bien Phu, and the Vietnam Decisions of 1965* (Princeton University Press, 1992); Richard Neustadt and Ernest May, *Thinking in Time: The Uses of History for Decision-Makers* (Free Press, 1988).

19. Indeed, in a broader sense, Cronin has noted that terrorist organisations 'display a kind of contagion effect, designed with the lessons of predecessors or contem-

poraries very much in mind... group leaders often look beyond their own narrow and specific context. If we want to understand them and what they are trying to do, so should we'. Audrey Kurth Cronin, *Ending Terrorism: Lessons for Defeating Al-Qaeda*, Adelphi Papers (International Institute for Strategic Studies, 2008), 25. On the 'contagion effect see: Crenshaw, "The Causes of Terrorism," 382; Manus Midlarsky, Martha Crenshaw, and Fumihiko Yoshida, "Why Violence Spreads," *International Studies Quarterly* 24 (1980).

20. Kepel, *Jihad: The Trail of Political Islam*, 110.
21. Scheuer, *Through Our Enemies' Eyes: Osama Bin Laden, Radical Islam, and the Future of America, Revised Edition*, 147.
22. PBS News, "Bin Laden's Fatwa Aug. 23, 1996".
23. Although the US would not use Aden as a base for Operation Restore Hope, but by the time of the attacks on the hotels there was little need to do so, as the US had established a working infrastructure in Mogadishu.
24. Kahneman, *Thinking, Fast and Slow*, 201.
25. Select Committee on Intelligence United States Senate, *Attempted Terrorist Attack on Northwest Airlines Flight 253: Unclassified Executive Summary of the Congressional Report* (US Goverment Printing Office, 2010), 2.
26. Kahneman, *Thinking, Fast and Slow*, 199.
27. Taleb, *The Black Swan*; Freedman, *Strategy: A History*.
28. Kahneman, *Thinking, Fast and Slow*, 201.

A NOTE ON DEFINITIONS

1. The same is true in Arabic. The word for extremism in Arabic, *tatarruf* comes from the root *tā-rā-fā*, 'to be on the extreme side, hold an extreme viewpoint or position, to go to extremes, be radical, have radical views' and the noun (*taraf*) refers to an outermost point, a fringe or limit and even comes to mean the tip of the tongue. Hans Wehr, *Arabic-English Dictionary: The Hans Wehr Dictionary of Modern Written Arabic* (Spoken Language Services).
2. Malik suggests: '[Extremism is] increasingly used to include non-violent groups who support ideas about political organization (e.g. the idea of the caliphate) or social and personal life (e.g. gender equality norms) that are deemed to be incompatible with liberal democracy... However the precise criteria for identifying who is a "Muslim extremist" remain surprisingly undertheorised'. Maleiha Malik, "Engaging with Extremists," *International Relations* 22, no. 1. Robert Lambert, "Salafi and Islamist Londoners: Stigmatised Minority Faith Communities Countering Al-Qaida," *Crime, Law and Social Change* 50, no. 1; Basia Spalek and Robert Lambert, "Muslim Communities, Counter-Terrorism and Counter-Radicalisation: A Critically Reflective Approach to Engagement," *International Journal of Law, Crime and Justice* 36, no. 4; Munira Mirza, Abi Senthilkumaran,

and Zein Ja'far, *Living Apart Together: British Muslims and the Paradox of Multiculturalism* (Policy Exchange).

3. For some, *jihad* has a violent element which is either defensive in nature, when required to protect Muslim territory from invasion, or offensive, to spread the word of Islam. See Quintan Wiktorowicz, "A Genealogy of Radical Islam," *Studies in Conflict & Terrorism* 28, no. 2: 83–6.

4. Marc Sageman, *Understanding Terror Networks* (University of Pennsylvania Press, 2008), 1. See also Antoine Sfeir, *The Columbia World Dictionary of Islamism* (Columbia University Press, 2007), 182f.; David Cook, "Jihad and Martyrdom in Classical and Contemporary Islam," in *The Blackwell Companion to Religion and Violence*, ed. Andrew Murphy (Blackwell, 2011).

5. Hegghammer phrases the difficulties of its use in an academic environment neatly; 'While Western academics (and liberal Muslim writers) use the term descriptively, mostly as a synonym for "violent Islamist", conservative Muslims see it as having normative implications that unfairly associate Islam with terrorism'. Thomas Hegghammer, "Jihadi-Salafis or Revolutionaries? On Religion and Politics in the Study of Militant Islamism," in *Global Salafism: Islam's New Religious Movement*, ed. Roel Meijer (Columbia University Press, 2009), 246.

6. Gilles Kepel, *Jihad: The Trail of Political Islam* (Belknap Press of Harvard University Press, 2003), 219–22. Bernard Haykel, "On the Nature of Salafi Thought and Action," in *Global Salafism: Islam's New Religious Movement*, ed. Roel Meijer (Columbia University Press, 2009).

7. A point also made by Malik, "Engaging with Extremists." On three 'types' of Salafi—purists, politcos and *jihadi*s, see Quintan Wiktorowicz, "Anatomy of the Salafi Movement," *Studies in Conflict & Terrorism* 29, no. 3. On typologies based on targeting, see Fawaz Gerges, *The Far Enemy: Why Jihad Went Global* (Cambridge University Press, 2009), ch. 1.

8. Hegghammer, "Jihadi-Salafis or Revolutionaries." See also, Madawi al-Rasheed, *Contesting the Saudi State: Islamic Voices from a New Generation* (Cambridge University Press, 2006); *Kingdom without Borders: Saudi Arabia's Political, Religious and Media Frontiers* (C. Hurst & Co., 2008).

9. Hegghammer provides a more complex argument of five types of Islamist, depending on their orientation; it is a valuable argument, but one which tends to unwieldiness from over-compartmentalization, bearing in mind that many of the organisations he mentions fit into multiple categories. "Jihadi-Salafis or Revolutionaries," 244–65.

10. This is a simple but effective definition based on that of Olivier Roy, *Globalised Islam: The Search for a New Ummah* (C Hurst & Co., 2004), 58. Kepel echoes this definition in Kepel, *Jihad: The Trail of Political Islam*, 4f. The ideology of Islamism is an enormous topic. On Egypt, see e.g. Saad Eddin Ibrahim, *Egypt, Islam and Democracy: Critical Essays* (The American University in Cairo Press, 2002); Kepel,

Roots of Radical Islam; *Jihad: The Trail of Political Islam*; Olivier Roy, *The Failure of Political Islam* (I. B. Tauris, 1994); *Globalised Islam: The Search for a New Ummah*; Quintan Wiktorowicz, *Islamic Activism: A Social Movement Theory Approach* (Indiana University Press, 2004); "A Genealogy of Radical Islam"; "Anatomy of the Salafi Movement." On Saudi Arabia, see Mamoun Fandy, *Saudi Arabia and the Politics of Dissent* (Palgrave Macmillan, 2001); Thomas Hegghammer, "Terrorist Recruitment and Radicalization in Saudi Arabia," *Middle East Policy* 13, no. 4; Stéphane Lacroix and Thomas Hegghammer, *Saudi Arabia Backgrounder: Who Are the Islamists* (Amman: International Crisis Group, 2004). On Yemen, see: Laurent Bonnefoy, "Varieties of Islamism in Yemen: The Logic of Integration under Pressure," *Middle East* 13, no. 1 (2009); "How Transnational Is Salafism in Yemen," in *Global Salafism: Islam's New Religious Movement*, ed. Roel Meijer (Colombia University Press, 2009); Jillian Schwedler, *Faith in Moderation: Islamist Parties in Jordan and Yemen* (Cambridge University Press, 2007).

11. As Freedman puts it, the term 'terrorist' can be seen as 'as a form of political abuse to delegitimize a range of political claims and deny the possibility of serious dialogue': Lawrence Freedman, "Terrorism as a Strategy," *Government and Opposition* 42, no. 3: 315; see also Alex Schmid, "Terrorism—the Definitional Problem," *Case Western Reserve Journal of International Law* 36: 396; Brian Michael Jenkins, *The Study of Terrorism: Definitional Problems* (RAND, 1980). The problem, as both point out, is that 'terrorist' and 'terrorism' are inherently value-laden and subjective. For two violently opposed portrayals, see the sharp moral contrast between Doris Lessing's image of the 'virtuous' terrorist who 'pulls down the shitty rubbish we live in' (Doris Lessing, *The Good Terrorist* (Fourth Estate, 2013), 354) and George Bush's characterisation of al-Qa'ida as 'the heirs of all the murderous ideologies ... follow[ing] in the path of fascism, and Nazism and totalitarianism' (George Bush, "President Declares Freedom at War with Fear," (Washington).

BIBLIOGRAPHY

'Cassandra'. "The Impending Crisis in Egypt." *The Middle East Journal* 49, no. 1 (1995): 9–27.

'M.J.S.' "The Killing of Al-Awlaqi: A Crippling Blow." Clausewitz: The Economist's Defence, Security and Diplomacy Blog, http://www.economist.com/blogs/clausewitz/2011/10/killing-anwar-al-awlaki.

Abelson, Robert. "Psychological Status of the Script Concept." *American Psychologist* 36, no. 7 (1981): 715–29.

———. "Script Processing in Attitude Formation and Decision-Making." In *Cognition and Social Behavior*, edited by John S. Carroll and John W. Payne. Oxford: Lawrence Erlbaum, 1976.

Abrahms, Max. "The Political Effectiveness of Terrorism Revisited." *Comparative Political Studies* 45, no. 3 (2012): 366–93.

———. "What Terrorists Really Want: Terrorist Motives and Counterterrorism Strategy." *International Security* 32, no. 4 (Spring 2008): 78–105.

———. "Why Terrorism Does Not Work." *International Security* 31, no. 2 (Fall 2006): 42–78.

Ackerman, Bruce. "Obama's Death Panel." *Foreign Policy*, 7 October 2011.

Agence France Presse. "Bomber Targets S Koreans in Yemen." http://www.aljazeera.com/news/middleeast/2009/03/200931871130679609.html.

———. "Drone Attack Kills 10 Qaeda Suspects in South Yemen." http://www.google.com/hostednews/afp/article/ALeqM5igSCJQYllvvvaI-70o66azhP9JwA?docId=CNG.0d3bf3dd466de4d0317f3f205dba2ee1.2f1.

———. "Yemen 'Al-Qaeda Fighters' Killed in Air Raids." http://www.aljazeera.com/news/middleeast/2012/05/2012511145648893973.html.

———. "Yemen Air Force, U.S. Drone Kill 24 Qaeda Suspects." http://english.alarabiya.net/articles/2012/04/08/206235.html.

Akhavi, Shahrough. "The Impact of the Iranian Revolution on Egypt." In *The Iranian Revolution: Its Global Impact*, edited by John Esposito. Miami: Florida International University Press, 1990.

al-Awlaqi, Anwar. "44 Ways to Support Jihad." n.p., 2009.

al-Hammadi, Khalid. "The inside Story of Al-Qa'ida." *al-Quds al-Arabi*, 22 March 2005.

al-Jazeera. "Profile: Al Qaeda in the Arabian Peninsula." http://www.aljazeera.com/news/middleeast/2012/05/2012597359456359.html.

al-Qa'ida in the Arabian Peninsula. "Abu Mu'sab Al-Suri: *Jihadi* Experiences." In *Inspire 2*: al-Malahim Media, 2010.

———. "Communiqué #4: Expel the Infidels from the Arabian Peninsula." al-Malahim Media, 2008.

———. "The Descendents of Muhammad Bin Maslamah." edited by Sada al-Malahim. Translated by NEFA Foundation 2009.

———. "The Fragility of the Administration and the Loss of Control." al-Malahim Media, 2008.

———. "From Here We Start and in Al-Aqsa We Shall Meet." al-Malahim Media, 2009.

———. *Inspire 2*. al-Malahim Media, 2010.

———. *Inspire 3*. al-Malahim Media, 2010.

———. "An Interview with One of the Most Wanted Men: Abu Hummam Al-Qahtani (Translated by the Nefa Foundation)." al-Malahim Media, 2008.

———. "Letter from the Editor,Yahya Ibrahim." In *Inspire 9*: al-Malahim Media, 2012.

———. "Masha'l Al-Shadukhi: Limadha Nuqatil Fi Jazirat Al-'Arab?" *Sada al-Malahim* 10 (2009).

———. "Yahya Ibrahim: $4200." In *Inspire 3*, al-Malahim Media, 2010.

al-Qaradawi, Yusuf. *The Lawful and the Prohibited in Islam*. Islamic Books, 1997.

al-Rahman, Hamdi, Ibrahim Najih, Ali Sharif, and Karam al-Zuhdi. *Taslit Al-Adwa Ala Ma Waqa'a Fil-Jihad Min Akhta* (Shining a Light on the Mistakes of the Jihad). Cairo: Maktabat al-Turath al-Islami, 2002.

al-Rasheed, Madawi. *Contesting the Saudi State: Islamic Voices from a New Generation*. Cambridge: Cambridge University Press, 2006.

———. *A History of Saudi Arabia*. Cambridge: Cambridge University Press, 2010.

———. *Kingdom without Borders: Saudi Arabia's Political, Religious and Media Frontiers*. London: C. Hurst & Co., 2008.

al-Saud, Prince Bandar bin Sultan bin Abdulaziz. "A Diplomat's Call for War." *Washington Post*, 6 June 2004.

al-Sharif, Sayyid Imam. *Wathiqat Tarshid Al-Jihad Fi Misr Wal-Alam* (Document for Guiding Jihad in Egypt and the World). Al-Jarida, 2007.

al-Zayyat, Montasser. *The Road to Al-Qaeda: The Story of Bin Laden's Right-Hand Man*. London: Pluto Press, 2004.

al-Zuhdi, Karam. *Istiratijiyat Wa Tafjirat Al-Qa'idah: Al-Akhta' Wal-Akhtar* (The Strategy and Bombings of al-Qa'ida: Dangers and Mistakes). Cairo: Maktabat al-Turath al-Islami, 2004.

BIBLIOGRAPHY

Alexander, Dean. "Al Qaeda and Al Qaeda in the Arabian Peninsula: Inspired, Homegrown Terrorism in the United States." *Journal of Applied Security Research* 6, no. 4 (2011): 467–82.

Ali, Rafid. "The Jihadis and the Cause of South Yemen: A Profile of Tariq Al-Fadhli." *Terrorism Monitor* 7, no. 35 (2009).

Alley, April Longley. "The Rules of the Game: Unpacking Patronage Politics in Yemen." *The Middle East Journal* 64, no. 3 (2010): 385–409.

———. "Shifting Light in the Qamariyya: The Reinvention of Patronage Networks in Contemporary Yemen." Unpublished doctoral dissertation, Georgetown University, 2008.

———. "Yemen's Multiple Crises." *Journal of Democracy* 21, no. 4 (2010): 72–86.

Almasmari, Hakim. "Suspected U.S. Drone Strike Kills Civilians in Yemen, Officials Say." http://www.cnn.com/2012/09/03/world/meast/yemen-drone-strike/index.html.

Almasmari, Hakim, Margaret Coker, and Siobhan Gorman. "Drone Kills Top Al Qaeda Figure." *Wall Street Journal*, 1 October 2011.

Almond, Gabriel, Scott Appleby, and Emmanuel Sivan. *Strong Religion: The Rise of Fundamentalisms around the World*. Chicago: University of Chicago Press, 2003.

Amnesty International. "Amnesty International Report 2002—Yemen." 2002.

———. "Amnesty International Report 2003—Yemen." 2003.

———. "Egypt: Arbitrary Detention and Torture under Emergency Powers." 1989.

———. "Egypt: Grave Human Rights Abuses Amid Political Violence." 1993.

———. "Yemen: The Rule of Law Sidelined in the Name of Security." 2003.

Ansari, Hamied N. "The Islamic Militants in Egyptian Politics." *International Journal of Middle East Studies* 16, no. 1 (1984): 123–44.

Araj, Bader. "Harsh State Repression as a Cause of Suicide Bombing: The Case of the Palestinian–Israeli Conflict." *Studies in Conflict & Terrorism* 31, no. 4 (2008): 284–303.

Arce, Daniel, and Todd Sandler. "Terrorist Signalling and the Value of Intelligence." *British Journal of Political Science* 37, no. 4 (2007): 573–86.

Aristotle. "Poetics." In *Complete Works of Aristotle, Volume 2*, edited by Jonathan Barnes. Princeton: Princeton University Press, 1984.

Ashour, Omar. "De-Radicalization of Jihad? The Impact of Egyptian Islamist Revisionists on Al-Qaeda." *Perspectives on Terrorism* 2, no. 5 (2010).

———. *The De-Radicalization of Jihadists: Transforming Armed Islamist Movements*. London: Routledge, 2009.

Associated Press. "Americans Targeted Again in Riyadh." http://www.cbsnews.com/8301-224_162-622798.html.

Atwan, Abdel Bari. *The Secret History of Al Qaeda: Updated Edition*. London: Abacus, 2008.

Axelrod, Robert. *The Evolution of Co-Operation*. Penguin, 1990.

Axelrod, Robert, and William D. Hamilton. "The Evolution of Cooperation." *Science* 211, no. 4489 (1981): 1390–96.

Ayubi, Nazih. *Political Islam: Religion and Politics in the Arab World*. Routledge, 1993.

———. "The Political Revival of Islam: The Case of Egypt." *International Journal of Middle East Studies* 12, no. 4 (1980): 481–99.

Bakier, Abdul Hameed. "Lessons from Al-Qaeda's Attack on the Khobar Compound." *Terrorism Monitor* 4, no. 16 (2006).

Bakunin, Mikhail. "Letters to a Frenchman on the Present Crisis." In *Bakunin on Anarchy. Selected works by the Activist-Founder of World Anarchism*, edited by Sam Dolgoff. London: Allen and Unwin, 1973.

Barfi, Barak. "Yemen on the Brink? The Resurgence of Al Qaeda in the Arabian Peninsula." In *Counterterrorism Strategy Initiative Policy Paper*: New America Foundation, 2010.

Barthes, Roland. "An Introduction to the Structural Analysis of Narrative." *New Literary History* 6, no. 2 (1975).

———. *Mythologies*. Translated by Dr Annette Lavers. Vintage Classics, 2009.

———. *S/Z*. Translated by Richard Miller. Oxford: Wiley-Blackwell, 1990.

BBC. "'Al-Qaeda Gulf Chief' Held by US." http://news.bbc.co.uk/1/hi/world/middle_east/2501121.stm.

———. "Profile: Al-Qaeda in the Arabian Peninsula." http://www.bbc.co.uk/news/world-middle-east-11483095.

———. "Profile: Umar Farouk Abdulmutallab." http://www.bbc.co.uk/news/world-us-canada-11545509.

———. "Tourists Die in Yemen Explosion." http://news.bbc.co.uk/1/hi/7945013.stm.

———. "Two BBC Men Shot in Saudi Capital." http://news.bbc.co.uk/1/hi/world/middle_east/3781803.stm.

———. "Yemen Bomb Kills Spanish Tourists." http://news.bbc.co.uk/1/hi/6262302.stm.

Beall, Jo, Thomas Goodfellow, and James Putzel. "Introductory Article: On the Discourse of Terrorism, Security and Development." *Journal of International Development* 18, no. 1 (2006): 51–67.

Beinin, Joel, and Frédéric Vairel. *Social Movements, Mobilization, and Contestation in the Middle East and North Africa*. Stanford University Press, 2011.

Benford, Robert, and David Snow. "Framing Processes and Social Movements: An Overview and Assessment." *Annual Review of Sociology* (2000): 611–39.

Bergen, Peter. *Holy War, Inc.: Inside the Secret World of Osama Bin Laden*. London: Free Press, 2002.

———. *The Osama Bin Laden I Know: An Oral History of Al Qaeda's Leader*. London: Free Press, 2006.

Bergen, Peter, and Paul Cruickshank. "Revisiting the Early Al Qaeda: An Updated

Account of Its Formative Years." *Studies in Conflict & Terrorism* 35, no. 1 (2012): 1–36.

Berger, J. M. "Anwar Al-Awlaki's Links to the September 11 Hijackers." *The Atlantic*, 9 September 2011.

———. "Exclusive: U.S. Gave Millions to Charity Linked to Al Qaeda, Anwar Awlaki." http://news.intelwire.com/2010/04/us-gave-millions-to-charity-linked-to.html.

———. "Two E-Mails from Anwar Awlaki.", http://news.intelwire.com/2012/06/two-e-mails-from-anwar-awlaki.html.

Berman, Paul. *Terror and Liberalism*. W.W. Norton, 2004.

Bethlehem, Daniel. "Mopping up the Last War or Stumbling into the Next?" *Harvard Law School National Security Journal* (2011). Published electronically 7 October.

Betts, Richard K. "Is Strategy an Illusion?" *International Security* 25, no. 2 (2000): 5–50.

bin Laden, Osama. "Letter to 'Sheikh Mahmood' (Socom-2012–0000003)." Combatting Terrorism Centre at West Point, 2010.

Birk, Ane Skov. "Incredible Dialogues: Religious Dialogue as a Means of Counter-Terrorism in Yemen." In *Developments in Radicalisation and Political Violence*. London: ICSR, 2009.

Blaydes, Lisa. "Makram Mohammed Ahmed Interviews the Historic Leadership of Al-Gama'a Al-Islamiyya inside the 'Scorpion' Prison." n.p., 2004.

Blaydes, Lisa, and Lawrence Rubin. "Ideological Reorientation and Counterterrorism: Confronting Militant Islam in Egypt." *Terrorism and Political Violence* 20, no. 4 (2008): 461–79.

Blomberg, Brock, Gregory Hess, and Akila Weerapana. "Economic Conditions and Terrorism." *European Journal of Political Economy* 20, no. 2 (2004): 463–78.

Blomfield, Adrian. "Analysis: Awlaki's Death Is a Boost for the West." http://www.telegraph.co.uk/news/worldnews/al-qaeda/8799991/Analysis-Awlakis-death-is-a-boost-for-the-West.html.

Bloom, Mia. *Dying to Kill: The Allure of Suicide Terror*. Columbia University Press, 2005.

———. "Palestinian Suicide Bombing: Public Support, Market Share, and Outbidding." *Political Science Quarterly* 119, no. 1 (2004): 61–88.

Bonnefoy, Laurent. "How Transnational Is Salafism in Yemen." In *Global Salafism: Islam's New Religious Movement*, edited by Roel Meijer: Colombia University Press, 2009.

———. "Muqbil Al-Wadi'i." In *Global Salafism: Islam's New Religious Movement*, edited by Roel Meijer, 2009.

———. *Salafism in Yemen: Transnationalism and Religious Identity*. London: C. Hurst & Co., 2012.

———. "Varieties of Islamism in Yemen: The Logic of Integration under Pressure." *Middle East* 13, no. 1 (2009): 26–36.

Borger, Julian. "Protesters Storm Us Embassy in Yemen over Anti-Islam Film." *The Guardian*, 13 September 2012.

Borum, Randy. "Psychological Vulnerabilities and Propensities for Involvement in Violent Extremism", *Behavioral Sciences & the Law* 32, no. 3 (2014): 286–305.

Boucek, Chris. "Extremist Re-Education and Rehabilitation in Saudi Arabia." In *Leaving Terrorism Behind: Individual and Collective Disengagement*, edited by Tore Bjørgo and John Horgan. London: Routledge, 2009.

———. "The New Face of Al-Qaeda?" *Foreign Policy*, 18 May 2011.

———. "Saudi Arabia's 'Soft' Counterterrorism Strategy: Prevention, Rehabilitation, and Aftercare." In *Carnegie Papers 97*: Carnegie Endowment for International Peace, 2008.

———. "Yemen: Avoiding a Downward Spiral." In *Yemen on the Brink*, edited by Chris Boucek and Marina Ottaway. Washington D.C.: Carnegie Endowment for Peace, 2010.

Boucek, Chris, Shazadi Beg, and John Horgan. "Opening up the *Jihadi* Debate: Yemen's Committee for Dialogue." In *Leaving Terrorism Behind: Individual and Collective Disengagement*, edited by Tore Bjørgo and John Horgan. London: Routledge, 2009.

Boucek, Chris, and Marina Ottaway, eds. *Yemen on the Brink*: Carnegie Endowment for International Peace, 2010.

Boukhars, Anouar. "At the Crossroads: Saudi Arabia's Dilemmas." *Journal of Conflict Studies* 26, no. 1 (2006).

Brehony, Noel. *Yemen Divided: The Story of a Failed State in South Arabia*. London: I. B. Tauris, 2011.

Brown, Nathan J., and Amr Hamzawy. *Between Religion and Politics*. Carnegie Endowment, 2010.

Brym, Robert, and Bader Araj. "Palestinian Suicide Bombing Revisited: A Critique of the Outbidding Thesis." *Political Science Quarterly* 123, no. 3 (2008): 485–500.

Burgat, François. *Face to Face with Political Islam*. London: I. B. Tauris, 1999.

———. *L'islamisme Au Maghreb: La Voix Du Sud*. Payot, 2008.

Burgat, François, and Mu'hammad Sbitli. "Les Salafis Au Yémen Ou... La Modernisation Malgré Tout." *Chroniques Yéménites*, no. 10 (2002).

Burke, Jason. *Al-Qaeda: The True Story of Radical Islam*. Penguin, 2007.

Burkeman, Oliver. "US Captures Key Al-Qaida Suspect." *The Guardian*, 22 November 2002.

Burns, John. "Yemen Links to Bin Laden Gnaw at F.B.I. In Cole Inquiry." *New York Times*, 26 November 2000.

Burns, Robert. *Poems of Robert Burns Selected by Ian Rankin*. Penguin Classics, 2008.

Burrowes, Robert D. *The Yemen Arab Republic: The Politics of Development 1962–1986*. Westview Special Studies on the Middle East. London: Boulder, 1987.

Bush, George. "President Declares Freedom at War with Fear." Address to a Joint Session of Congress and the American People, Washington, 20 September 2001; https://georgewbush-whitehouse.archives.gov/news/releases/2001/09/20010920–8.html.

Byman, Daniel. "Do Targeted Killings Work." *Foreign Affairs* 85 (2006): 95–111.

Calvert, John. *Sayyid Qutb and the Origins of Radical Islamism*. Columbia University Press, 2010.

Cannon, Walter Bradford. *Bodily Changes in Pain, Hunger, Fear and Rage: An Account of Recent Researches into the Function of Emotional Excitement*. New York: Appleton, 1915.

———. "The Emergency Function of the Adrenal Medulla in Pain and the Major Emotions." *American Journal of Physiology* 33, no. 2 (1914): 356–72.

Carapico, Sheila. *Civil Society in Yemen: The Political Economy of Activism in Modern Arabia*. Cambridge: Cambridge University Press, 2007.

———. "No Quick Fix: Foreign Aid and State Performance in Yemen." In *Rebuilding Devastated Economies in the Middle East*, edited by Leonard Binder, p. 153–76. New York: Palgrave MacMillan, 2007.

Carroll, Rory. "Terrorists or Tourists?" *Guardian* Article Reprinted at http://www.al-bab.com/yemen/artic/gdn42.htm.

Carvin, Stephanie. "The Trouble with Targeted Killing." *Security Studies* 21, no. 3 (2012): 529–55.

Chesney, Robert. "Al-Awlaki as an Operational Leader Located in a Place Where Capture Was Not Possible." http://www.lawfareblog.com/2011/09/al-awlaki-as-an-operational-leader-located-in-a-place-where-capture-was-not-possible/.

———. "Who May Be Killed? Anwar Al-Awlaki as a Case Study in the International Legal Regulation of Lethal Force." *SSRN eLibrary* (2011). http://papers.ssrn.com/sol3/papers.cfm?abstract_id=1754223.

Cigar, Norman. *Al-Qaida's Doctrine for Insurgency: Abd Al-Aziz Al-Muqrin's "a Practical Course for Guerrilla War"*. Potomac Books Inc., 2009.

Ciluffo, Frank, and Clinton Watts. "Countering the Threat Posed by Aqap: Embrace, Don't Chase Yemen's Chaos." Selected Wisdom Blog, http://selectedwisdom.com/?p=352.

———. "Yemen & Al Qaeda in the Arabian Peninsula: Exploiting a Window of Counterterrorism Opportunity." In *HSPI Issue Brief Series*: Homeland Security and Policy Institute, 2011.

Clark, Janine. "Islamist Women in Yemen: Informal Nodes of Activism." In *Islamic Activism: A Social Movement Theory Approach*, edited by Quintan Wiktorowicz, 164–85. Bloomington: Indiana University Press, 2004.

Clark, Victoria. *Yemen: Dancing on the Heads of Snakes*. Yale University Press, 2010.

Clarke, Michael, and Valentina Soria. "Terrorism: The New Wave." *RUSI Journal* 155, no. 4 (2010): 24–31.

Clutterbuck, Lindsay. "Law Enforcement." In *Attacking Terrorism: Elements of a Grand Strategy*, edited by Audrey Kurth Cronin and James Ludes: Georgetown University Press, 2004.

CNN. "Most Wanted: Anwar Al-Awlaki." CNN Security Clearance [Blog], http://security.blogs.cnn.com/2011/06/17/most-wanted-anwar-al-awlaki/.

———. "Yemeni Defense Minister Survives Apparent Assassination Attempt." 11 September 2012.

Coll, Steve. *The Bin Ladens: Oil, Money, Terrorism and the Secret Saudi World*. Penguin, 2008.

Colton, Nora Ann. "Yemen: A Collapsed Economy." *The Middle East Journal* 64, no. 3 (2010): 410–26.

Cook, David. "Jihad and Martyrdom in Classical and Contemporary Islam." In *The Blackwell Companion to Religion and Violence*, edited by Andrew Murphy, 282–92: Blackwell, 2011.

Cordesman, Anthony, and Nawaf Obaid. "Al-Qaeda in Saudi Arabia: Asymmetric Threats and Islamist Extremists." Washington: Centre for Strategic and International Studies, 2005.

Cordesman, Anthony, and Nawaf Obaid. *National Security in Saudi Arabia: Threats, Responses, and Challenges*. Praeger Security International, 2005.

Council on Foreign Relations. "U.S. Policy toward Yemen: A Transcript of John O. Brennan on Pbs Newshour." 2012.

Cowell, Alan. "Mideast Tensions: Egypt's Parliament Speaker Is Assassinated by Gunmen." *New York Times*, 13 October 1990.

Cozzens, Jeffrey B. "Al-Takfir Wa'l Hijra: Unpacking an Enigma." *Studies in Conflict & Terrorism* 32, no. 6 (2009): 489–510.

Craig, Gordon A. "Delbrück: The Military Historian." In *Makers of Modern Strategy from Machiavelli to the Nuclear Age*, edited by Peter Paret, Gordon A. Craig and Felix Gilbert: Oxford: OUP, 1986.

Craig, Iona. "13 Die in Blast Targeting Yemen's Defense Minister." *USA Today*, 11 September 2012.

Crenshaw, Martha. "The Causes of Terrorism." *Comparative Politics* 13, no. 4 (1981): 379–99.

———. "The Logic of Terrorism: Terrorist Behavior as a Product of Strategic Choice." In *Origins of Terrorism: Psychologies, Ideologies, Theologies, States of Mind*, edited by Walter Reich. Woodrow Wilson Center Press, 1998.

———. "Terrorism and Global Security." In *Leashing the Dogs of War: Conflict Management in a Divided World*, edited by Chester A. Crocker, Fen Osler Hampson and Pamela R. Aall: US Institute of Peace Press, 2007.

———. "Terrorism, Strategies and Grand Strategies." In *Attacking Terrorism: Elements of a Grand Strategy*, edited by Audrey Kurth Cronin and James Ludes: Georgetown University Press, 2004.

Cronin, Audrey Kurth. *Ending Terrorism: Lessons for Defeating Al-Qaeda*. Adelphi Papers. International Institute for Strategic Studies, 2008.

———. *How Terrorism Ends: Understanding the Decline and Demise of Terrorist Campaigns*. Princeton: Princeton University Press, 2009.

———. "Introduction." In *Attacking Terrorism: Elements of a Grand Strategy*, edited by Audrey Kurth Cronin and James Ludes: Georgetown University Press, 2004.

Culler, Jonathan. *The Pursuit of Signs*. London: Routledge, 2001.

Dekmejian, R. Hrair. *Islam in Revolution: Fundamentalism in the Arab World*. Syracuse University Press, 1994.

Dershowitz, Alan. *Why Terrorism Works: Understanding the Threat, Responding to the Challenge*. New edition: Yale University Press, 2003.

Dessouki, Ali. *Islamic Resurgence in the Arab World*. New York: Praeger, 1982.

Devji, Faisal. *Landscapes of the Jihad*. London: C. Hurst and Co., 2005.

Dixon, Paul. "'Hearts and Minds'? British Counter-Insurgency Strategy in Northern Ireland." *Journal of Strategic Studies* 32, no. 3 (2009): 445–74.

Doran, Michael Scott. "The Saudi Paradox." *Foreign Affairs* 83, no. 1 (2004): 35–51.

Dresch, Paul. *A History of Modern Yemen*. Cambridge University Press, 2001.

Dresch, Paul, and Bernard Haykel. "Stereotypes and Political Styles: Islamists and Tribesfolk in Yemen." *International Journal of Middle East Studies* 27, no. 4 (1995): 405–31.

Duffield, Mark. "Human Security: Linking Development and Security in an Age of Terror." *New Interfaces between Security and Development* (2006): 11–38.

Durac, Vincent. "The Joint Meeting Parties and the Politics of Opposition in Yemen." *British Journal of Middle Eastern Studies* 38, no. 3 (2011): 343–65.

Eckstein, Harry. *Internal War: Problems and Approaches*. Greenwood Press, 1980.

Egyptian Organisation for Human Rights. "When Will the Crime of Torture Stop?", 2009.

El-Awaisi, Abd al-Fattah M. *The Muslim Brothers and the Palestine Question 1928–1947*. I. B. Tauris, 1998.

El-Said, Hamed. "De-Radicalising Islamists: Programmes and Their Impact in Muslim Majority States." The International Centre for the Study of Radicalization and Political Violence (ICSR), 2012.

El-Said, Hamed, and Jane Harrigan. *Deradicalising Violent Extremists: Counter-Radicalisation and Deradicalisation Programmes and Their Impact in Muslim Majority States*. Routledge, 2012.

Enders, Walter, and Todd Sandler. *The Political Economy of Terrorism*. Cambridge: Cambridge University Press, 2011.

———. "Transnational Terrorism 1968–2000: Thresholds, Persistence, and Forecasts." *Southern Economic Journal* (2005): 467–82.

Euben, Roxanne, and Muhammad Zaman. *Princeton Readings in Islamist Thought: Texts and Contexts from Al-Banna to Bin Laden.* Princeton: Princeton University Press, 2009.

Evans, Jonathan St B. T. "Dual-Processing Accounts of Reasoning, Judgment, and Social Cognition." *Annual Review of Psychology* 59, no. 1 (2008): 255–78.

Faksh, Mahmud A. *The Future of Islam in the Middle East: Fundamentalism in Egypt, Algeria and Saudi Arabia.* Greenwood Press, 1997.

Fandy, Mamoun. "Egypt's Islamic Group: Regional Revenge?". *Middle East Journal* 48, no. 4 (1994): 607–25.

———. *Saudi Arabia and the Politics of Dissent.* Palgrave Macmillan, 2001.

Fanon, Frantz. *The Wretched of the Earth* (Les Damnés de la Terre). Translated by Constance Farrington. New York: Grove Press, 2005 [1961].

Fearon, John. "Bargaining, Enforcement, and International Cooperation." *International Organization* 52, no. 2 (1998): 269–305.

Fink, Naureen, and Ellie Hearne. "Beyond Terrorism: Deradicalization and Disengagement from Violent Extremism." *International Peace Institute Report* (2008).

Fiske, Susan, and Shelley Taylor. *Social Cognition.* McGraw-Hill, 1991.

Fleming, Marie. "Propaganda by the Deed: Terrorism and Anarchist Theory in Late Nineteenth-Century Europe." *Studies in Conflict & Terrorism* 4, no. 1 (1980): 1–23.

Freedman, Lawrence. "Prevention, Not Preemption." *The Washington Quarterly* 26, no. 2 (2003): 105–14.

———. "The Revolution in Strategic Affairs." *The Adelphi Papers* 38, no. 318 (1998).

———. "Strategic Terror and Amateur Psychology." *The Political Quarterly* 76, no. 2 (2005): 161–70.

———. *Strategy: A History.* OUP, 2013.

———. "Terrorism as a Strategy." *Government and Opposition* 42, no. 3 (2007): 314–39.

Freedman, Lawrence, and Jeffrey Michaels, eds. *Scripting Middle East Leaders: The Impact of Leadership Perceptions on US And UK Foreign Policy.* London: Bloomsbury Academic, 2013.

Fromkin, David. "The Strategy of Terrorism." *Foreign Affairs* 53, no. 4 (1975): 683–98.

Frontline. "Al Qaeda in Yemen.", PBS, 2012.

Gamson, William A. "An Experimental Test of a Theory of Coalition Formation." *American Sociological Review* (1961): 565–73.

———. "A Theory of Coalition Formation." *American Sociological Review* (1961): 373–82.

Ganor, Boaz. "Terrorism as a Strategy of Psychological Warfare." In *The Trauma of Terrorism: Sharing Knowledge and Shared Care, an International Handbook*, edited by Yael Danieli, Danny Brom and Joe Sills, 33–43. Binghampton, NY: Hawthorne Press, 2005.

Gause III, F. Gregory. *The International Relations of the Persian Gulf*. Cambridge: Cambridge University Press, 2009.

Gearson, John. "Deterring Conventional Terrorism: From Punishment to Denial and Resilience." *Contemporary Security Policy* 33, no. 1 (2012): 171–98.

Gellner, Ernest. *Islamic Dilemmas: Reformers, Nationalists, Industrialization: The Southern Shore of the Mediterranean*. Walter de Gruyter, 1985.

Gentry, Caron. "The Relationship between New Social Movement Theory and Terrorism Studies: The Role of Leadership, Membership, Ideology and Gender." *Terrorism and Political Violence* 16, no. 2 (2004): 274–93.

Gerges, Fawaz. *The Far Enemy: Why Jihad Went Global*. Cambridge: Cambridge University Press, 2009.

Geva, Nehemia, and Alex Mintz. *Decision-Making on War and Peace: The Cognitive-Rational Debate*. New York: Lynne Rienner 1997.

Ghosh, Bobby. "Has the Alleged Fort Hood Gunman's Imam Been Silenced?" *Time*, 24 November 2009.

———. "How Dangerous Is the Cleric Anwar Al-Awlaki?" *Time*, 13 January 2010.

Gioia, Dennis, and Peter Poole. "Scripts in Organizational Behavior." *Academy of Management Review* (1984): 449–59.

Goerzig, Carolin. *Talking to Terrorists: Concessions and the Renunciation of Violence*. Routledge, 2010.

Golding, Bruce. "Times Sq. Bomber's Vile Rant as He Gets Life in Jail." *New York Post*, 6 October 2010.

Gould, Eric, and Esteban Klor. "Does Terrorism Work?". *The Quarterly Journal of Economics* 125, no. 4 (2010): 1459–510.

Grenier, Robert. "Yemen and the US: Down a Familiar Path." al-Jazeera, http://www.aljazeera.com/indepth/opinion/2012/05/201251071458557719.html.

Gunaratna, Rohan, and Mohamed Bin Ali. "De-Radicalization Initiatives in Egypt: A Preliminary Insight." *Studies in Conflict & Terrorism* 32, no. 4 (2009): 277–91.

Gunning, Jeroen. "Social Movement Theory and the Study of Terrorism." In *Critical Terrorism Studies: A New Research Agenda*, edited by Richard Jackson, Marie Breen Smyth and Jeroen Gunning: Routledge, 2009.

Hafez, Mohammed M. "Radicalization in the Persian Gulf: Assessing the Potential of Islamist Militancy in Saudi Arabia and Yemen." *Dynamics of Asymmetric Conflict* 1, no. 1 (2008): 6–24.

———. *Why Muslims Rebel: Repression and Resistance in the Islamic World*. New York: Lynne Rienner Publishers, 2004.

Hafez, Mohammed M., and Joseph Hatfield. "Do Targeted Assassinations Work? A Multivariate Analysis of Israel's Controversial Tactic During Al-Aqsa Uprising 1." *Studies in Conflict & Terrorism* 29, no. 4 (2006): 359–82.

BIBLIOGRAPHY

Hafez, Mohammed M., and Quintan Wiktorowicz. "Violence as Contention in the Egyptian Islamic Movement." In *Islamic Activism: A Social Movement Theory Approach*, edited by Quintan Wiktorowicz, 61–88. Bloomington: Indiana University Press, 2004.

Hafiz, Usamah, Muhammad Asim Abd al-Majid, and Karam al-Zuhdi. *Mubadarat Waqf Al-Unf: Ru'yah Waqi'iyah Wa Nazrah Shar'iyah* (An Initiative for Stopping Violence: A Practical Vision and Legal Framework). Cairo: Maktabat al-Turath al-Islami, 2002.

Halliday, Fred. *Revolution and Foreign Policy: The Case of South Yemen, 1967–1987*. Cambridge: Cambridge University Press, 2002.

———. "The Third Inter-Yemeni War and Its Consequences." *Asian Affairs* 26, no. 2 (1995): 131–40.

Hammond, Kenneth. *Human Judgment and Social Policy: Irreducible Uncertainty, Inevitable Error, Unavoidable Injustice*. Oxford: Oxford University Press, 2000.

Hamzawy, Amr, and Sarah Grebowski. "From Violence to Moderation: Al-Jama'a Al-Islamiya and Al-Jihad." In *Carnegie Papers*. Washington DC: Carnegie Endowment for International Peace, 2010.

Harris, Alistair. "Exploiting Grievances: Al-Qaeda in the Arabian Peninsula." In *Yemen on the Brink*, edited by Chris Boucek and Marina Ottaway. Carnegie Endowment for International Peace, 2010.

Haykel, Bernard. "On the Nature of Salafi Thought and Action." In *Global Salafism: Islam's New Religious Movement*, edited by Roel Meijer, 33–55. New York: Columbia University Press, 2009.

Hegghammer, Thomas. "The Case for Chasing Al-Awlaki." In *Foreign Policy*, 2010.

———. "Deconstructing the Myth About Al-Qa'ida and Khobar." Combating Terrorism Centre at Westpoint, http://www.ctc.usma.edu/posts/deconstructing-the-myth-about-al-qaida-and-khobar.

———. "The Failure of Jihad in Saudi Arabia." DTIC Document, 2010.

———. "Islamist Violence and Regime Stability in Saudi Arabia." *International Affairs* 84, no. 4 (2008): 701–15.

———. *Jihad in Saudi Arabia: Violence and Pan-Islamism since 1979*. Cambridge: Cambridge University Press, 2010.

———. "Jihad, Yes, but Not Revolution: Explaining the Extraversion of Islamist Violence in Saudi Arabia." *British Journal of Middle Eastern Studies* 36, no. 3 (2009): 395–416.

———. "Jihadi-Salafis or Revolutionaries? On Religion and Politics in the Study of Militant Islamism." In *Global Salafism: Islam's New Religious Movement*, edited by Roel Meijer: New York: Columbia University Press, 2009.

———. "Saudi and Yemeni Branches of Al-Qaida Unite." *Jihadica* 2009.

———. "Terrorist Recruitment and Radicalization in Saudi Arabia." *Middle East Policy* 13, no. 4 (2006): 39–60.

BIBLIOGRAPHY

Hegghammer, Thomas, and Stéphane Lacroix. "Rejectionist Islamism in Saudi Arabia: The Story of Juhayman Al-Utaybi Revisited." *International Journal of Middle East Studies* 39, no. 1 (2007): 103–22.

Heikal, Mohamed. *Autumn of Fury: The Assassination of Sadat*. Corgi, 1984.

Hellmich, Christina. "Fighting Al Qaeda in Yemen? Rethinking the Nature of the Islamist Threat and the Effectiveness of U.S. Counterterrorism Strategy." *Studies in Conflict & Terrorism* 35, no. 9 (2012): 618–33.

Herridge, Catherine. "Awlaki Tops Bin Laden as Top Terror Threat to U.S., Counterterrorism Official Says." Fox News, http://www.foxnews.com/us/2011/02/09/awlaki-tops-bin-laden-terror-threat-counterterrorism-official-says/.

Heyworth-Dunne, James. *Religious and Political Trends in Modern Egypt*. 1950.

Hill, Ginny. "Yemen: Fear of Failure." Chatham House, 2010.

Hill, Ginny, and Gerd Nonneman. "Yemen, Saudi Arabia and the Gulf States: Elite Politics, Street Protests and Regional Diplomacy." In *Chatham House Briefing Paper*. London: Chatham House, 2011.

Hoffman, Bruce. *Inside Terrorism*. New York: Columbia University Press, 2006.

Home Office. "Contest: The United Kingdom's Strategy for Countering Terrorism." London: The Stationery Office, 2011.

———. "Countering International Terrorism: The United Kingdom's Strategy." London: The Stationery Office, 2006.

———. "The United Kingdom's Strategy for Countering International Terrorism." Home Office. London: The Stationery Office, 2009.

Honig, Or. "Explaining Israel's Misuse of Strategic Assassinations." *Studies in Conflict & Terrorism* 30, no. 6 (2007): 563–77.

Horgan, John, and Kurt Braddock. "Rehabilitating the Terrorists?: Challenges in Assessing the Effectiveness of De-Radicalization Programs." *Terrorism and Political Violence* 22, no. 2 (2010): 267–91.

Hosenball, Mark. "Secret Panel Can Put Americans on Kill List." Reuters, http://www.reuters.com/article/2011/10/05/us-cia-killlist-idUSTRE79475C20111005.

Hoyt, Thomas. "Military Force." In *Attacking Terrorism: Elements of a Grand Strategy*, edited by Audrey Kurth Cronin and James Ludes: Georgetown University Press, 2004.

Huband, Mark. *Warriors of the Prophet: The Struggle for Islam*. Basic Books, 1999.

Human Rights Watch. "Abd Al-Rahim Al-Nashiri." http://www.hrw.org/news/2012/10/26/abd-al-rahim-al-nashiri.

———. "Behind Closed Doors: Torture and Detention in Egypt." 1992.

———. "Human Rights and Saudi Arabia's Counterterrorism Response: Religious Counseling, Indefinite Detention, and Flawed Trials." 2009.

———. "Human Rights Watch World Report 1993." 1993.

———. "Human Rights Watch World Report 1994." 1994.

———. "Human Rights Watch World Report 2002—Yemen." 2002.

———. "No Direction Home: Returns from Guantanamo to Yemen." 2009.

———. "Precarious Justice: Arbitrary Detention and Unfair Trials in the Deficient Criminal Justice System of Saudi Arabia." Human Rights Watch, 2008.

Ibrahim, Saad Eddin. *Egypt, Islam and Democracy: Critical Essays.* The American University in Cairo Press, 2002.

———. "Egypt's Islamic Militants." *MERIP Reports*, no. 103 (1982): 5–14.

Ingrams, William Harold. *The Yemen: Imams, Rulers & Revolutions.* London: J. Murray, 1963.

International Federation for Human Rights (FIDH). "Egypt: Counter-Terrorism against the Background of an Endless State of Emergency." FIDH, 2010.

Jackson, Sherman. "Beyond Jihad: The New Thought of the Gamāʿa Islāmiyya." *Journal of Islamic Law and Culture* 11, no. 1 (2009): 52–69.

Jansen, Johannes *The Neglected Duty: The Creed of Sadat's Assassins and Islamic Resurgence in the Middle East.* New York: Macmillan, 1986.

Jasper, James. "A Strategic Approach to Collective Action: Looking for Agency in Social Movement Choices." *Mobilization: An International Quarterly* 9, no. 1 (2004): 1–16.

Jenkins, Brian Michael. "International Terrorism: A New Mode of Conflict." In *International Terrorism and World Security*, edited by David Carlton and Carlo Schaerf. London: Croom Helm, 1975.

———. *The Study of Terrorism: Definitional Problems.* RAND, 1980.

Johnsen, Gregory. "The Al-Awlaki Debate Continues." Waq al-Waq, http://bigthink.com/waq-al-waq/the-al-awlaki-debate-continues.

———. "Al-Qaida in the Arabian Peninsula in Yemen." In *Talk of the Nation*: NPR, 2010.

———. "Aqap in Yemen and the Christmas Day Terrorist Attack." In *CTC Sentinel*: Combatting Terrorism Centre at West Point, 2010.

———. "A False Target in Yemen." http://www.nytimes.com/2010/11/20/opinion/20johnsen.html.

———. "Frontline: Al-Qaeda in Yemen." Waq al-Waq, http://bigthink.com/waq-al-waq/frontline-al-qaeda-in-yemen?page=all.

———. "Is Al-Qaeda in Yemen Regrouping." *Terrorism Focus* 4, no. 15 (2007).

———. *The Last Refuge: Yemen, Al-Qaeda, and America's War in Arabia.* W. W. Norton & Company, 2012.

———. "The Resiliency of Yemen's Aden-Abyan Islamic Army." In *Global Terrorism Analysis*: The Jamestown Foundation, 2006.

———. "Tracking Yemen's 23 Escaped Jihadi Operatives Part I." *Terrorism Monitor* 5, no. 18 (2008).

———. "Tracking Yemen's 23 Escaped Jihadi Operatives Part II." *Terrorism Monitor* 5, no. 19 (2008).

———. "Yemen's Passive Role in the War on Terrorism." *Terrorism Monitor* 4, no. 4 (2006).

Johnston, Patrick B. "Does Decapitation Work?: Assessing the Effectiveness of Leadership Targeting in Counterinsurgency Campaigns." *International Security* 36, no. 4 (2012): 47–79.

Johnston, Philip. "Anwar Al Awlaki: The New Osama Bin Laden?" *The Telegraph*, 17 September 2010.

Jones, Toby C. "Social Contract for Saudi Arabia." *Middle East Report* 228 (2003).

Jonsson, Patrik. "Will Yemen Air Strike Change View of Fort Hood Shooting?" *Christian Science Monitor*, 24 December 2009.

Jordan, Jenna. "When Heads Roll: Assessing the Effectiveness of Leadership Decapitation." *Security Studies* 18, no. 4 (2009): 719–55.

Joscelyn, Thomas. "Another Former Gitmo Detainee Killed in Shootout." The Long War Journal http://www.longwarjournal.org/archives/2009/10/another_former_gitmo.php.

———. "Awlaki's E-Mails to Terror Plotter Show Operational Role." Long War Journal, http://www.longwarjournal.org/archives/2011/03/anwar_al_awlakis_ema.php—ixzz1HXMb3Cp, 2 March 2012.

———. "Former Gitmo Detainee Killed in Shootout." The Long War Journal, http://www.longwarjournal.org/archives/2009/09/former_gitmo_detaine.php

Kahneman, Daniel. *Thinking, Fast and Slow*. Penguin, 2012.

Kahneman, Daniel, and Shane Frederick. "A Model of Heuristic Judgment." In *The Cambridge Handbook of Thinking and Reasoning*, edited by Keith Holyoak and Robert Morrison: Cambridge: Cambridge University Press, 2005.

———. "Representativeness Revisited: Attribute Substitution in Intuitive Judgement." In *Heuristics and Biases: The Psychology of Intuitive Judgment*, edited by Thomas Gilovich, Dale Griffin and Daniel Kahneman: Cambridge: Cambridge University Press, 2002.

Kahneman, Daniel, Paul Slovic, and Amos Tversky. *Judgment under Uncertainty: Heuristics and Biases*. Cambridge: Cambridge University Press, 1982.

Kapiszewski, Andrzej. "Saudi Arabia Steps toward Democratization or Reconfiguration of Authoritarianism?". *Journal of Asian and African Studies* 41, no. 5–6 (2006): 459–82.

Kassel, Rudolf. *Aristotelis De Arte Poetica Liber*. repr. of 1966 ed. Oxford: Clarendon Press, 1968.

Kassem, Maye. *Egyptian Politics: The Dynamics of Authoritarian Rule*. Lynne Rienner Publishers Inc, 2004.

Katz, Mark. "U.S.-Yemen Relations and the War on Terror: A Portrait of Yemeni President Ali Abdullah Salih." *Terrorism Monitor* 7, no. 2 (2005).

Kepel, Gilles. *Jihad: The Trail of Political Islam*. Belknap Press of Harvard University Press, 2003.

————. *Muslim Extremism in Egypt: The Prophet and Pharaoh, with a New Preface for 2003*. University of California Press, 2003.

————. *Roots of Radical Islam*. Saqi Books Publishers, 2005.

Kepel, Gilles, Jean-Pierre Milelli, Pascale Ghazaleh, Omar Saghi, Thomas Hegghammer, and Stéphane Lacroix. *Al Qaeda in Its Own Words*. Harvard University Press, 2010.

Khong, Yuen Foong. *Analogies at War: Korea, Munich, Dien Bien Phu, and the Vietnam Decisions of 1965*. Princeton: Princeton University Press, 1992.

Klein, Gary. *Sources of Power: How People Make Decisions*. MIT Press, 1999.

Knickmeyer, Ellen. "Attack against U.S. Embassy in Yemen Blamed on Al-Qaeda." http://www.washingtonpost.com/wp-dyn/content/article/2008/09/17/AR2008091700317.html.

Koehler-Derrick, Gabriel. *A False Foundation? AQAP, Tribes and Ungoverned Spaces in Yemen*. Combatting Terrorism Centre, 2011.

Kohlmann, Evan. "'The Eleven': Saudi Guantanamo Veterans Returning to the Fight." NEFA Foundation, 2009.

Kurzman, Charles. "The Qum Protests and the Coming of the Iranian Revolution, 1975 and 1978." *Social Science History* 27, no. 3 (2003): 287–325.

Kydd, Andrew, and Barbara Walter. "Outbidding and the Overproduction of Terrorism." n.p., 2009.

————. "Sabotaging the Peace: The Politics of Extremist Violence." *International Organization* 56, no. 2 (2002): 263–96.

————. "The Strategies of Terrorism." *International Security* 31, no. 1 (2006): 49–80.

Lacey, Robert. *Inside the Kingdom*. Arrow, 2010.

Lacroix, Stéphane. *Awakening Islam: The Politics of Religious Dissent in Contemporary Saudi Arabia*. Edited by George Holoch: Harvard University Press, 2011.

Lacroix, Stéphane, and Thomas Hegghammer. *Saudi Arabia Backgrounder: Who Are the Islamists*. Amman: International Crisis Group, 2004.

LaFranchi, Howard. "US Covert Attacks in Yemen: A Better Template for the War on Terror?" *Christian Science Monitor*, 15 June 2011.

Lahood, Nelly, Stuart Caudill, Liam Collins, Gabriel Koehler-Derrick, Don Rassler, and Muhammad al-'Ubaydi. "Letters from Abbottabad: Bin Ladin Sidelined." In *Harmony Program*: Combatting Terrorism Center at West Point, 2012.

Lake, David. "Rational Extremism: Understanding Terrorism in the Twenty-First Century." *Dialog-IO* 1, no. 1 (2002): 15–28.

Lambert, Robert. "Salafi and Islamist Londoners: Stigmatised Minority Faith Communities Countering Al-Qaida." *Crime, Law and Social Change* 50, no. 1 (2008): 73–89.

Lapan, Harvey, and Todd Sandler. "Terrorism and Signalling." *European Journal of Political Economy* 9, no. 3 (1993): 383–97.

———. "To Bargain or Not to Bargain: That Is the Question." *The American Economic Review* 78, no. 2 (1988): 16–21.

Larson, Deborah Welch. "The Role of Belief Systems and Schemas in Foreign Policy Decision-Making." *Political Psychology* 15, no. 1 (1994): 17–33.

Lessing, Doris. *The Good Terrorist*. Fourth Estate, 2013.

Lévi-Strauss, Claude. *Myth and Meaning: Cracking the Code of Culture*. Schocken Books, 1995.

———. *The Raw and the Cooked: Introduction to a Science of Mythology*. Translated by John Weightman and Doreen Weightman. Penguin Books Ltd, 1986.

Lewis, Bernard. *What Went Wrong?: The Clash between Islam and Modernity in the Middle East*. Harper Perennial, 2003.

Lia, Brynjar. *The Society of the Muslim Brothers in Egypt: The Rise of an Islamic Mass Movement, 1928–1942*. Ithaca Press, 2006.

Lia, Brynjar, and Thomas Hegghammer. "Jihadi Strategic Studies: The Alleged Al Qaida Policy Study Preceding the Madrid Bombings." *Studies in Conflict & Terrorism* 27, no. 5 (2004): 355–75.

Lieberman, Joseph. *Ticking Time Bomb: Counter-Terrorism Lessons from the Us Government's Failure to Prevent the Fort Hood Attack*. DIANE Publishing, 2011.

Linschoten, Alex Strick van, and Felix Kuehn. *An Enemy We Created: The Myth of the Taliban/Al-Qaeda Merger in Afghanistan, 1970–2010*. London: C. Hurst & Co., 2012.

Liska, George. *Nations in Alliance: The Limits of Interdependence*. The Johns Hopkins University Press, 1962.

Lister, Tim. "Killing of Al Qaeda Leader in Yemen Evidence of New U.S.-Yemeni Offensive." CNN Security Clearance [Blog], http://security.blogs.cnn.com/2012/05/07/killing-of-al-qaeda-leader-in-yemen-evidence-of-new-u-s-yemeni-offensive/.

Loidolt, Bryce. "Managing the Global and Local: The Dual Agendas of Al Qaeda in the Arabian Peninsula." *Studies in Conflict & Terrorism* 34, no. 2 (2011): 102–23.

Longley, April. "The High Water Mark of Islamist Politics? The Case of Yemen." *The Middle East Journal* 61, no. 2 (2007): 240–60.

Luttwak, Edward. *Strategy: The Logic of War and Peace*. 2nd ed.: Harvard University Press, 2002.

MacEoin, Denis. "Anwar Al-Awlaki: 'I Pray That Allah Destroys America.'" *Middle East Quarterly* XVIII, no. 2 (2010).

MacFarquhar, Neil. "Among the Saudis, Attack Has Soured Qaeda Supporters." *New York Times*, 11 November 2003.

Maher, Shiraz. "Instant Analysis: New Issue of Inspire Magazine." FreeRad!cals Blog, International Centre for the Study of Radicalisation, http://icsr.info/2010/11/instant-analysis-new-issue-of-inspire-magazine-2/.

Malik, Maleiha. "Engaging with Extremists." *International Relations* 22, no. 1 (2008): 85–104.

Mannes, Aaron. "Testing the Snake Head Strategy: Does Killing or Capturing Its Leaders Reduce a Terrorist Group's Activity?". *The Journal of International Policy Solutions* 9 (2008).

Mansfield, Peter. *A History of the Middle East.* Penguin, 2004.

Marighella, Carlos. *Minimanual of the Urban Guerrilla.* Red and Black Publishers, 2008.

Masters, Jonathan. "Al Qaeda in Arabian Peninsula (Aqap)." http://www.huffington-post.com/jonathan-masters/yemen-al-qaeda_b_1028389.html.

———. "Al-Qaeda in the Arabian Peninsula (Aqap)." http://www.cfr.org/yemen/al-qaeda-arabian-peninsula-aqap/p9369.

McAdam, Doug, Sidney Tarrow, and Charles Tilly. *Dynamics of Contention.* Cambridge: Cambridge University Press, 2001.

McCormick, Gordon. "Terrorist Decision Making." *Annual Review of Political Science* 6, no. 1 (2003): 473–507.

McGreal, Chris. "Ibrahim Hassan Al-Asiri: The Prime Bombmaking Suspect." 31 October 2010.

McGreal, Chris, and Vikram Dodd. "Cargo Bombs Plot: Us Hunts Saudi Extremist." *The Guardian*, 31 October 2010.

———. "Cargo Plane Bomb Plot: Saudi Double Agent 'Gave Crucial Alert'." *The Guardian*, 1 November 2010.

Mearsheimer, John. *Conventional Deterrence.* Ithaca: Cornell University Press, 1983.

Meijer, Roel. "Commanding Right and Forbidding Wrong as a Principle of Social Action: The Case of the Egyptian Al-Jama'a Al-Islamiyya." In *Global Salafism: Islam's New Religious Movement*, edited by Roel Meijer. New York: Columbia University Press, 2009.

———. "The Cycle of Contention and the Limits of Terrorism in Saudi Arabia." In *Saudi Arabia in the Balance: Political Economy, Society, Foreign Affairs*, edited by Paul Aarts and Gerd Nonneman. London: C. Hurst & Co., 2005.

———. "Re-Reading Al-Qaeda Writings of Yusuf Al-Ayiri." *ISIM Review* 18 (2006).

———. "Yusuf Al-'Uyairi and the Making of a Revolutionary Salafi Praxis." *Die Welt des Islams* 47, no. 3–4 (2007): 422–59.

———. "Yusuf Al-Uyairi and the Transnationalisation of Saudi Jihadism." In *Kingdom without Borders: Saudi Arabia's Political, Religious and Media Frontiers*, edited by Madawi al-Rasheed. London: C. Hurst & Co., 2008.

Ménoret, Pascal. *The Saudi Enigma: A History.* Translated by Patrick Camiller. Zed Books Ltd, 2005.

Meyer, Josh. "Fort Hood Shooting Suspect's Ties to Mosque Investigated." *Los Angeles Times*, 9 November 2009.

Midlarsky, Manus, Martha Crenshaw, and Fumihiko Yoshida. "Why Violence Spreads." *International Studies Quarterly* 24 (1980): 262–98.

Mirza, Munira, Abi Senthilkumaran, and Zein Ja'far. *Living Apart Together: British Muslims and the Paradox of Multiculturalism*. Policy Exchange, 2007.

Mitchell, Richard P. *The Society of the Muslim Brothers*. Oxford University Press, USA, 1993.

Morgenthau, Hans J., Kenneth W. Thompson, and David Clinton. *Politics among Nations*. McGraw-Hill Higher Education, 2005.

Mubarak, Hisham. "What Does the *Gama'a Islamiyya* Want? Tal'at Fu'ad Qasim, Interview with Hisham Mubarak." Translated by Souhail Shadoud and Steve Tamari. In *Political Islam: Essays from Middle East Report*, edited by Joel Beinin and Joe Stork, 40–46: University of California Press, 1997.

Munson, Ziad. "Islamic Mobilization: Social Movement Theory and the Egyptian Muslim Brotherhood." *The Sociological Quarterly* 42, no. 4 (2001): 487–510.

Najih, Ibrahim. *Hurmat Al-Ghulu Fi Al-Din Wa Takfir Al-Muslimin* (The Illegality of Excess in Declaring Muslims Apostate). Edited by Ali Sharif and Karam al-Zuhdi. Cairo: Maktabat al-Turath al-Islami, 2002.

Najih, Ibrahim, and Ali Sharif. *Tafjirat Al-Riyad: Al-Ahkam Wal-Athar* (The Bombings in Riyadh: Rulings and Effect). Cairo: Maktabat al-Turath al-Islami, 2003.

National Commission on Terrorist Attacks. *The 9/11 Commission Report: Final Report of the National Commission on Terrorist Attacks Upon the United States*. W. W. Norton & Company, 2004.

"National Consortium for the Study of Terrorism and Responses to Terrorism (Start)." Global Terrorism Database 2011.

Neumann, Peter. "Negotiating with Terrorists." *Foreign Affairs* 86, no. 1 (2007): 128–38.

Neumann, Peter, and Brooke Rogers. "Recruitment and Mobilisation for the Islamist Militant Movement in Europe." London: ICSR, 2007.

Neumann, Peter, and M. L. R. Smith. "Strategic Terrorism: The Framework and Its Fallacies." *Journal of Strategic Studies* 28, no. 4 (2005): 571–95.

Neustadt, Richard, and Ernest May. *Thinking in Time: The Uses of History for Decision-Makers*. Free Press, 1988.

Niblock, Tim. *Saudi Arabia: Power, Legitimacy and Survival*. Routledge, 2006.

Ochs, Molly. "Yemen: New Government, Same Challenges to Press Freedom." International Press Institute, 2012.

Okruhlik, Gwenn. "Making Conversation Possible: Islamism and Reform in Saudi Arabia." In *Islamic Activism: A Social Movement Theory Approach*, edited by Quintan Wiktorowicz. Bloomington: Indiana University Press, 2004.

Overgaard, Per Baltzer. "The Scale of Terrorist Attacks as a Signal of Resources." *Journal of Conflict Resolution* 38, no. 3 (1994): 452–78.

Page, Michael, Lara Challita, and Alistair Harris. "Al Qaeda in the Arabian Peninsula: Framing Narratives and Prescriptions." *Terrorism and Political Violence* 23, no. 2 (2011): 150–72.

Pape, Robert. *Dying to Win: The Strategic Logic of Suicide Terrorism.* Random House, 2005.

———. "The Strategic Logic of Suicide Terrorism." *American Political Science Review* 97, no. 3 (2003): 343–61.

Pargeter, Alison. *The Muslim Brotherhood: The Burden of Tradition.* Saqi Books, 2010.

PBS News. "Bin Laden's Fatwa Aug. 23, 1996." http://www.pbs.org/newshour/updates/military/july-dec96/fatwa_1996.html.

PBS Newshour. "American Hostage in Saudi Arabia Beheaded by Captors." 18 June 2004.

Pedahzur, Ami, and Magnus Ranstorp. "A Tertiary Model for Countering Terrorism in Liberal Democracies: The Case of Israel." *Terrorism and Political Violence* 13, no. 2 (2001): 1–26.

Peraino, Kevin. "The Reeducation of Abu Jandal." Newsweek Magazine, http://www.thedailybeast.com/newsweek/2009/05/28/the-reeducation-of-abu-jandal.html.

Perez, Evan. "U.S. Terror Suspect Arrested." *Wall Street Journal*, 3 June 2010.

Peterson, J. E. *Yemen: The Search for a Modern State.* The Johns Hopkins University Press, 1982.

Phillips, Sarah. "Al-Qaeda and the Struggle for Yemen." *Survival* 53, no. 1 (2011): 95–120.

———. *Yemen and the Politics of Permanent Crisis.* Routledge, 2011.

———. "Yemen: Developmental Dysfunction and Division in a Crisis State." In *Developmental Leadership Program Research Paper*, 2011.

———. *Yemen's Democracy Experiment in Regional Perspective: Patronage and Pluralized Authoritarianism.* Palgrave Macmillan, 2008.

Porges, Marisa. "The Saudi Deradicalization Experiment." *Council on Foreign Relations, Expert Brief* (2010).

Porter, Gareth. "Khobar Towers Investigated: How a Saudi Deception Protected Osama Bin Laden." 2009.

Post, Jerrold M. "The Generation of Vipers: The Generational Provenance of Terrorists." *SAIS Review* 31, no. 2 (2011): 111–22.

Price, Bryan C. "Targeting Top Terrorists: How Leadership Decapitation Contributes to Counterterrorism." *International Security* 36, no. 4 (2012): 9–46.

Propp, Vladimir. *Morphology of the Folktale.* Translated by Louis Wagner. University of Texas for the American Folklore Society, 1968.

Qutb, Sayyid. *Milestones.* Islamic Book Service, 1964 (tr. 2006).

Rabasa, Angel, Stacie Pettyjohn, Jeremy Ghez, and Christopher Boucek. "Deradicalizing Islamist Extremists." In *RAND Corporation Monograph Series*: RAND, 2010.

Raghavan, Sudarsan. "In Yemen, U.S. Airstrikes Breed Anger, and Sympathy for Al-Qaeda." *The Washington Post*, 30 May 2012.

Ranstorp, Magnus. "Mapping Terrorism Studies after 9/11: An Academic Field of Old Problems and New Prospects." In *Critical Terrorism Studies: A New Research Agenda*, edited by Richard Jackson, Marie Breen Smyth and Jeroen Gunning: Routledge, 2009.

Raphaeli, Nimrod. "Ayman Muhammad Rabi' Al-Zawahiri: The Making of an Arch-Terrorist." *Terrorism and Political Violence* 14, no. 4 (2002): 1–22.

Rashid, Ahmed. *Descent into Chaos: The World's Most Unstable Region and the Threat to Global Security*. Penguin, 2009.

Rashwan, Dia'a. "The Obstacle Course of Revisions: Gamaah Versus Jihad." In *al-Ahram Commentary*. Cairo: al-Ahram Centre for Political and Security Studies, 2007.

———. "The Renunciation of Violence by Egyptian Jihadi Organizations." In *Leaving Terrorism Behind: Individual and Collective Disengagement*, edited by Tore Bjørgo and John Horgan. London: Routledge, 2009.

Reid, Donald. "Political Assassination in Egypt, 1910–1954." *International Journal of African Historical Studies* 15, no. 4 (1982): 625–51.

Reuters. "Yemen Says Deployment of U.S. Marines Is Temporary." 17 September 2012.

Riedel, Bruce. *The Search for Al Qaeda: Its Leadership, Ideology, and Future*. 2nd ed.: Brookings Institution, 2010.

Riedel, Bruce, and Bilal Saab. "Al Qaeda's Third Front: Saudi Arabia." *Washington Quarterly* 31, no. 2 (2008): 33–46.

Riker, William H. *Theory of Political Coalitions*. Greenwood Press, 1984.

Rinehart, Christine Sixta. "Volatile Breeding Grounds: The Radicalization of the Egyptian Muslim Brotherhood." *Studies in Conflict & Terrorism* 32, no. 11 (2009): 953–88.

Roggio, Bill, and Bob Barry. "The Covert US Air Campaign in Yemen." Long War Journal http://www.longwarjournal.org/multimedia/Yemen/code/Yemen-strike.php.

Roy, Olivier. *The Failure of Political Islam*. I. B. Tauris, 1994.

———. *Globalised Islam: The Search for a New Ummah*. London: C. Hurst & Co., 2004.

Rubin, Barry. *Islamic Fundamentalism in Egyptian Politics*. Palgrave Macmillan, 2002.

———. *The Muslim Brotherhood: The Organization and Policies of a Global Islamist Movement*. Palgrave Macmillan, 2010.

Sageman, Marc. *Leaderless Jihad: Terror Networks in the Twenty-First Century*. Philadelphia: University of Pennsylvania Press, 2008.

———. *Understanding Terror Networks*. Philadelphia: University of Pennsylvania Press, 2004.

Saleh, Heba. "Egyptian Report Denounces Torture." BBC, http://news.bbc.co.uk/1/hi/world/middle_east/4433303.stm.

Sandler, Todd. "The Analytical Study of Terrorism." *Journal of Peace Research* 51, no. 2 (2014): 257–71.

Sandler, Todd, John Tschirhart, and Jon Cauley. "A Theoretical Analysis of Transnational Terrorism." *The American Political Science Review* 77, no. 1 (1983): 36–54.

Sartre, Jean-Paul. *Nausea* [La Nausée]. Translated by Robert Baldick. Penguin, 1965 [1938].

———. "Preface." In Fanon, *The Wretched of the Earth*. New York: Grove Press, 2005 [1961].

Saussure, Ferdinand de. *Course in General Linguistics*. Translated by R. Harris. 2nd ed.: Gerald Duckworth & Co Ltd, 1995.

Scahill, Jeremy. "Why Is President Obama Keeping a Journalist in Prison in Yemen?" *The Nation*, 13 March 2012.

Schank, Roger, and Robert Abelson. "Scripts, Plans, and Knowledge." In *Proceedings of the 4th International Joint Conference on Artificial intelligence*, 151–7. Tblisi: Morgan Kaufmann 1975.

———. *Scripts, Plans, Goals, and Understanding: An Inquiry into Human Knowledge Structures*. Psychology Press, 1977.

Schanzer, Jonathan. "Yemen's War on Terror." *Orbis* 48, no. 3 (2005): 517–31.

Schelling, Thomas. *Arms and Influence*. Yale University Press, 1967.

———. "What Purposes Can 'International Terrorism' Serve?". In *Violence, Terrorism and Justice*, edited by Raymond Gillespie Frey and Christopher W. Morris. Cambridge: Cambridge University Press, 1991.

Scheuer, Michael. *Through Our Enemies' Eyes: Osama Bin Laden, Radical Islam, and the Future of America, Revised Edition*. Potomac Books Inc., 2006.

Schmid, Alex. "Terrorism—the Definitional Problem." *Case Western Reserve Journal of International Law* 36 (2004): 375–419.

Schwedler, Jillian. *Faith in Moderation: Islamist Parties in Jordan and Yemen*. Cambridge: Cambridge University Press, 2007.

———. "The Islah Party in Yemen: Political Opportunities and Coalition Building in a Transitional Polity." In *Islamic Activism: A Social Movement Theory Approach*, edited by Quintan Wiktorowicz, 205–30. Bloomington: Indiana University Press, 2004.

Select Committee on Intelligence United States Senate. *Attempted Terrorist Attack on Northwest Airlines Flight 253: Unclassified Executive Summary of the Congressional Report*. US Goverment Printing Office, 2010.

Sfeir, Antoine. *The Columbia World Dictionary of Islamism*. New York: Columbia University Press, 2007.

Shane, Scott. "U.S. Approves Targeted Killing of American Cleric." *The New York Times*, 7 April 2010.

Sharif, Ali. *Nahr Al-Dhirkrayat: Al-Muraja'at Al-Fiqhiyah Lil-Jama'a Al-Islamiya* (The River of Memories: Interpretative Revision in the Gama'a Islamiyya). Cairo: Maktabat al-Turath al-Islami, 2003.

Shenon, Philip. "Threats and Responses: Terror Network; a Major Suspect in Qaeda Attacks Is in U.S. Custody." *The New York Times*, 22 November 2002.

Shepard, William. "Sayyid Qutb's Doctrine of Jahiliyya." *International Journal of Middle East Studies* 35, no. 04 (2003): 521–45.

Silke, Andrew. *Research on Terrorism: Trends, Achievements and Failures*. Routledge, 2004.

Simon, Herbert. "From Substantive to Procedural Rationality." In *Method and Appraisal in Economics*, edited by Spiro Latsis. Cambridge: Cambridge University Press, 1980.

———. *Models of Bounded Rationality, Vol. 3: Empirically Grounded Economic Reason*. MIT Press, 1997.

Siqueira, Kevin, and Todd Sandler. "Terrorists Versus the Government: Strategic Interaction, Support, and Sponsorship." *Journal of Conflict Resolution* 50, no. 6 (2006): 878–98.

Sivan, Emmanuel. *Radical Islam: Medieval Theology and Modern Politics*. Yale University Press, 1990.

Smith, G. R. *The Yemens: The Yemen Arab Republic and the People's Democratic Republic of Yemen*. World Bibliographical Series. Oxford: Clio, 1984.

Smith, M. L. R., and Peter Neumann. *The Strategy of Terrorism: How It Works, and Why It Fails*. Routledge, 2009.

Soage, Ana Belen, and Jorge Fuentelsaz Franganillo. "The Muslim Brothers in Egypt." In *The Muslim Brotherhood: The Organization and Policies of a Global Islamist Movement*, edited by B. Rubin. Palgrave Macmillan, 2010.

Spalek, Basia, and Robert Lambert. "Muslim Communities, Counter-Terrorism and Counter-Radicalisation: A Critically Reflective Approach to Engagement." *International Journal of Law, Crime and Justice* 36, no. 4 (2008): 257–70.

Spencer, James. "Al-Qa'ida in the Arabian Peninsula: Mos & Deductions." *Small Wars Journal* (2011).

Spencer, Ruth. "In Case You Missed It: The 'Al Qaeda in Yemen' Live Chat." http://www.guardian.co.uk/commentisfree/cifamerica/2012/may/29/frontline-al-qaida-yemen-live-chat.

Sprinzak, Ehud. "Rational Fanatics." *Foreign Policy* 120 September–October (2000).

Stanovich, Keith, and Richard West. "Individual Differences in Reasoning: Implications for the Rationality Debate?". *Behavioral and Brain Sciences* 23, no. 5 (2000): 645–65.

Stein, Ewan. "An Uncivil Partnership: Egypt's Jama'a Islamiyya and the State after the Jihad." *Third World Quarterly* 32, no. 5 (2011): 863–81.

Stern, Jessica, and Marisa L. Porges. "Getting Deradicalization Right." *Foreign Affairs*, 2010.

Stewart, Frances. "Development and Security." *Conflict, Security & Development* 4, no. 3 (2004): 261–88.

Stone, John. "Al Qaeda, Deterrence, and Weapons of Mass Destruction." *Studies in Conflict & Terrorism* 32, no. 9 (2009): 763–75.

Stracke, Nicole. "Arab Prisons: A Place for Dialogue and Reform." *Perspectives on Terrorism* 1, no. 4 (2010).

Suskind, Ron. *The One Percent Doctrine: Deep inside America's Pursuit of Its Enemies since 9/11.* Simon and Schuster, 2006.

Taber, Robert. *The War of the Flea.* London: Paladin, 1977.

Taleb, Nassim Nicholas. *The Black Swan: The Impact of the Highly Improbable.* Penguin, 2008.

Talmadge, Caitlin. "Deterring a Nuclear 9/11." *Washington Quarterly* 30, no. 2 (2007): 21–34.

Tarnoff, Curt. "Millennium Challenge Corporation." In *CRS Report for Congress*: Congressional Research Service, 2012.

Tawil, Camille. *Brothers in Arms: Al Qa'ida and the Arab Jihadists.* Saqi Books, 2010.

Taylor, Peter. "Generation Jihad." BBC 2, 2011.

———. "Yemen Al-Qaeda Link to Guantanamo." BBC, http://news.bbc.co.uk/1/hi/programmes/newsnight/8454804.stm.

Teitelbaum, Joshua. *Holier Than Thou: Saudi Arabia's Islamic Opposition.* Brookings Institution, 2000.

Thornton, Thomas. "Terror as a Weapon of Political Agitation." In *Internal War: Problems and Approaches*, edited by Harry Eckstein. Greenwood Press, 1980.

Tilly, Charles. "Terror as Strategy and Relational Process." *International Journal of Comparative Sociology* 46, no. 1–2 (2005): 11–32.

———. "The Trouble with Stories." In *Stories, Identity and Political Change*, edited by Charles Tilly. New York: Rowman & Littlefield, 2002.

Tilly, Charles, and Sidney G. Tarrow. *Contentious Politics.* Paradigm Publishers, 2007.

Toth, James. "Islamism in Southern Egypt: A Case Study of a Radical Religious Movement." *International Journal of Middle East Studies* 35, no. 4 (2003).

Trager, Robert, and Dessislava Zagorcheva. "Deterring Terrorism: It Can Be Done." *International Security* 30, no. 3 (2006): 87–123.

Tversky, Amos, and Daniel Kahneman. "Judgment under Uncertainty: Heuristics and Biases." *Science* 185, no. 4157 (1974): 1124–31

U.S. House of Representatives. *Report of the Joint Inquiry into the Terrorist Attacks of September 11, 2001—by the House Permanent Select Committee on Intelligence and the Senate Select Committee on Intelligence, Volume I.* 2005.

U.S. Department of State. "2000 Country Report on Human Rights in Egypt." Bureau of Public Affairs, 2001.

U.S. Treasury. "Treasury Designates Al Haramain Islamic Foundation." 2008.

UNESCO. "Old Walled City of Shibam." http://whc.unesco.org/en/list/192.

"Us Embassy Cables: Yemen Trumpets Strikes on Al-Qaida That Were Americans' Work." http://www.guardian.co.uk/world/us-embassy-cables-documents/240955.

Vandenbroucke, Lucien. "Why Allah's Zealots? A Study of the Causes of Islamic Fundamentalism in Egypt and Saudi Arabia." *Middle East Review* 16, no. 1 (1983): 31.

Voice of America. "Al-Awlaki's Death Leaves Gap in Al-Qaida." 29 Septmber 2011.

Waardenburg, Jacques. "Islam as a Vehicle of Protest." In *Islamic Dilemmas: Reformers, Nationalists, Industrialization: The Southern Shore of the Mediterranean*, edited by Ernest Gellner. Amsterdam: Mouton, 1985.

Walt, Stephen M. "Alliance Formation and the Balance of World Power." *International Security* 9, no. 4 (1985): 3–43.

———. *The Origins of Alliances*. Cornell University Press, 1990.

Waterbury, John. *The Egypt of Nasser and Sadat: The Political Economy of Two Regimes*. Princeton: Princeton University Press, 1992.

Waterman, Harvey. "Reasons and Reason: Collective Political Activity in Comparative and Historical Perspective." *World Politics* 33, no. 4 (1981): 554–89.

Waugh, William. "The Values in Violence: Organizational and Political Objectives of Terrorist Groups." *Journal of Conflict Studies* 3, no. 4 (1983).

Weaver, Matthew. "Britain's Deputy Ambassador to Yemen Survives Rocket Attack." *The Guardian*, 6 October 2010.

Weber, Max. *The Theory of Social and Economic Organization*. Translated by Talcott Parsons and A. M. Henderson. Martino Fine Books, 2012 [1947].

Wehr, Hans. *Arabic-English Dictionary: The Hans Wehr Dictionary of Modern Written Arabic*. Spoken Language Services, 1993.

Weiser, Benjamin, and Colin Moynihan. "A Guilty Plea in Plot to Bomb Times Square." *The New York Times*, 22nd June 2010.

Westervelt, Eric. "Growing Repression in Yemen May Feed Al Qaeda." In *All Things Considered*: National Public Radio, 2005.

Whewell, Tim. "Yemeni Anti-Terror Scheme in Doubt." In *Crossing Continents*: BBC, 2005.

Whitaker, Brian. "Abu Al-Hassan and the Islamic Army of Aden-Abyan", http://www.al-bab.com/yemen/hamza/hassan.htm.

———. "Abu Hamza and the Islamic Army." http://www.al-bab.com/yemen/hamza/day.htm.

———. "Extracts from Supporters of Shari'a Newsletters." Yemen Gateway, http://www.al-bab.com/yemen/hamza/sos3.htm.

———. "Saudis Brandish 'Iron Fist' against Militants Who Threaten Foreigners." *The Guardian*, 5 May 2004.

Whiteneck, Daniel. "Deterring Terrorists: Thoughts on a Framework." *Washington Quarterly* 28, no. 3 (2005): 187–99.

Wikileaks: The Guantánamo Files. "Abd Al Rahim Hussein Mohammed Al Nashiri." 2011.

———. "Al-Qa'ida Escape: Update." Embassy Sanaa (Yemen): Wikileaks, 2006.

———. "Ali Yahya Al-Raimi." http://wikileaks.org/gitmo/prisoner/167.html.

———. "Ambassador Presses Foreign Ministry on Badawi Case." Embassy Sanaa (Yemen): Wikileaks, 2007.

———. "August 29, 2003, Security Environment Profile Questionnaire Response." Embassy Sanaa (Yemen): Wikileaks, 2003.

———. "Diplomatic Security Daily." Department of State: Wikileaks, 2009.

———. "Embassy Follow-up to Mcc Signing Ceremony Postponement." Embassy Sanaa (Yemen): Wikileaks, 2007.

———. "Mohamed Atiq Awayd Al-Harbi." http://wikileaks.org/gitmo/prisoner/333.html.

———. "Royg Operation against Terrorists in Abyan." Embassy Sanaa (Yemen): Wikileaks, 2003.

———. "Sa'id Ali Jabir Al Khathim Al Shihri." http://wikileaks.org/gitmo/prisoner/372.html.

———. "Sanaa Security Environment Profile Questionnaire—Spring 2009." Embassy Sanaa (Yemen): Wikileaks, 2009.

———. "Yemen: 2003 Annual Terrorism Report." Embassy Sanaa (Yemen): Wikileaks, 2003.

Wiktorowicz, Quintan. "Anatomy of the Salafi Movement." *Studies in Conflict & Terrorism* 29, no. 3 (2006): 207–39.

———. "A Genealogy of Radical Islam." *Studies in Conflict & Terrorism* 28, no. 2 (2005): 75–97.

———. *Islamic Activism: A Social Movement Theory Approach*. Bloomington: Indiana University Press, 2004.

Wilkinson, Benedict. "What Is the Link between Ansar Al-Sharia and Al-Qa'ida in the Arabian Peninsula?" RUSI Analysis, https://www.rusi.org/commentary/what-link-between-ansar-al-sharia-and-al-qaida-arabian-peninsula.

Wilkinson, Benedict, and Jack Barclay. *The Language of Jihad: Narratives and Strategies of Al-Qa'ida in the Arabian Peninsula and UK Responses*. RUSI Whitehall Report. London: Royal United Services Institute, 2012.

Wilkinson, Paul. *Terrorism and the Liberal State*. Basingstoke: Macmillan, 1986. 2nd Edition.

———. *Terrorism Versus Democracy: The Liberal State Response*. Frank Cass Publishers, 2000.

William H. Webster Commission. "The Federal Bureau of Investigation, Counterterrorism Intelligence, and the Events at Fort Hood, Texas on November 5, 2009." 2012.

Woods, Ngaire. "Reconciling Effective Aid and Global Security: Implications for the Emerging International Development Architecture." In *Global Economic Governance Programme*. University College, Oxford 2005.

World Bank. "Republic of Yemen—Poverty Reduction Strategy Paper Annual Progress Report and Joint Ida-IMF Staff Advisory Note." Washington D.C.: The World Bank, 2006.

Wright, Lawrence. "The Heretic." *The Guardian*, 13 July 2008.

———. *The Looming Tower: Al Qaeda's Road to 9/11*. Penguin, 2007.

Xinhua. "Yemenis Protest Botched U.S. Drone Strikes." 4 September 2012.

Yadav, Stacey. "Antecedents of the Revolution: Intersectoral Networks and Post-Partisanship in Yemen." *Studies in Ethnicity and Nationalism* 11, no. 3 (2011): 550–63.

Yamani, Mai. "The Two Faces of Saudi Arabia." *Survival* 50, no. 1 (2008): 143–56.

Zeidan, David. "Radical Islam in Egypt: A Comparison of Two Groups." *Middle East Review of International Affairs* 3, no. 3 (1999) (repr. in David Rubin ed. *Revolutionaries and Reformers: Contemporary Islamist Movements in the Middle East*. Albany: SUNY Press, 2003, 11–22).

Zollner, Barbara. *The Muslim Brotherhood: Hasan Al-Hudaybi and Ideology*. Taylor & Francis, 2009.

INDEX

223